To
Enjoy Is
to Live

To Enjoy Is to Live

PSYCHOTHERAPY EXPLAINED

Benjamin Fabrikant, Ph.D.
Jules Barron, Ph.D.
Jack D. Krasner, Ph.D.

Nelson-Hall nh Chicago

To Laurine, Nina, and Selma

Library of Congress Cataloging in Publication Data

Fabrikant, Benjamin.
  To enjoy is to live.

  Includes index.
    1. Psychotherapy.   2. Mental health education
I. Barron, Jules, joint author.   II. Krasner, Jack D.,
joint author.   III. Title.
RC480.F3   616.8'914   76-40141
ISBN 0-88229-148-3

Contents

Preface

Several years ago the three of us were charged by the executive board of the Division of Psychotherapy of the American Psychological Association with the task of writing a booklet on psychotherapy. This booklet was intended to present various aspects of psychotherapy to the general public. Reader response to this booklet and our personal observations led us to believe that a more comprehensive work would be of value on a public information and educational level.

To Enjoy Is to Live is the title and the theme of this book, even though these words are rarely mentioned. It may even seem incongruous to write a serious book on psychotherapy with such a title. Yet for us this theme expresses the purpose of psychotherapy. Psychotherapy is a path towards meaningfulness, particularly for those who have been unable to achieve it in their natural course of development.

Clinically we have learned that significant vital psychological signs that are critical for sanity are experiences of satisfaction, fulfillment, and humor—that is, the ability to *enjoy*. It is the old Greek theme of tragedy and comedy in a mixture or balance that makes survival possible in a world that can be harsh and hurtful. (However gentle the psychotherapist may be, the patient is still there with the pain with which he has lived and suffered for many years.) If amidst the struggle it is still possible to experience moments of enjoyment, there is greater hope for effecting an improvement in emotional health. The direction of psychotherapy is towards a growth process that will include more creative ways of living and increased ability to enjoy the creativity.

And in the therapeutic process itself, meaningful signs of healthy change are the increasing ability to laugh at others and at ourselves, to enjoy what we do, and to do what we enjoy.

There is no one path. We each have to find our own path and choose between heaven and hell. Or, more realistically, we must find a better balance between the two.

In this book we seek to be as uncomplicated as possible without sacrificing accuracy, and to remove the mystique of psychotherapy without losing its substance. We have made an effort to present our perceptions of psychotherapy with an awareness of our biases, which are necessarily present here. At the same time we feel a real sense of conviction about our own orientations, but without the kind of arrogance we believe can close off openness. In our opinion any therapist, any professional, or any scientist who professes to hold the only truth suffers from a myopic view that can become dangerous to himself and others.

Part of the struggle we had in writing this text was that each of us has areas of difference as well as common grounds of agreement. However similar our theoretical orientations may be we have different styles of applying our skills. Our artistic inclinations are probably more diverse than our scientific foundations. A common purpose motivated us to combine our efforts in this endeavor.

If this volume serves to add a little more to a general understanding of psychotherapy, if a few more people can in some way benefit from our endeavor, our efforts will have been worthwhile. The mental health movement has progressed a long way in the twentieth century. We still have far to go in providing adequate services, training more people, changing attitudes towards people in trouble, and in general, improving the human condition.

There are many misconceptions about psychotherapy. With the proliferation of theories and techniques in a rapidly expanding field, the existing confusion is easy to understand. Although we have tried to present the broad spectrum of psychotherapy, it would be both arrogant and illusory to believe that we have achieved complete success. Our differences clearly appear when we talk about the psychotherapeutic process and how we work with people. However, we do share a psychodynamic orientation which is quite different from behavior modification.

We suspect that if each of us had written this volume by himself, each result would be different in both obvious and subtle ways. The advantage of a three-way writing, we believe, is the built-in set of checks and balances on more personalized biases. Omissions and commissions are both intentional and unintentional.

We have been fortunate in being exposed to a relatively large number of people from whom we have gained experience and knowledge which directly and indirectly influenced this book. We appreciate their contribution to our personal lives and the flavor of our writing. We especially wish to thank Naomi B. Levine for the many hours spent in assisting us with the editing of this volume.

We begin this book with a dialogue between two friends, one of whom is a psychotherapist. The purpose of this approach is to create a living situation from which questions are raised that are responded to in the substance of some of the chapters that follow. The chapters are written as if Joe, the psychotherapist, is continuing to talk to his friend Ed. Therefore we have merged the three authors into the single identity of Joe and use the first person singular "I." "We" is used in a literary sense. Since the dialogue primarily serves as a vehicle for beginning this book much of the content goes well beyond the questions that are provoked by the interaction between Joe and Ed.

We hope that you enjoy this book in addition to learning more about psychotherapy.

Introduction:
Have You Seen
a Shrink Lately?

The sinking feeling in the pit of the stomach experienced by most people when hearing "psychotherapy" unfortunately results too often in running away. The prefix "psycho" has been associated with being crazy or insane, when in fact it simply refers to the mind. Thus, to try to temper their fright, many people have condensed the term to "therapy." The veil of anxiety and skepticism which clouds "therapy" has been instrumental in perpetuating the fuzziness of this treatment procedure. The definitions and ideas attributed to psychotherapy have ranged anywhere from a "bull" or "rap" session between two or more people to a Svengali-like manipulation or brainwashing of one person by another. The anxiety which usually accompanies the unknown, especially when the unknown deals with human relationships, has produced many jokes that are both humorous and too deep for tears. This humor, however, has not stunted the growth and recognition of a form of treatment which has been of invaluable help to many people.

A stigma continues to be attached to emotional problems and to the treatment used to help a person resolve his debilitating conflicts. Apprehension related to being identified as "psycho" has sorely limited people's efforts to gain understanding of psychotherapy. Even in a casual discussion, pertinent questions which might lead to clarification and enlightenment are rare. Some people remain silent to avoid being viewed as ignorant or stupid. There are also some people with misconceptions of psychotherapy who ask questions which appear irrelevant and unanswerable.

Thus vague and/or irrelevant questions result in ambiguous answers, reinforcing the threatening mystique of psychotherapy.

Our endeavor in this book is to remove the mystique surrounding psychotherapy by exploring the many questions often implied but rarely asked. We shall elaborate on the what, when, how, and by whom of psychotherapy. We hope to explain the concept of psychotherapy as a treatment process.

[*Joe opens door and greets Ed.*]

JOE: Hi, Ed, it was good to hear from you. Glad we could get together. How are things at home?

ED: Not too bad!

JOE: Meaning what? Your face and the call don't say that!

ED: Well, some things are fine. Of course, as with everybody, some things just aren't. I suppose I could go on and on talking, but you—how about you? How's your family?

JOE: Fine, fine, doing well.

ED: Well I wish it were going like that for me. I said, "Not too bad," but things aren't what I'd like them to be. In fact, it's been a pretty long time since things have been really good.

JOE: Let's go into the study where we can relax and talk.

[*Both walk into the study and sit facing each other.*]

ED: Joe, I know you're my friend as well as a psychotherapist. I really wanted to talk to you because you know about other people's problems and I thought you could help me think through a couple of things. I think I'm going to find it hard to get started even though I usually feel confortable with you. I'm not sure where to begin, but here goes. I don't really want to talk about all my symptoms and the problems and the things that are going on in my life, because I'm not coming to you as my therapist. I think I've finally come to a decision that I need help and I want to do something about it, but I feel a lot of anxiety about what to do and where to go. Frankly, I don't have a clear idea of what really goes on in therapy. There are so many different ideas about psychotherapy and psychotherapists. I suppose I am asking you to help me clear up my confusion so I can go ahead and get the help I need.

JOE: I'm not sure I fully understand. You said that you had already come to a decision!

ED: Yes, I've decided I need help but I don't know where to go from there.

JOE: Can you give me some idea of what went into this decision, some background so I can be more helpful?

ED: Well, that's where I have the most difficulty—talking about myself. I think that's why I feel so upset about taking the next step and carrying out my decision. *(Pause)* You've known me for some time, Joe, and obviously you've noticed that I wasn't feeling too great. I suppose the problem is really me—the way I relate to people, the dissatisfaction I feel in my job and at home. It's hard for me to feel close to anybody and I've begun to feel more and more hopeless, as though I'm in a trap and can't get out. I feel as though there are two parts to me. One part is the outside that goes along and says all the right things, while the other is inside needing something that I'm not getting. I feel like a fraud. As a matter of fact, I feel that I'm acting in a way that's not real. I think this affects me at home. I know it affects my relationship with my wife and my children. Even sex isn't what it used to be!

JOE: *(Sympathetic)* Sounds like these problems have been developing for some time now.

ED: For an awfully long time! I think I kept denying things and kept telling myself everything would work out. I'd take a vacation and it would be better. While I'm away, I'm fine, but when I come back—wow! My wife has been very understanding, even when I take it out on her. I get angry with her and I get irritable with the kids. Then I start feeling guilty about it, because I know I can be a bastard! Even my job no longer provides me with satisfaction.

JOE: *(In a soft compassionate voice)* Gee, Ed, you have been going through a miserable period. *(Pause)* I also get the feeling that you have gone through a lot of self-questioning and suddenly come up with a conclusion, but without going through some of the preliminary steps. I don't know all of what you've gone through, and I'm not sure of what's going on now—as you said, I'm your friend, not your therapist. At the moment I don't want to get into that, but I'm really puzzled. You sound as if you're trying to ask me something, as well as yourself.

ED: I really don't understand you, Joe. You asked me to tell you what's been going on, and I'm telling you what I've been feeling, and that I decided I need help.

JOE: You've already decided you need help. However, you want something of *me!* What puzzles me is *what?* If you've already made the decision, then—

ED: *(Interrupting)* I suppose I haven't made myself clear. This is a trouble I sometimes have with people, when I think I'm making myself clear and it turns out I'm not. I thought I was telling you that I feel a lot of anxiety about getting help. *(Pause)* Joe, I'm not really sure if I'm afraid of going into therapy or that I don't really understand psychotherapy or how it might help me.

JOE: Ed, something strikes me—what I have heard so far is a series of negatives. As you describe the situation, nothing is working for you. But I haven't heard anything to balance this. Is there anything positive in your life?

ED: I don't know. When I get to feeling this way it seems that there is nothing good. I'm making money and things like that, but I don't feel that these things are of much worth to me right now.

JOE: Are you saying that when you get into this mood, you can't experience the good things, or get any enjoyment out of them?

ED: That's right. I just can't *feel* them!

JOE: Let's go back a little. I'm still stuck on one point. You're looking for something, and not just some *thing* but for some*one.* Now, you came to me first, and even though we're friends and you usually feel at ease with me, you're having trouble talking to me. Several times I've raised questions and you seem to have glided around them. Actually, how do you feel about discussing these very personal problems with me!

ED: That's where I'm having trouble. I know you're my friend, and I guess I'm afraid I might hurt your feelings. Psychotherapy is your profession, after all. The question in my mind is whether there's really anything worthwhile in therapy. What is it all about? Does it really help anybody?

JOE: Are you asking whether therapy can help you?

ED: I guess what I need from you is reassurance, because right now, I find it hard to believe that anything or anyone can help me. I need to understand more about psychotherapy. How can it help me? Right now, I've got to trust someone, and I don't trust myself or my judgment. I suppose I feel that I trust you more than anyone else and even there I have my doubts. Maybe you can help me or at least set me in the right direction.

JOE: Ed, you are quite distraught and I think we ought to try to see clearly just exactly what's happening here. Are you seeking reassurance and direction from me as a friend, as your potential psychotherapist, or as a friend who is a psychotherapist?

ED: I came to you because you're a friend and I felt you would be honest with me.

JOE: Then, what you want primarily is information?

ED: I don't know exactly what I want. All I know is that I need help! *(Pause)* And there's something more than that. I also need someone to help me get started, because if I don't get moving I'm afraid I'll crack up.

JOE: You want information that can be helpful to you, you want to know how psychotherapy applies to you, and you're looking for some reassurance about your decision. You also want some help in getting started.

ED: I sometimes wonder whether I'm coming to you because you'll help me find a way *out* of doing something. That's how *bad* I've been feeling. I suppose I really haven't made a decision.

JOE: That's what I've been sensing. Maybe you grabbed for the conclusion too fast. *(Pause)* The best procedure might be to discuss the questions you've raised. Then you'll be in a better position to think about where to go from here.

ED: Maybe I am asking you to be my psychotherapist. Knowing you as a friend, I know you would be good. I suppose I'm also asking you to do something that would make everything all right. If nothing more, you can give me information and that would be a help to me.

JOE: Well, let's take a look at some of the questions you've raised and clear up some of the doubts you have. When we're through we'll be in a much better position to discuss the question, "How do you get the help you need and from whom?"

ED: I feel kinda funny. I'm asking an awful lot of you, making a lot of demands of you. Maybe it's more than I have the right to ask of you. But I *need* to get this stuff clear in my mind. Sometimes I don't even know what to think or say or ask.

JOE: You have always been the kind of person who takes one thing at a time. You're an organizer. You like to put things together.

ED: That's part of my problem. I like to organize and everything seems so disorganized.

JOE: One of the things that I sense is that you keep shifting my role from being "your friend" to being a "psychotherapist." There doesn't have to be an incompatibility.

ED: That's what I don't understand. What is the difference between a friend and a psychotherapist? If I can talk to a friend, I don't know why I should go to a psychotherapist.

JOE: There is often a great deal of similarity in that both may understand, console, sympathize, and share with you. A couple of major differences are that while a friend is available for advice and doing things for you, a therapist helps you to uncover and understand the basis of your existing disturbing emotional problems. He also helps you to learn how to develop methods for understanding and effectively coping with conflicts that arise.

ED: The thought that keeps coming to me is that I can talk to you more easily because I feel you care. I don't know if a stranger is going to care about me.

JOE: You seem quite concerned about how important you may be to the psychotherapist.

ED: Yes! I'm afraid that if I feel I'm unimportant I'm going to have to try to impress him until he feels I *am* important. *(Pause)* Hell, I'm afraid that I may react with a therapist the same way I do with other people I don't know well. Boy, when I go to a party, do I have to impress every new person there!

JOE: You're not sure how you will react to a therapist whom you don't know well?

ED: You're right! I have trouble with that. *(Ed becomes calmer.)* I also question what happens in psychotherapy. Tell me something of what goes on, and what it's all about. What am I supposed to do when I get into the therapist's office? And what does the psychotherapist do? I'm scared of what he's going to do to me.

JOE: Do to you? Why must he do something to you?

ED: Well, he's a doctor!

JOE: What are you? Maybe I should ask, "Who are you?"

ED: I'm just a guy in trouble.

JOE: A guy? You're an entity—a thinking, feeling, doing person.

ED: Right now I feel less than a person. I can tell you a lot of things about how great I am and how successful I've been in my life. But that's not how I really feel. *(Pause)* I'm also wondering about something else. If I go into psychotherapy do I have to go with my wife and kids?

JOE: Ed, so far you've described yourself and some of your feelings. It comes across that you feel you're to blame for everything. If the kids or your wife were to become involved in psychotherapy you would still feel that you are at fault.

ED: *(Becoming tense)* That word "fault" gets to me. I'm always feeling like that.

JOE: But you're so ready to grab hold of this fault. Ed, this is the kind of pattern that one explores in therapy. However, in psychotherapy we're not looking to see who's at fault or who's right or wrong. We're seeking the most effective method of working out and resolving the problems. Sometimes the focus is on one person, sometimes on another, and at times on several people at the same time.

ED: As long as we're talking about all this, let me ask something else that's been bothering me for some time. If all therapists do different things, how do I know which one is *right* or *wrong* for me? How am I supposed to know? I wouldn't even know if a therapist was qualified.

JOE: Actually you've asked several questions. You raise the question of whether there are right or wrong ways of doing psychotherapy. Perhaps it's more a question of different ways of reaching the same goal. You also raise the question, "How do I know who's most effective for me?" It's quite true that someone who works effectively with one person may not do as well with somebody else. You may find yourself responding better to one kind of person than another. Therefore, it's also important to know the kind of person with whom you're going to be working. It is more than how technically capable and well-trained the therapist might be. In psychotherapy there are two human beings who are going to be relating to each other. What you're looking for is somebody who is very well qualified, who is well-trained, has good background and experience and attributes that go beyond that.

ED: You mean somebody who really cares!

JOE: Someone who's interested in you as a human being, as a person.

ED: That's the way I feel you are, Joe.

JOE: If I can do it, I'm quite sure there are others who can also become interested.

ED: Well, I don't know. You seem to be suggesting that you can't do it for me.

JOE: That's something we can work out a little later. Let me assure you that I'm not pulling away. But first let's talk about the most effective person for you. Knowing what we know about each other and considering our past relationship, am I the best psychotherapist for you? There's more to it than information and knowledge, and how much we know about each other. It's the kind of people we are, the way we feel, the way we feel about each other. These are very important elements to consider.

ED: One other thing, Joe. At times I have heard you talk about going to meetings and discussing techniques in psychotherapy. *(Pause)* I don't know why, but something about that bothered me. It's as if you're using something or the therapist will be using something on me and I really don't know what it is all about. It just sounds so strange when you talk about "techniques." I can picture what happens if I get my appendix removed and when I go to see my dentist, I understand what he's doing. But I don't know anything about techniques in psychotherapy.

JOE: Maybe the idea of technique sounds like a contradiction to what we have been discussing. Before, we talked about the therapist's concern about you as a person, and your working together. Now you're back to the idea that the therapist is going to do something to you as if you're a *thing* that's worked on. If you like we can talk about this some more—what we mean by techniques, how they are used, and what purpose they serve. Techniques always serve a purpose and are never an end in themselves. Techniques are methods or ways of enhancing the treatment in the direction of the desired goals. For example, many therapists explore the meaning of their patient's dreams as an aid in understanding the basis for existing conflicts. There is really no mystery or secret to these procedures.

ED: I suppose I was upset when I heard you talk about—oh well, it sounded kind of cold and foreboding, as if I would become some kind of guinea pig in an experiment. I feel much easier about the whole thing now.

JOE: Good! Perhaps I can be more helpful now if we explore some of the questions you've raised. Let's start with psychotherapy and what it is.

1

What Is Psychotherapy?

As we move through the second half of the twentieth century we see increased concern for and interest in mental health. A basic part of the growth of the mental health movement has been the development of psychotherapy. Today "psychotherapy" has become a popular and acceptable term in millions of homes, social institutions, and schools. At the same time it has been frequently misunderstood and seems to hold different meanings for different people. For some, psychotherapy is thought of in terms of its scientific origins in the work of Sigmund Freud. Although he created the concept of psychoanalysis as a means of studying the human mind, Freud was only a beginning and his work has been affected by the currents of time and progress. Freudian psychoanalysis gave birth to many new ideas which became varied and took many new and different directions. Nonetheless, the Freudian idea had its impact not only by helping people but also by creating images of psychotherapy.

I may have already confused you by using two similar terms—"psychoanalysis" and "psychotherapy." Although some psychoanalysts may disagree, I would like you to consider for our momentary purpose that the two are relatively interchangeable. It may help to know that Freud was primarily interested in investigating and analyzing the workings of the mind. Hence the word "psychoanalysis." Literally, "psychotherapy" means the treatment of the mind. It should be added that "psycho-" has Greek origins and means, "mind, soul, or spirit." Today the practice of psychotherapy involves working with the emotions, thoughts, and other aspects of personality. Let us therefore regard "psychotherapy" as the broader and most practical term for us to use.

For a long time psychotherapy remained somewhat of a mystery for many professionals, as well as for laymen. Much curiosity was stirred up. Questions were asked directly and indirectly, publicly and privately. In the absence of adequate knowledge the imagination was provoked into creating its own fantasies about what psychotherapy is and what happens in the course of treatment. In Freud's day it was common for men to grow beards and so the bearded face of Freud became part of the image of the therapist. The bearded man plus the couch within the confines of some inner sanctum where the unconscious or inner depths of the patient were unearthed, brought to consciousness, and explored, were part of the picture of psychotherapy.

Today, after a period of short hair and crew cuts, the beard has regained its status as an acceptable style. However, the couch has diminished in use and the therapist and patient are often found in face-to-face communication with each other. Along with great social change and the multiplying ideas about the nature of man there has grown a wide spectrum of definitions of psycho-therapy. The experience has become less imbued with magic or secrecy and regarded more as a human experience.

In the light of historic events and changes in the field of psychotherapy it would seem presumptuous to come up with any single definition of psychotherapy or any single answer to the question of what psychotherapy is. If my purpose were to present one point of view, my task would be simplified. However, I am one of many psychotherapists who have differences in orientation. It is my wish to provide you with a statement about psychotherapy that will help clarify the nature of psychotherapy in a most basic way. Perhaps I can contribute to your understanding and minimize any ambiguity and confusion.

I do believe that there are significantly common elements to all of psychotherapy. Therefore it is possible to come up with a useable and understandable explanation. My explanation may not be agreeable or fully satisfactory to all psychotherapists but I am not trying to deal in absolutes that do not exist or be a pretender to grandiose goals. What counts is that I can confidently give you what is truly important.

Psychotherapy is designed to be a helping procedure. It is an activity in which people with special backgrounds of training and experience help others to live more comfortably, more fully, and more productively. Psychotherapy is a form of interaction between two or more people wherein the therapist uses his skills and person to creatively influence those who seek his help.

Let us look at the various ingredients that enter into an understanding of psychotherapy.

Psychotherapy is a form of interaction

An interaction takes place when two or more people act upon each other. It is an interchange in which there are actions and reactions. For example, if I hit you over the head with a mallet this is an action. If you scream or strike back that is a reaction. To the best of my knowledge such interaction would not be psychotherapeutic. Therefore it is not likely that a therapist would engage in such behavior. I would also hope that no patient would take such action. It does not inspire me with a feeling of friendliness. The therapist is more inclined to influence the interaction in the direction of health or growth. This is best accomplished in the context of a good relationship.

Psychotherapy is a relationship

An interaction is not necessarily a relationship but a relationship is always an interaction. The interaction provides the ground in which a relationship may develop. The relationship is usually regarded as the basic aspect of therapy that promotes change. Of course a relationship may be pleasant or painful, creative or destructive. People often seek help because of relationships in their past that have been destructive to some degree or that have interfered with their ability to function or grow adequately. In therapy, as in other human relationships, there is likely to be hurt, pain, and imperfection as part of the experience of change. A good relationship between therapist and patient is beneficial to this process of change. Nevertheless, the relationship does not constitute the whole of psychotherapy.

Psychotherapy is learning

As long as you live and are exposed to the world, you learn. The learning may be primarily through your intellect or your emotions but both are always involved. It may be direct and indirect, verbal and nonverbal, conscious and unconscious. You learn when you study at school, when you read, and when you solve problems. However you apply your intellect, it is never unaffected by your emotional state. You also learn as you are exposed to various experiences and relationships. This experiential learning affects the way you feel and think. In psychotherapy you have an opportunity to explore and experience your feelings and thoughts in an effort to reach a greater awareness of yourself and the nature of your being and existence. Awareness is the step that opens the doors to resolution and change. It is a step towards learning new, alternative, and productive ways of living. The therapeutic interactions help to form a relationship that allows the awareness to occur; this makes it possible for you and the therapist to share and search for new and more fulfilling ways of being. The learning is reciprocal, for the therapist learns as well as the patient.

Psychotherapy is communication

If psychotherapy is learning, there must be communication that permits it to take place. Communication may occur through the media of words, gestures, postures, or other forms of body language. You speak with your eyes as well as with your mouth. Your manner, tone of voice, and even manner of dress are part of your communication system. Essential to this system are your senses, perceptions, and sensibilities. Your senses include your abilities to see, hear, taste, smell, and touch, and to feel movement, heat, cold, and pain. These senses are your contact, your lifeline to your inner world and the world about you. Your senses are located throughout your entire body. Perception is the process by which the brain interprets and understands the messages received through the senses. Most of us rely primarily on the senses of sight and hearing. Communication and learning are effective to the degree that our whole person is involved in what takes place.

More recognition and acceptance are now being given to the fact that touch and the other senses are critical to human growth. For example, research done over the past years has demonstrated the importance of physical contact as a means of achieving feelings of security. At one time there were therapists who would not even shake hands with a patient. Today it is not regarded as unseemly for the human action of hugging or embracing to take place. There is a strong movement towards a more humanistic approach that regards the patient as a person rather than an object. This is resulting in a larger system of communication. Many of the earlier taboos in psychotherapy were reflections of the prohibitions in a society that was born of the Victorian ethic. In the past, and to a large extent in the present, affectionate behavior between two people of the opposite sex was necessarily regarded as indication of sexual motivation. If the affection was between people of the same sex, homosexuality was suspected. There would be little room for affectionate contact if all contact was considered sexual and if sexuality was seen as bad. Of course in psychotherapy there must always be good clinical judgment combined with spontaneity and humanness to determine what would be most appropriate and therapeutic in any given situation. The appropriateness of when and how to communicate is always an important consideration in terms of what would facilitate rather than impede the healing or growth of the patient.

The therapist tunes into the patient by listening. Listening is one of the hardest things for most people to learn. The "third ear" is the expression frequently used to speak of the special tuning in by the therapist that makes hearing possible. Hearing is more than that which occurs through the ears. I hear you with my eyes, my touch, and so on. If I am willing and able to hear you, and if you try to be open and honest with me, a two-way bridge of communication may be formed between us. When we can find a common language of understanding, therapeutic movement is fostered.

Psychotherapy is a process

Life in motion is a process. It is ongoing, changing, and dynamic. As we grow we are continually affected by all the forces operating within and outside of us. Hence there are internal and external processes going on simultaneously. We affect each other overtly and subtly. With our personal resources we modify our natural and human environment in order to meet our needs and facilitate our adaptation. In this way we continue to create new conditions to which adaptations must be made. Interaction, relationship, and communication are all essential to this continuing process of living and growing. As a therapist I must be aware of this process and the ways in which my behavior influences its direction. Out of my training and experience has evolved for me an integration of concepts and feelings that serve as a guide or frame of reference in my psychotherapeutic work. The frame(s) of reference so applied are referred to as theories.

Psychotherapy is based on theories

In therapy the nature of the interaction, relationship, learning, communication, and process will vary in small or large ways in accordance with the theoretical orientation of the psychotherapist. The theory is the philosophy or combination of principles that determines the therapist's style, way of being, and techniques that he applies. In all sciences theories may be found in abundance. The fact that there are many theories may sometimes be confusing. However, the various ways of looking and knowing keep us on our toes and contribute to progress and the continual improvement in our work. So do not be disheartened by the differences in theories or disagreements between therapists, for they keep the doors open to new knowledge and understanding. As a psychotherapist I select my theories because of what I have learned and what I am as a person. As the patient must be open to change I, too, must be prepared to change and not become a slave to a theory. The theory must be in the service of people.

Psychotherapy and techniques

There is a wide range of attitudes regarding techniques in psychotherapy. Some therapists believe that the style or nature of the relatedness is the only or primary means of influencing positive change. Others believe that specific techniques are either necessary or beneficial to the therapeutic process. There are different attitudes about the importance of the therapist as a person. Some of us believe that all of these are appropriate and important depending upon the individual patient and where he is in the therapeutic process. Techniques are methods or specific procedures that are deliberately and purposefully used to elicit particular reactions, attitudes, or behavior. The potential list of techniques available is so long that I will discuss them later.

Discussion

Through the years the many theoretical orientations in psychotherapy have attracted followers or adherents of specific points of view. Some of these groups have started centers or schools where a particular theory is promoted and taught. Most psychotherapists, however different or individualized their approaches, draw from the basic concepts of Sigmund Freud.

The psychotherapist utilizes psychological theories and techniques for the purpose of helping persons with disturbances in their intellectual and emotional growth to achieve a higher level of personality and human development. The psychotherapeutic process draws from a multitude of psychological areas including personality, motivation, perception, sensation, conditioning, learning, thinking, feeling, dreaming, and so forth.

As we can see, the knowledge of psychotherapy is drawn from the many aspects of human behavior and functioning that are synthesized to result in a more total understanding of the person. In addition to an understanding of the specifically psychological ingredients that make up psychotherapy, knowledge is also drawn from such fields as anthropology, biology, physics, sociology, and literature.

If we put together the ingredients of psychotherapy as discussed, we can say what it is.

Psychotherapy is an interactive process wherein therapist(s) and patient(s) form a relationship that facilitates the kind of communication and learning resulting in improved functioning, relatedness, healing, or growth on the part of the patient.

Sometimes people say that psychotherapy is artificial or contrived because the sessions are by appointment and the relationship is a professional one. In some situations this might be the case, but the degree of authenticity is controlled by the individuals involved. And by the way, aren't most meetings between people in everyday life arranged by appointment! The primary purposes may differ; they may be social, business, or other. The critical difference is in the purpose and the agreed upon nature of the meeting. All relationships have rules, be they apparent or hidden, explicit or implicit, conscious or unconscious. Psychotherapy is a helping service. It is a science and a discipline by virtue of training and an art by virtue of the therapist's person and sensitivities. An authentic therapist can sell his skills and his time. He cannot sell his feelings, his friendship, or his person. What he gives and invests of himself is a matter of individual and personal response. No two relationships in psychotherapy are any more alike than relationships outside psychotherapy.

It seems clear that psychotherapy is a unique experience requiring a genuine caring and personal investment on the part of the psychotherapist, in addition to many years of study and training. Psychotherapy as a profession and special process of helping people has continued to grow for over a century now. Yet its origins are even older. What were its beginnings and how did they develop to fill an important human need?

2

Development of Psychotherapy

The history of psychotherapy may look like a maze at first. But it is more like a number of roads all gradually leading to the same place. Some of these roads were built about the same time; others came later and from different sources. Let us see if we can get some idea of each in a sequence and follow it through time.

I know that this is going to be very sketchy, with quite a bit left out. The history of the field of psychotherapy might include dozens of names and events, but I am going to try to stay with the highlights. If there is a specific area you would want to explore further, look up one of the names, and explore that in more depth.

Black magic, religion, faith healing, superstition, philosophy, medicine, witch doctors, demons, honest men and charlatans, Greek, Roman, Hebrew, Arab, Christian and pagan, lord and commoner—these are some of the parts of the psychotherapy map. We will mention some familiar and unfamiliar names and dates which offer some idea of the road markers.

Let us start with the fear of the unknown, one of the strongest fears people have. Imagine the cave man trying to figure out the meaning of thunder and lightning, and to control himself in a world of volcanoes, hurricanes, day and night, eclipses, and sudden and unexpected death. A man usually fears what he does not understand. Who does this primitive man turn to for help and understanding? His neighbor? The neighbor probably knows little more than he does. Someone from another group or tribe? Never! They were also unknowns and by definition most likely enemies.

In turning to someone who might possibly explain these things, and so calm him, the cave man turned to one who seemed to wear the mantle of authority. Thus, the first witch doctor, priest, or in our own modern terms, psychotherapist appeared. The two did not have a relationship, but there was faith on the part of the frightened one; an "aura" on the part of the other. The function of the doctor or priest was not to explain as much as to calm the individual and to remove the fear of the unknown.

Somewhere along the way he began to capitalize on his patient's fear of the unknown in order to direct and modify behavior. He attributed this to the laws of magic as he, the doctor/priest, understood them. Interestingly enough the history of magic indicates that women did not function as witch doctors in the earliest times. We can trace this use of magic through some of the ancient drawings that archaeologists have interpreted. Ancient Egyptian hieroglyphics and Babylonian writings and drawings show that many forms of magic existed thousands of years ago. In these documents there are many references to spirits and demons, significant magic words and numbers, and amulets and charms, together with a strong belief in the power of all of these. The Egyptians also believed that dreams could be interpreted as the will of the gods.

The belief in magic and superstition has never totally died out. We can still see its influences today. The number thirteen is bad luck. Medicines are taken either three or four times a day although the frequency may have little or no effect on their efficacy. People have "lucky" numbers. A rabbit's foot is good luck, but walking under a ladder or having a black cat cross your path is bad luck. Actors have their favorite superstitions, as do athletes and many others. A belief in astrology controls many people's decisions and sometimes their very lives.

The next group which might be considered are the Greeks. They developed a more naturalistic approach to healing and magic than did primitive man. They did not turn to magic or faith of any kind as the basis for either explaining behavior or treating deviant behavior. However, they still believed in the healing power of the gods and used dreams in diagnosis and treatment. The Greeks felt that the god Asclepius would reveal himself to the patient in a dream (but only within the temple walls) and then the patient would enter into personal contact with the god. Thus the patient's disease would be cured or the patient helped in the treatment process. The patient's dreams were also used to divine the nature of the illness and to foretell the future. The Greek approach was that of empiricism—knowledge based on experience of things that could be seen, touched, or heard—influenced by their religious ideas. The Greeks rejected the supernatural and turned to the more rational and objective. This approach slowly drifted to Rome.

The Romans were even more pragmatic than the Greeks, accepting as real only what they could literally see and touch. Moreover, believing that work of any kind was beneath the pursuit of the Roman patrician, they allowed only slaves and foreigners to practice the healing arts. The patrician was forbidden to become involved in such healing work or treatment. In their pragmatic approach the Romans depended much on the power of herbs, specific household gods for each different disease, and specific religious observances for the treatment of illness. The naturalistic ideas of the Greeks were at first resisted by the Romans. Gradually the Greek ideas took hold. Around the second century of the common era, the rational naturalistic approach of the Greeks was finally accepted by the Romans as it related to physical illness. However, the understanding of emotional disturbance as expressed in psychotherapy was still almost nonexistent to the Romans. It was not until the fall of the Roman Empire and the spread of Christianity that this situation began to change.

The Bible permitted the dissection of animals that had been sacrificed. The influence of the Talmud was very strong on the Hebrews, and focused less on magical aspects of healing than did the medicine of Egypt and Babylon. The Bible also referred to "madness" including descriptions of epileptic seizures and catatonic furor. As early as 490 A.D. a hospital for the mentally ill existed in Jerusalem.

Christianity, of course, begins with Jesus. He taught that faith alone was sufficient to solve all problems, but that this ability was purely a gift. He added the "touch" or "laying on of hands" which was to become important later. Gradually his disciples added to faith, magic oils, potions, and the holy water used in purification. They felt that people needed more specific aspects of faith, formerly called magic, in order to respond.

Over the centuries the strength of the church increased and the priests continued to emphasize the forces of faith, magic oils, potions, and relics. The influence of priests in the healing area increased and expanded. By the ninth and tenth centuries, the Church took an important step and affirmed that it alone could work miraculous cures and took full responsibility for exorcism. Thereby the clergy became the psychotherapists of the Dark and Middle Ages. The priests emphasized the divine, and rejected all matters of the flesh. Together with the focus on faith, this contributed to the emphasis on the spiritual rather than on the material. All of these factors flowed together towards what we now call psychotherapy.

Priests put much faith in "relics," pieces of holy bone, wood, or cloth. The healing power Jesus is said to have handed down to his disciples was later transferred to relics and shrines. The shrine is the repository of the holy relic and is invested not only with healing power, but with a general aura of "spirituality." The spirit of the shrine is timeless. It carries a message of healing, hope, and peace. The patient experiences this healing power through faith in the relic and the atmosphere of the shrine. The modern hospital also is endowed with some of the same traditions as a haven of peace and humane treatment.

To summarize so far, we have a number of important forces leading towards the development of psychological healing, or psychotherapy.

1. The primitive supernaturalism, in which the person believed in magic, both good and bad. The witch doctor was the important individual although the focus was not on the relationship, but on the atmosphere of power and authority. The primitive man had to have faith that the other person would be able to explain, or at least protect him against the unknown forces.

2. The Greeks moved towards a more reality-based, natural explanation for events and behavior. The combination of this pragmatic explanation, together with some of the religious ideas, introduced the concept of the mind and its

influence on behavior in both diagnosis and treatment.

3. The church turned to the belief in faith as a major aspect of the healing process. There was an emphasis on potions, amulets, and aspects of magic including the spread of power to the words that were used during the incantation of ritual. In this process, the saying itself took on some of the power of the relic's ability to cure. It was not necessary to have the actual relic, but only to use the proper words and/or spell.

4. Probably the most significant contribution in the Western world at the time of the Middle Ages was the concept of faith used in the healing process as refined by the followers of Jesus. They turned to the spiritual and nonmaterial, rejecting empirical reality and the present in their beliefs. These ideas held sway until the rise of psychology in the eighteenth century.

Now we can introduce a specific name—Paracelsus—who lived in the later fifteenth and early sixteenth centuries. He was a dogmatic inflexible man who attacked the "medical establishment" of his time and pretty well demolished the blind acceptance of the authoritarianism of the physician in the Middle Ages. He disagreed with many of the ideas of the medieval priests and physicians. He had strong power drives of his own, as well as a strong belief in alchemy. He also believed in the stars, and combined astrology with inorganic chemistry. Perhaps the major effect he had on psychotherapy was through a follower of his who lived about two centuries later. This man was Anton Mesmer, who left his brand, mesmerism, on the technique he developed and used to cure illness. He believed that the flow of the magnetic force, through iron out of the body, took with it the illness itself. Mesmer's investigations with this approach eventually led to the development of what we now know as hypnotism.

The idea of the "touch" or "laying on of hands" which was discussed earlier was eventually transferred from the priests to the rulers. Clovis the Frank in the fifth century, and later, Henry IV and Louis IX of France used this approach. The English kings in the fourteenth and fifteenth centuries practiced this as well. Until about the seventeenth century, treatment and what we might call psychotherapy was left to the province of the clergy, to physicians, and to kings and rulers. One of the more important individuals who broke this particular line of power—Greatrakes—is little known outside of the various history books. We might say that the student of psychotherapy who recognizes his name is the unusual rather than the expected. Greatrakes was a commoner who demonstrated that healing power was not the sole province of kings, priests, and physicians, but could be accomplished by lord and commoner alike. He said that he could cure the King's evil, aches, and falling sickness successfully. Although he was investigated and discredited by "the establishment," people continued to invest him with a measure of divine power and flocked to him. His influence produced a series of followers. There are some healers today who trace their methods back to Greatrakes.

Let us now take a look at the history of hospitals or asylums for the emotionally disturbed. We have evidence that the Chinese and Hindus had these hospitals thousands of years ago. During the reign of Pope Innocent III in the twelfth century, the monasteries became the first places in the Western world for the treatment of individuals who were emotionally disturbed. Did you know that Sir Lancelot of the Round Table in the sixth century was said to have gone to a monastery for about a year and a half for treatment? Whether this is fact or fiction it offers evidence that this idea existed at that time, even before Pope Innocent III declared the monasteries official refuges for the emotionally disturbed.

Another approach to the mental hospital which also predates the monastery is the colony of Gheel, Belgium. Over a thousand years ago, patients here lived and worked together with the townspeople. This approach continues today in the same city in Belgium. Gheel, the monasteries, and the colonies of patients were all contributions to the development of the mental hospitals we have today.

Up to about the eighteenth century, mental hospitals were primarily custodial. Based on a belief in demons and spirits as the causes of emotional disturbance, treatment relied on stringent attempts to rid the person of the intruding demon or spirit. This sometimes resulted in the patient's death. The patients were chained and usually treated as distinct from the rest of humanity. Chiarugi of Italy, in the late eighteenth century, and Pinel of France, about the time of the French Revolution, used their own influence to have the chains taken off the "lunatiks," stopped the beatings, and replaced them with medicine and kindness. Benjamin Rush, the father of American psychiatry, made a number of important contributions towards the development of humane treatment of mental patients in the United States. His book on psychiatry, published in 1812, became the authoritative work until about 1890. Although essentially a humane person he used bleeding extensively on his patients, sometimes much to their discomfort. Dr. Eli Todd of the Hartford Retreat in Connecticut was another leader in the early nineteenth century in the fight to free patients of their restraints and to use kind and humane treatment. His hospital became the place to visit in the 1820s and 1830s if one wanted to see psychological approaches to treatment.

Dorothea Dix was a reformer who had a strong influence on mental hospital practices during the nineteenth century. Starting in Massachusetts she went on to influence the rest of the United States and then Europe. She was a strong believer in humane treatment. She fought for the removal of chains and restraints, for decent living quarters, good food, and decent medical and psychological attention. She also put forth the idea that the "insane" were wards of the nation, and not just "lost souls" to be disregarded. She was influential in the designing of new hospitals, treatment of patients, and even selection of personnel. She founded a number of major hospitals, including St. Elizabeth's, the federal hospital in Washington, D.C.

We have looked at the major positive aspects of the development of psychotherapy and treatment for the emotionally disturbed. We have mentioned the importance of the idea of "faith" for the new field of psychotherapy. However, the focus on faith was a mixed blessing. What can happen when faith and the belief in faith go astray? Let us briefly follow the strange change from a faith that healed to a faith that destroyed all who deviated and/or who would not profess a belief in the orthodoxy of the times. The obsession with witchcraft goes back to the Bible with the injunction that "Thou shalt not suffer a witch to live." During the Middle Ages there was a strong belief in witchcraft in Europe and a concerted move towards the hunting out and punishing of witches by the clergy. The concern with witchcraft moved to the Americas in the seventeenth century and came to its height in New England in the Salem trials. Witchcraft was used to explain madness, wrongdoing, misfortunes, and many physical symptoms. The evidence we have today shows that many of the people, mostly women, who were tried as witches, were most probably emotionally disturbed, as were many of their victims. Some of these people would now be considered either hysterics, psychotics, or bearers of psychosomatic symptoms. Some of these people were undoubtedly normal individuals who were themselves convenient targets for others in the community who were either hysterics or paranoid. The latter needed scapegoats, and accusing others of being witches enabled them to direct their fears and hatred. In hunting out the witches the inquisitors in the fourteenth to sixteenth centuries followed a medical model. The inquisitor saw the process as a problem in diagnosis. The evidence was the stigmata (symptoms), and the purging (treatment) of the individual followed. There was then the confession (cure), with or without the renunciation of the devil. The devil and his followers were very real to the people during that period. Gradually witchcraft lost its hold on the people because of a combination of discoveries in medicine, more liberal thinking in religious matters, and the development of psychology as a science. People began to look for a more rational and natural explanation for strange behavior.

Starting in the early nineteenth century physicians slowly came to the idea that emotional disturbance might well be an illness that was treatable, and probably curable. But medicine took a while to go from demons and devils of the religious medieval ages to the Greek naturalisic explanation, then back to demons again, and finally to the reality of the emotional disturbance. By the end of the nineteenth century psychiatry had become a branch of clinical medicine focusing on the diagnosis and treatment of emotional disturbances.

Let us return to Anton Mesmer. Even today it is difficult to understand whether he was a charlatan or a genius who combined some of the beliefs of his time with new ideas. He developed the idea that magnetic forces could cure illness and he built up a large practice using a combination of iron bars, faith, an imposing appearance, and the theory of "animal magnetism." The medical authorities did not go along with him and had him investigated by a royal commission that included Benjamin Franklin. The commission concluded that while what he did worked, his explanation was not acceptable. Thus he was banished and forbidden to practice Mesmerism. This prohibition lasted until James Braid and John Elliotson, both extremely reputable men, revived the use of suggestion in treatment in the 1840s. Through some of their work they developed the art and science of what is now known as hypnotism.

Continuing with a look at some of the faith healers, we ought to take a quick look at Dr. Franz G. Hall and his ideas of craniology. Early in the nineteenth century he, together with the phrenologist Dr. Johann Casper Spurzheim, said that the areas of the brain were related to certain specific behavioral patterns and traits and that these patterns were reflected in increased pressures on the skull. These pressures resulted in raised areas known as "bumps." One could then diagnose and understand personality through the readings of these raised areas. Despite an almost total lack of valid evidence this idea lasted a surprisingly long time. It wasn't until late in the nineteenth century that the scientific and medical professions finally gave up the belief in phrenology.

While faith as a method of healing began in a religious context, a series of important faith healers during the nineteenth century grew out of a lay group. During this period the influence of religion came back strongly to the scene. Phineas Quimby focused on the idea of using the impact of the scripture to heal the sick and disturbed. Out of some of his ideas Mrs. Mary Baker Eddy founded what is now known as Christian Science—a religion, a cosmology, and a method of psychotherapy. While some may have considered Quimby to have been a quack, he was both sincere and successful. A strong conflict still exists as to whether he or Mrs. Eddy developed the basic tenets of what is now Christian Science. Mrs. Eddy's contribution to the study of psychotherapy was her focus on the nonmedical treatment of emotional as well as physical disturbances. Practitioners known as "scientists" use the power of the scriptures and prayers to heal both the physical and emotional aspects of a disturbance. They are secular healers, not to be confused with priests, clergy, or physicians. While every scientist is able to heal, the practitioner is the one who devotes her full time and energy to the work of healing. Mrs. Eddy's concept that the "sick are terrified by their sick beliefs" is the forerunner of the idea that you are affected psychologically by what you believe.

Today pastoral counselors use the power of faith. They focus on the removal of tension and anxiety which interferes with the person's ability to respond to faith. Thus they free the individual from the denials and blindness of his own concerns so that he may be able to receive the healing power of God. One of the early forerunners of the shift from physical to verbal methods, done within the framework of the church, was Jonathan Edwards. He was a Puritan clergyman who in the eighteenth century used verbal psychotherapeutic methods with some of the disturbed parishioners in his New England congregation. As we have seen here, each major step has been pointed out by some earlier practitioners on the scene.

Early in the nineteenth century, psychology as a science and discipline began to show an interest in abnormal aspects of behavior. Experimental psychologists were interested in the investigation of specific psychophysical aspects of human behavior. Their concern was for the understanding of reaction time, conscious thinking, visual perception, the organization of perception and thought, and neurophysiological correlates of behavior. Gradually, experimentalists became interested in the differences between normal and abnormal behavior. Hugo Munsterberg was trained in experimental psychology by Wilhelm Wundt in Germany and was brought to Harvard to teach this course. He became interested not only in the experimental aspects of psychology but in the practical aspects and applications in the areas of law and industry. He also became interested in psychotherapy and practiced as a psychotherapist. Psychologists continued to focus their interest during the later years of the nineteenth century and early twentieth century on the study of the ultimate nature of the mind and its place in nature. Until the middle of the twentieth century, psychology as a field had expressed but minimal interest in a clinical science devoted to individual cases and to the scientific study of psychotherapy.

The American psychiatrists now turned to what could be seen and measured, primarily neurology. As an example of the work, the idea of the exhaustion of the nervous system reached its final point with the concept of the "neurasthenic" syndrome. The clinical picture included the languid movements, "vapours," inability to work for extended periods of time, and the fashionable lassitude of the person involved. Involving the idea of the exhausted nervous system as a basis for this now posited a medical-physical basis for what had seemed to be an emotional disturbance, and rendered the treatment as a medical problem. As a consequence, to be "neurasthenic" became popular with certain segments of "high" society.

Beneath the neurological emphasis, however, there were strong movements toward the idea of functional disturbances, that is, disorders which were not the effects of disturbances in the nervous system. As a result of the work done by several people, the system known as psychobiology was presented by Adolph Meyer. He stated that the patient's symptoms, his thinking, and his behavior were reactions to life's stress and could be treated in that light.

A familiar name, Mesmer, provides a direct link between the work and contributions of the faith healers and modern psychotherapy. Mesmer's original ideas concerning animal magnetism have been discarded. However, the results cannot be so readily overlooked. Today we would say that the power of suggestion was the more important part of his treatment process, as was the faith of the patient in the magical effects of the procedures. Even though Mesmer was discredited and had to return to a rural medical practice, his work did not simply fade away. Dr. James Esdaile, an English surgeon, wrote a book on a series of successful surgical procedures performed in India in the middle of the nineteenth century using only "mesmeric anesthesia." He reported excellent results, including cases of major surgical procedures, in producing either a reduction or total absence of pain. Dr. John Elliotson, one of the first practitioners to use the stethoscope, also had used mesmerism during surgery and reported on the positive results. The medical profession did everything possible to discredit both Esdaile and Elliotson by using terms "liar" and "fraud." However the concept of the "transference of thought" which was an important part of the mesmeric approach became more and more an acceptable area for research. James Braid, an English physician in the nineteenth century, continued his own work despite official medical opposition, and initiated the idea of "nervous sleep" or "neurohypnotism." He was attacked by both the proponents of hypnotism and those against it. For a while hypnotism was called "Braidism" in Europe. Then in the 1840s under the study and influence of the French neurologist, Jean-Martin Charcot, hypnotism became both an acceptable area to be studied and a useful method for patients with emotional disturbances and symptoms. Whether hypnosis is primarily physiological or psychological in nature is still under exploration and there are strong believers on both sides.

Freud was an Austrian neurologist who studied under Charcot later in the nineteenth century. Impressed by a number of the things he saw and learned in France, Freud began working with the hypnotic method during the last years of the nineteenth century. From these experiences, and with the collaboration of J. Breuer, a fellow physician, Freud published a series of case studies. These included "On the Psychical Mechanism of Hysterical Phenomena" in 1893, and "Studies in Hysteria," later translated into English by the American psychiatrist, A. A. Brill, which included the celebrated case of Anna O. In these studies Freud indicated that there was something either "beneath" or "behind" the overt symptoms of an emotional disturbance. As he explored more and more the subjective feelings and thoughts of the individual patient, Freud began to investigate the contents of dreams and fantasies. This led him into the development of the system of personality investigation and therapy known as "psychoanalysis."

During the same period of time, there was another direction developing out of neurology and physiology. Ivan Sechenov, a Russian neurophysiologist, during the late nineteenth century worked on the idea of the body as a machine, with the nervous system as the central regulator. Another Russian, Ivan Pavlov, is the best known in this area of study and research. Spanning the late nineteenth and early twentieth centuries, he developed the idea of the "conditioned reflex" and incorporated this idea into the basic concepts of classical conditioning. These concepts have become the foundations for the school of psychotherapy known as behavior modification. Pavlov was interested in the studies of the action of the brain on a physiological rather than on a psychological basis. The results of his work spanned both areas. He also contributed the idea of a "second signal system" which in the human is language. This enables the human to be conditioned or programmed through the use of words as a stimulus. We have been conditioned to react without hesitation to words like "fire," "help," "danger," "watch out," and so forth. We have also been conditioned to respond in other ways to words like "mother," "lover," and "child," depending on the kind of early conditioning used.

Watsonian behaviorism is the school of behavior study developed by John Watson, an American psychologist, in the 1920s. He studied the overt measurable aspects of behavior and felt that all of personality was encompassed by what could be seen and measured. He rejected the idea of the "unconscious" and of motivation other than that which fit into his system. A better-known follower of this behavioristic approach is another American, B. F. Skinner. Skinner's ideas of modifying behavior focus on the reinforcement of the desired behavior by appropriate rewards. This method, known as "operant conditioning," is now becoming an important aspect of the psychotherapeutic approach of a segment of American psychologists and psychiatrists. There are a number of controversial aspects to the use of the behavior modification approach that we might discuss later. This approach has been less successful in influencing psychotherapy in Europe and Asia than in the United States.

In the twentieth century there has been a marked increase in the number of psychologists involved in both the theoretical and practical aspects of psychotherapy, starting with William James, Morton Prince, and G. Stanley Hall. More recently, the outstanding people have been Carl Rogers, Frederick Allen, Abraham Maslow, and Rollo May. These psychologists have continued the emphasis on research, innovations in practice, and exploration of new aspects of the field of psychotherapy. Psychiatrists William A. White and Harry Stack Sullivan founded and contributed greatly to the development of the interpersonal school of psychotherapy.

The field of applied psychology, known as clinical psychology, had focused primarily on intelligence testing and research during the decades preceding World War II. In the period during and after World War II, clinical psychology was given a strong push towards deeper involvement in psychotherapy. The combination of increased demand for services, both in and out of the armed forces, the small number of therapists available, and the improved training of psychologists were factors in this push. Today clinical psychologists are found on all levels in the practice of psychotherapy, both in private practice and in the hospital/clinic setting.

In recent years Abraham Maslow has contributed to a new orientation in American psychology and psychotherapy. He introduced the concept of the "third force" wherein the concern is for the patient as a person with unique subjective problems rather than either a machine or battleground for unresolved conflicts. Maslow combines the phenomenological emphasis on the "here and now" experience, the existential ideas of the purpose of life and man's search for a meaning to his existence, and the humanistic approach of man as the center of the experience and the importance of the relationship between humans. The other approaches he considered as either *mechanistic,* in that man is seen as a machine that needs to be put back into proper operating sequence, or *reductionistic,* in that man is broken down into small specific pieces, gatherings of habits, and learned rejections, to be reprogrammed back into a proper whole. He rejected both of these interpretations.

Let us introduce other areas of the world and the brief story of their developments in psychotherapy. The Japanese showed only a peripheral interest in psychology and psychoanalysis in the early part of the twentieth century. After World War II, however, Japanese psychological thinking was strongly influenced by American psychologists such as Carl Rogers and by some of their psychoanalytic ideas. In their haste to adopt things Western the Japanese rather uncritically took up what seemed to be accepted Western ideas of psychotherapy and psychological thought. At the same time that the client-centered approach was being investigated, another group of Japanese psychologists and psychiatrists were investigating Jung's ideas, particularly with respect to the emphasis on religion and mysticism. A recent development is Morita therapy which combines some aspects of Western-oriented psychotherapy, Zen philosophy, the emphasis on the individual as a social yet independent organism, and overtones of psychoanalysis. The Japanese are trying to work out their own particular approach to psychotherapy but have been hindered by their rush to adopt Western ideas. It may well turn out that some of Jung's ideas may be the most effective "link" between the Asian and Western approaches in psychotherapy.

In Russia dynamic psychotherapy developed slowly until Josef Stalin's death. Emphasis was placed on the importance of the state. There was a ban on Sigmund Freud and psychoanalytic ideas. Thus the emphasis was placed upon a Pavlovian and biological approach. Recently, while still opposed to Freud and many of his ideas, the Russians have indicated their acceptance of the unconscious as a force in understanding human behavior and as a part of the process of psychotherapy. Also, after many years of experience with the conditioning and biological approaches, the Russians have swung somewhat more towards dynamic aspects of psychotherapy. They now hold that the totality of human behavior can neither be explained nor explored and reconstituted by focusing only on the overt behavior/biological approach.

Germany offers psychotherapists little in the way of formal training. The psychotherapy that is done is based primarily on the ideas of Adler and Jung. From Adler, these would include the ideas of the will to power, lifestyle, compensation and overcompensation for inferiorities, the inferiority complex, and the life plan as therapy. From Jung came the ideas of the racial unconscious, religion as a creative force, symbolism, the idea of the extrovert-introvert approach to life, and the therapy/educational approach to learning to cope with one's problems in life. Kurt Koffka, Wolfgang Kohler, and Max Wertheimer presented the idea that the individual learns behavior in total units, and not by adding together or combining specific bits and pieces. They worked primarily in the areas of perception and conscious experience. They contributed the idea of insight, in that a person learns a task as a meaningful whole, and not in a dismembered, piecemeal manner. Despite the early contributions of the Gestalt group, there is not a strong Gestalt group in Germany.

From European philosophy comes a strong concern for the human condition, the questions of "Who am I?" and "What am I in

life?" and being and nonbeing. Viktor Frankl is a therapist concerned with the goal of human existence. He is involved with the
purpose and meaning of life to the individual. He sees his therapy as providing both an alternative and a supplement to other
methods of psychotherapy.

Now that we have some idea of how and where this all came
about, let us go on to the next question, "For whom is
psychotherapy?"

3

Psychotherapy for Whom?

There are two ideas that we often hear regarding the question of who ought to be in psychotherapy. On one hand there is a popular idea that everyone can benefit from psychotherapy. On the other hand, some people believe that anyone in psychotherapy is *crazy*—that the patient has had or is having a "nervous breakdown," is unable to function, and has to be put back together. Which of these points of view is valid? When either is taken as an absolute, it is misleading. Let's take each idea separately and see how it fits into the overall question of who becomes a patient.

Almost anyone can enrich his life by a variety of experiences. Thus any positive personal relationship has a beneficial effect. However, a person does not have to enter a psychotherapeutic situation in order to have an interpersonal relationship—a close, emotional involvement with one or more persons. If you think about your own experiences, you will recognize that therapeutic effects may be obtained from members of one's own family, friends, fellow workers and others. Psychotherapy usually involves an investment of energy, time, and money. A person who experiences satisfaction in his relationships with others and achieves success in his endeavors will not ordinarily need psychotherapy.

The meaning of "nervous breakdown" is usually unclear. The variety of reactions to which this label may be attached ranges from a person's being consistently tired to being unable to function at all. Taking either extreme we may see that psychotherapy, per se, may not be the treatment of choice. The "tiredness" may be a result of a physiological condition requiring only a change of working, sleeping, or eating habits. It can also be a symptom of depression. On the other hand the immobilized person may be so out of contact with reality that no interpersonal contact can be established. Psychotherapy can take place only when communication can be developed between two or more individuals. Regretfully there are still people who mistakenly believe that to seek psychological assistance may mean that they are weak or perhaps even insane. Although the stigma attached to psychological problems has not been completely erased, more and more people are willing to seek and benefit from psychotherapy.

Now to the issue of "For Whom?" Psychotherapy is for those who are unable to experience themselves as worthwhile individuals, who are unable to establish and to achieve realistic success in their endeavors, and/or to maintain mutually satisfying interpersonal relationships as a consequence of emotional conflicts or personality disturbances. To help understand these conditions, perhaps some clarification is in order. What does it mean to experience oneself as worthwhile? This condition exists when a person feels that there is purpose and value to his existence—when he experiences adequate fulfillment from an activity in which he participates. Often we hear of someone being labeled as having "an identity crisis." This person usually cannot adjust to uncertainty or trust himself or others. He is uncertain as to who he is, where he is going, or why. He continually questions why he was put on this earth. Although he may be able to follow through with other people's expectations and assignments, he can rarely, if ever, take the initiative or "think for himself." This lack of self-assurance and self-determination is an example of a person who does not see himself as a total person or experience himself as worthwhile.

The inability of a person to achieve success in his endeavors may occur in one or more areas of his living experiences. Difficulties in learning and other forms of intellectual functioning may be a consequence of emotional conflict. A distressing problem for some parents is to have a bright child who does poorly and is a constant underachiever in school. Conferences with a teacher and educational testing indicate that the child has the capacity for working at an above average level, but he just doesn't produce at that level. Often psychological evaluation will reveal that the child's failure is the expression of an emotional problem, rather than an intellectual deficit. Sometimes educational problems are the only means bright children have of expressing hostile feelings towards parents or other significant authority figures. A need to maintain a dependency relationship may result in the child's demonstration of his "helplessness." The psychotherapeutic approaches in such a situation may include both parents and child in the treatment program. The parents' goal may be to resolve their need to hold onto the child by fostering ineffectual functioning. The child needs to remove the conflict between the natural growth process and the desire to remain dependent. Thus he will be able to find more constructive means of achieving approval, rather than blunting his emotional and intellectual development. A psychotherapeutic approach fosters the development of better communication and a sharing of responsibility between parents and child.

The problem of succeeding in a work experience may be illustrated by the following life history of a fifty-year-old business man: Harry R. is a hard-working, talented business executive who has spent the last thirty years of his life striving for success. At least six times during this period he has been on the verge of financial success. However, each time at the critical moment he has made decisions that have led to catastrophic results and eventual failure. Experiences of severe depression have appeared after each failure and these finally pressured him into psychotherapy. The repetitiveness of his behavior patterns suggested a direct relationship between the "smell of success" and his self-defeating actions. Exploration of his emotional development revealed a continual need to fail. In order to conceal his own emotional involvement, Harry R. had always convinced himself that his failures were due to external conditions or "bad luck." It was as if the "gods" were against him. After a period of treatment, Harry R. began to realize that the connection between his self-defeating behavior and the depressions involved his own emotional needs. As he developed the ability to accept his responsibility in determining his life pattern, he became more effective in using his talents to achieve his desired goals.

The inability to find satisfaction or experience happiness in interpersonal relationships is often a signal of emotional problems. An individual's personality develops over the years and shapes his thinking and his emotional and behavior patterns. The person who develops a sense of security and a good self-image in his early formative years is usually able to adapt more readily to stressful changes during later years. On the other hand those who harbor a sense of inadequacy tend to seek out and attach themselves to situations and people who provide them with a feeling of being worthwhile, a feeling which they are unable to attain on their own. An illustration of this pattern is the experience of a middle-aged woman, widowed for two years. Mrs. Mary S. had been married to a professional man who became ill soon after their marriage. As long as the husband needed her care, she had a *raison d'être,* a meaning to her life. The birth and rearing of a son gave her a temporary sense of accomplishment. The child grew up and the mother attempted to hold onto him by moving to the town where he attended college. The son completed his education and married. At this point the husband died suddenly. The mother tried to overcome the traumatic effect of her husband's death by developing a more possessive attitude towards her son. She began "to do small things for him," such as buying his clothes. Her attempt to attach herself to him was resented by her daughter-in-law, with whom a conflict ensued. At this time, the son's job seemed to require his moving from the East to the West Coast. The timing of this move away from the mother raises the question as to whether the job relocation was purely coincidental.

The loss of her husband and the separation from her son left Mrs. S. feeling lost. She began to develop symptoms of a pulmonary condition for which her physician could find no physiological basis. He advised her to "get away" and she began to travel. She toured the Orient and took a Caribbean cruise to meet people. However, she was preoccupied with thoughts and feelings of being deprived by the death of her husband and the behavior of her son. Clinging contacts with others resulted in a failure to form satisfying relationships, increasing her feelings of frustration and deprivation.

The increased feelings of loneliness and isolation and the failure to find a dependent person to substitute for the dead husband and the departed son forced her back to her family physician. Recognizing the existence of an emotional problem, he recommended a psychological consultation. Although she was unable to recognize the nature of her problem, she was willing to follow the physician's advice.

Psychotherapy was used by Mrs. Mary S. to explore her rigid dependent way of living. She was helped to recognize and use her intellectual and social potentials. With appropriate therapeutic support she developed a sense of security and realistic feelings of self-worth by successfully putting her potentials into action. Her successful utilization of psychotherapy has placed her in a position of replacing ineffectual dependency attachments with mutually satisfying relationships.

From our discussion we may readily see that personality disturbances of persons who may benefit from psychotherapy are exhibited in different areas of functioning. The severity of the problem or disturbance, however, may be quite blatant in the behavior exhibited or may be concealed by the person's behavior. There is little doubt as to the severity of the personality disturbance in a person who believes himself to be Napoleon, or who believes he can perform magical feats such as flying through the air without the aid of mechanical means.

A less obvious manifestation of a personality disturbance might be termed a "good girl" syndrome. The underlying dynamics of this behavior pattern have been observed in both females and males of various backgrounds. Sophie A., a thirty-two-year-old single Protestant, described dissatisfaction with most of her activities and involvements. Although she had achieved relative success in her professional career, she was unable to accept her role in a supervisory capacity. She was bright, but experienced herself as being intellectually inferior. Her social relationships were generally good. However, as she became more intimately involved she always developed the feeling that the other person (male or female) was "using her," that she was being abusively exploited to gratify "their selfish needs." Whether at work or play she eventually experienced herself as being "put down." She felt that others, rather than appreciating and reciprocating, saw her warmth and giving nature as "weakness," and would accept her only if she unconditionally submitted to their demands. She had

had several sexual affairs during her adult life and had been engaged three times. Each of these relationships had a disastrous ending. When she felt ready to get married, the man would terminate the relationship; if the man pushed for marriage, she always found some reason for dissolving the relationship. The repetitive format of her love life might fit into the old concept of "I'm really not good enough for someone worthwhile. If they want *me*, there must be something awfully wrong with *them.*"

In exploring her personality development and the significant people involved, Sophie A. began to become aware that her value system was identical to her mother's. This awareness proved traumatic for it appeared paradoxical to her. To Sophie, her mother symbolized everything negative in a woman and she was always determined to be different from "Mother." To illustrate this determination, Sophie A. described how her mother rejected sex, even to the point of refusing to sleep with her father. On the other hand Sophie A. had allowed herself "the pleasures of sexual intercourse" since her early twenties. During psychotherapy, there appeared a confession that she did not always experience pleasure in her sexual activities. "It seemed that whenever I felt secure in a relationship and considered really getting married, I would freeze up sexually. As I think of it, this was the beginning of the end of our relationship . . . " Further exploration of her fantasies brought out that she could enjoy sex only when there was an absence of "love and affection" for the man. She associated these feelings with her mother's attitude that "only tramps" had sexual drives and enjoyed having intercourse. Sex was an obligation in marriage and had to be tolerated in order to have children. "Good girls" had neither strong sexual drives nor enjoyed intercourse. Having unconsciously adopted her mother's value system, she experienced sexual drives in association with feelings of being a tramp. Thus she was able to gratify her sexual desires only with men who would not marry. Whenever she developed a warm, loving relationship, she began to experience extreme guilt and, as a result, "froze."

Recognizing that she had internalized her mother's value system, Sophie A. was then in a better position to work through her former dependency ties to her mother. She let go of her formerly held antiquated value system and developed values based on her conscious, rational understanding of reality. Further analysis of the relationship between her self-concept and her behavior (emotional and overt actions) allowed her to change her total living pattern. She began to use her intellectual abilities in an effective manner. Her interpersonal relationships with others became more and more fulfilling. She then was able to bring her desire for marriage to fruition.

The question now arises as to what signs or signals a person might pick up that would suggest the need for evaluation and possible psychotherapy. As we look at this situation we might realize that most people are perceptive in recognizing emotional disturbance in others, such as members of their family, friends, fellow workers, and so forth. However we also find that people frequently fail to recognize these signs in themselves. Hesitancy to admit that something is "wrong" acts to prevent a person from seeking help. This limitation is related to the false belief that to seek aid to overcome emotional conflicts or personality problems may mean that one is "insane."

A few examples have been given showing who may benefit from psychological treatment. The number of symptoms suggesting the need for evaluation and possible psychotherapy is too numerous to elaborate in a single volume or chapter. However there are a number of frequent, although not always obvious, signs which are important and should be mentioned. Difficulties in learning and other intellectual functioning and dissatisfaction with oneself have, in part, already been described. Included here are people who suffer from feelings of inferiority. There is an old sad joke about the individual who sought help because of what he considered an "inferiority complex." After professional evaluation he was informed, "Sir, you do not have an inferiority complex, you *are* inferior!" To cope with the problem of "inferiority" would be to help the indiviudal to develop the greatest use of his potential and capacities. However, there are many people who actually perform relatively well but continue to experience themselves as "never doing well enough." The standards which they have set for themselves usually turn out to be higher than their performances. There are also those who demonstrate a significant difference between their functioning ability and their potential. In considering people of your acquaintance you can likely select that bright capable person whose performance never quite measures up to what might be anticipated from him.

In looking around, one recognizes that *success* is a persistent value in our society. On occasion our achievements do fall short of our desired goals and expectations. There are those, however, who consistently are unable to exert appropriate effort to carry through the desired or assigned tasks. These failures are often the result of debilitating emotional conflicts. Some people have a *fear of success* related to a foreboding of the demands and responsibilities that often accompany the ability *to do*. Because of a need to punish themselves, hurt others by disappointing them or, at times, to reinforce or prove their *ineptness* some people tend to engage in what may be labeled as *self-defeating behavior*. An example of this behavior is the person who continually forces the bolt an extra turn, stripping the threads and thereby spoiling all his efforts. Others engage in what Jack Krasner has termed "defeat by default." Have you ever noticed how some people almost always avoid facing opposition or undertaking a competitive task? They use the rationalization that they do not want to get into a useless argument or that the rewards are not worth the effort. Usually these individuals are trying to avoid the anxiety that results from expected defeat. However, the absence of real effort actually results in the failure that the person attempts to avoid, that is, defeat by default. Perfectionistic tendencies—"Am I doing the right thing?" or "Is this good enough?"—are attempts to prevent or to relieve anxiety which results in the wasteful expenditure of energy. Rather than completing an activity which has been undertaken, the individual has become overly involved in his need to attain approval.

Unnecessary unhappiness as well as the failure to experience the joys and sometimes exhilarations from personal satisfaction frequently result from a person's inability to establish and maintain an emotionally involved relationship with others. The conscious and unconscious feelings related to these disturbances are many. They may include feelings of inadequacy or the feelings of having "nothing of value" to offer another person, concern about being taken advantage of unfairly (abused) by others, the fear of being falsely accused and blamed whenever a disagreement arises, or anxiety related to the possibility of hurting or causing someone else pain. The fear of involvement and approaching others may often be denied, resulting in feelings of being left out or not liked. Emotional conflicts may also be displayed in recurrent persistent feelings of hate and contempt for others. To hate and have contempt justifies avoidance and protects one from the fear of approaching another person. These antagonistic feelings may also result in destructive, competitive drives and sometimes overt aggressive actions. There is the fear that to accept one's own destructive or hostile feelings may result in "something bad happening." Thus the individual avoids involved personal relationships and in so doing protects himself from his fear of these destructive drives.

Two extreme behavior patterns warrant psychological evaluation and psychotherapy. Both patterns involve the individual's inability to control his actions or thinking. In one instance, we have the impulse ridden person whose feelings or thoughts are immediately put into action without prior evaluation or consideration of consequence. Impulsiveness should be differentiated from spontaneity. Spontaneity refers to an individual's freedom to respond (to select from a variety of options or choices) without feeling oppressed or "tied up." Impulsiveness, on the other hand, is the *spilling out* of the experienced feeling or thought with no choice or controls. Impulsive behavior may range anywhere from uncontrolled histrionics to indiscriminate or promiscuous sexual activity. At the other end of the continuum we may find the extremely inhibited person who has severe difficulty in putting any thought or feeling into action. An illustration of the latter is the young woman who condemns sexual activity as "dirty and repulsive," as a means of justifying her inability to put her own strong sexual desires into action.

The ability to consider and evaluate the appropriateness of thoughts, feelings, and actions may be a positive sign of health. However, when persistent deliberation and doubt take the place of or prevent action, the psychological status of the person is in doubt. Any persistent pattern of behavior which interferes with the effective functioning of the individual may as a rule of thumb be taken as a sign of emotional disturbance that warrants professional evaluation. As already indicated, these patterns may be exhibited in undue impulsiveness, obsessiveness, and/or compulsion.

Questions related to various aspects of sleep often are raised as indications of emotional health and disturbances. The amount of sleep required varies from individual to individual and may even vary within the same person at different times. However, sleep is necessary for the physical as well as psychological well-being of the individual. Therefore, disruption or prevention of the required amount of sleep may be considered a sign of a problem. Where no environmental or physiological factors are involved, we usually find that the inability to benefit effectively from sleep is caused either by not being able to sleep (insomnia), or by sudden or continued awakening during the night and/or nightmares. Why we dream and the meaning of dreams will be discussed later. However, it may be helpful to bear in mind a rule of thumb regarding disruptive sleeping patterns—hostility prevents one from falling asleep; anxiety interferes with the healthful sleeping process. Consideration of these ideas may help you in evaluating whether professional psychological aid is needed.

The loss of a dear friend or family member as a result of separation or death brings about uncomfortable feelings of sadness or mourning. These feelings are usually most appropriate and are related to the feelings of loss of an important person. However, if the feelings develop into persistent depression, one might suspect the presence of emotional conflicts or personality disturbance. The same consideration applies when a person experiences persistent or frequent periods of loneliness without appropriate reason. There are occasions when a person desires or chooses to be alone in order to do something important for himself. Being or feeling alone when separated from others is quite different from the experience of loneliness or being alone even if in a crowd or with others. These latter feelings usually result from emotional isolation or the feeling that no one really cares.

An often occurring although not an obvious symptom of emotional disturbance is having frequent accidents. There are people who consistently, although seemingly inadvertently, find themselves involved in accidents. A typical example is the young woman who over a period of years seemed to have "the worst of luck." Walking across the floor of a nightclub she slipped and broke her ankle. While placing garbage in a sunken container she succeeded in putting a hole in her leg. While mowing the lawn she severed and almost lost a finger. During psychotherapy her injuries appeared to be more than purely accidental. More intensive exploration was undertaken. Descriptions of the patient's activities and related feelings prior to and at the time of the "accidents" revealed the presence of guilt feelings. She was aware of some but not all of these feelings. Each accident became a means of punishing herself to make up for the guilt she suffered. As she became aware of the relationship between guilt and the accidents the patient took advantage of the opportunity to evaluate her difficulty. She learned that guilt and self-condemnation had become automatic reactions to "unapproved" behavior. Understanding the meaning of this conflict and finding more realistic values allowed her to cope more effectively with self-created pressures. The occurrences of unwarranted guilt feelings became less and less frequent. On the rare occasions when these feelings did appear she was able to face and cope with them on a more realistic basis, rather than punishing herself by bringing about an accident.

There are also occasions when a person continues to be involved in accidents where other persons suffer bodily or property damage. Several unconscious motivating factors may be considered. There are two common reasons. First, this activity may be a means of self-punishment in which the individual creates an objective way of doing penance for persistent internalized guilt feelings. The internalized guilt is dealt with by becoming involved in an accident and the individual is then able to lessen his anxiety by compensating others financially. The second unconscious motivating force may be hostile feelings which the person cannot accept. Unable to accept these feelings, he acts out his unconscious wishes by getting into accidents.

Over 70 percent of the patients crowding physicians' offices and hospital rooms have physical symptoms or maladies which are directly or indirectly related to emotional disturbances. Often there is a misunderstanding and sometimes confusion of two psychological terms regarding physical symptoms, *psychogenic* and *psychosomatic*. *Psychogenic* symptoms are those of a physiological nature with no apparent organic basis or cause. Can you recall when, as a child, you would awake with an excruciating headache or severe stomach pain and around noontime these would disappear? Perhaps some time later you or someone else connected these physical symptoms to a test or some other unpleasant school situation which you wished to avoid.

The following is a composition written by a fourth grade student in response to the teacher's request to write about the things the pupils worry about:

WHAT I WORRY ABOUT

I worry about schoolwork because I do not know if the papers are going to turn out right or wrong. When I get more than three answers wrong I get sharp pains in my stomach, and when I get one or two wrong, or all right, I am glad. My brain does not mind school at all. It's my stomach that hates it!

It is common for adults to carry over from childhood the use of physical symptoms to avoid facing an unpleasant situation, or as a reaction to emotional conflicts which the individual is unable to cope with effectively. Often these physical signs may not be quite so dramatic. Some people experience ever-present feelings of tiredness or sleepiness even though they have gotten sufficient rest the night before and no organic illness is present. You may recall that man or woman who always seemed to fall asleep whenever a frustrating or other anxiety-provoking situation occurred. Sleep in these instances becomes a "cop-out," a means of withdrawing and hopefully either preventing or avoiding anxiety.

Psychosomatic illnesses are those with actual physical signs or changes which are initiated, triggered, or intensified by emotional conflicts. An example of these maladies may be peptic ulcers or other digestive problems which result from persistent hyperacidity. In these cases ulceration is an eating away of body tissues by an overabundance of hydrochloric acid within the body. The overproductive rather than the normal acid condition may result from disturbances related to emotional pressures which the individual cannot effectively handle. Some dental problems may result from hyperacidity within the mouth or other malfunctioning which, in turn, is related to the emotional status of the individual. Some allergic reactions may also be related to psychosomatic problems. Although the allergy itself may be congenital (potentiality present at birth), the resistance to the allergic reaction is dependent upon the emotional state of the person. You may have known people with hay fever who react differently at various times even though the pollen count might be the same. The difference, as already indicated, is not due to the pollen count but is affected by the individual's expectations and emotional state. Another common area of psychosomatic difficulty involves dermatological problems or symptomatic conditions of the skin.

In our discussion of who becomes a patient, we have mentioned some of the more obvious as well as lesser symptoms which warrant professional evaluation to determine if psychotherapy might be the treatment of choice. However, more evident signs of emotional or personality disturbances should also be mentioned. Hallucination, which may be visual, auditory, olfactory, or even tactile, is one. In these instances, the individual may see visions of things or persons which in reality do not exist, hear voices when there are no auditory stimuli, smell odors which do not exist, or experience physical pounding on his body when he is not being touched. Actual feelings of losing touch with reality are also ineffective means of coping with internal or environmental pressures. Here we may have feelings of *loss of identity* (dissolving of one's own personality related to the *who, what,* and *why* of the "I"), depersonalization (loss of sense of reality as to oneself and, at times, of others—the extreme being the amnesia victim), or grandiosity. The latter may be shown by a feeling of omniscience (having infinite knowledge as well as the ability to see all) or omnipotence (unlimited authority, ability, and power). Although relatively rare, there are people who experience and portray themselves as having "X-ray eyes," or being Jesus Christ.

Perhaps one of the greatest difficulties that some people have is to differentiate between fear and anxiety, and to know whether these reactions are healthy self-preservation or unhealthy feelings unrelated to reality. Fear may be defined as apprehension and caution in situations perceived as dangerous. The development of apprehension and caution towards dangers which may result in injury or death is important and necessary. Children must learn to avoid running in front of automobiles or jumping off high buildings by personal experience or from others. Even though such adventures might appear to be exciting, the development of fears in these and similar situations increases the likelihood of survival. However, if the emotional reaction progresses to the point where the individual is unable to cross the street or to walk down stairs in the absence of real danger, then his ability to function is curtailed, resulting in a miserable life.

Anxiety is related to fear of *anticipated* events which are experienced as threats to the individual. Here again, anxiety may be classified as healthy or unhealthy, depending upon its intensity as well as what the person does about it. Taking a final examination in a required college course may determine whether an individual is able to pursue his professional aspirations. Thus the anticipated results would naturally cause some concern. An emotionally healthy individual would recognize the sign of approaching danger. He would review his notes and other material which would increase his chances of doing well on the examination. The emotionally unhealthy person, on the other hand, might develop anxiety to a point of immobilization. Thus rather than preparing himself to meet the threatening situation he would find himself overburdened and unable to function effectively.

Now that some clarification has been offered with regard to who might become a patient, there is another important question which arises. Recognizing that there are certain signs that something is amiss and that you ought to do something about it, what do you do? Whom do you see? How do you go about finding the *right* person for you? Are there ways of evaluating a psychotherapist? Is one psychotherapist different from another or are they all the same? Do all psychotherapists work as well with everyone or is there a *best* person for a specific problem? Or is the real question "Who is the person most effective for you?"

4 Theories of Personality Development and Psychotherapeutic Procedures

The concept of simplicity has a magnetic quality because it offers a sense (although sometimes false) of security. Thus people seek to "cubbyhole" concepts, objects, and people in order to experience the comfort of "knowing where they belong." Although this tendency may result in misleading stereotypes, the professional as well as the general public has tended to label the psychologist-psychotherapist according to the type of therapy he practices. The classification may or may not adequately describe the theoretical education, training, and clinical practice of the therapist. For example, one may be labeled "psychoanalytically oriented therapist," "reality therapist," or "behavior therapist." It is hoped that these classifications adequately describe the therapist's major theoretical orientation regarding psychological issues. These issues include specific theories about development of the individual's personality and the therapist's preferred psychotherapeutic approach.

The foundation of any psychotherapeutic procedure is usually a theory of personality. This theory encompasses the process by which learning takes place and behavior patterns develop. Most people have their own conception of a theory of personality, that is, what a person is really like. Such a concept permits an individual to assign characteristics to the people he meets and helps him to predict their behavior under varied conditions.

Psychologists construct theories of personality, that is, sets of assumptions about human behavior accompanied by a group of empirical definitions of data concerning that behavior. These data are based on observation and experiment. People's individual concepts are highly subjective and colored by their own experiences, values, feelings, and attitudes. Psychologists attempt to make statements about what people are like and how they arrived at their behavior pattern based on formally stated sets of logical assumptions about human behavior and its development. Such theories enable psychologists to make predictions adequate to cope with a wide variety of human behavior. An important consideration is that different theories may focus on different aspects of human behavioral experiences. Calvin Hall and Gardner Lindzey have described over fifty definitions of "personality." One working definition of "personality" may be described as that which integrates a person's experience of behavior and helps him to adapt to his environment.

Once having selected a theoretical orientation that is a basis for the development of intellectual, emotional, and physical activity, procedures and techniques may then be devised to modify or eliminate activity in any of these areas. Theory and technique of psychotherapy are not synonymous. Nor is each technique exclusively utilized by therapists of a single theoretical orientation. For example, a history of the patient's life may be obtained in different ways by different therapists. Many psychotherapists spend most of the initial session in securing historical information about the patient. Some even require the patient to complete a detailed questionnaire regarding his past and such persons closely related to him as parents and siblings. Other therapists obtain these historical data by having the patient relate present activities to the past. There are some therapists who believe that the past is irrelevant and focus on the "here and now." The information acquired also may be used selectively in an effort to achieve different goals.

A brief description of some of the theories of personality may help to clarify these differences.

The idea that emotional problems have their origin in the individual's early psychological development has been widely studied within several accepted theories. These theories are the psychoanalytical view of emotional difficulties, arising from Freudian concepts (Freud, Adler, Jung, Horney, Fromm, Erikson), social learning or behaviorist concepts (Hull, Pavlov, Dollard,

Miller, Skinner), and Gestalt or perceptual concepts (Perls, Meyer). Recent transactional analysis explanations have examined possible alternative causation within family and interpersonal interactions (Berne, Spiegel).

Other current therapeutic approaches that draw from several philosophies include client-centered therapy (Rogers), rational-emotive therapy (Ellis), cognitive therapy (Beck), and logotherapy (Frankl).

Psychodynamic concepts have evolved from psychoanalytic theory. Freud, the founder of psychoanalysis, conceived the first theory of personality as a developmental process of successive stages of psychosexual growth. The psychoanalytic concept proposes that personality is composed of three interacting systems— the id, the ego, and the superego. Each of these systems has specific functions as well as various other characteristics. The individual's behavior usually results from the interaction among these systems. One system rarely functions alone to the exclusion of the others.

The id is the primal system which continues to function throughout life and from which the ego and superego are developed. The id, which supplies the power for all of the systems, is composed of psychological and inherited traits. Its activity is primarily related to the body functions. Since it is essentially a part of the inner world the id has no direct contact with outer reality. The system serves to discharge tension, or energy, which then returns the body to a state of equilibrium and comfort. This is referred to as the pleasure principle. This principle consists of two processes—innate automatic reflex action and primary process. An example of innate automatic reflex action is the sucking response of infants when the lips are stimulated. In the primary process, the id forms a memory picture of the object that will relieve the prior tension. This is the id's only link to reality.

The ego comes into being because the needs of the individual require a transition into reality. The ego is able to distinguish between fantasy and reality. The ego tends to obey the reality principle by utilization of secondary processes which prevent the release of tension until the needed object is found. The secondary process is the realistic thinking which can delay and plan for the satisfaction of the need. The ego is the organized portion of the id which integrates the id, superego, and the external world. The ego functions carry out the aims of the id, while acting as a mediator between the purely pleasurable needs of the id and the reality expectations of the environment. In other words, the ego is responsible for the survival of the individual and thus the ego serves as a bridge between the inner self of the individual and the outside world.

The superego, which includes the conscience, is the last system to develop and contains the initial network of morals and standards for the individual. The superego consists of the traditional value judgments and ideas which have been taken over and incorporated from the parents. Value judgments and standards tend to be ideal rather than realistic. As a result the goal is perfection instead of pleasure. This system consists of two parts: (1) the experiencing of guilt as a result of inappropriate action, thoughts or feelings, and (2) the feeling of pride which is a reward when performing in an ego ideal direction. The superego inhibits the impulses of the id. It may cause the ego to perform moral goals rather than realistic ones. With the development and formation of the superego system, self-control replaces the parental control. A healthy superego allows enjoyment, however, while maintaining the expected societal mores.

In orthodox psychoanalytic thinking, psychic energy is considered to be that energy which is used for psychological activity. There is the belief that physiological energy can be transformed into psychic energy as well as the reverse. The id with its instincts is believed to form the bridge between the two types of energy. In this case an instinct such as sexual drives may be viewed as an inborn psychological representation of an inner somatic, or bodily, source of excitation. The instinct is thus represented both psychologically by wish, and bodily by a need. So an instinctual drive, which Freud referred to as a cathexis, possesses four characteristic features: (1) the source is the bodily need, (2) the aim is removal of the bodily excitation, (3) the object is the activity which occurs between the appearance of the need and its fulfillment, (4) the impetus is the intensity of the need which determines the force of the strength. If the exact object is not found a substitute or displacement may be used. This substitute activity is called an instinct derivation. Freud grouped instincts into two general headings: (1) life instincts, or survival and propagation, and (2) death instincts, or those leading to destruction. He believed in death consistency, which means all living processes eventually return to the stability of the inorganic world.

The energy within the body is originally contained within the id. It goes from the id to the ego when the mental representation is matched with physical reality. The ego, in touch with the outside world, uses restraining forces called anticathexis to keep the id in line. Thus, conflicts within a personality structure are provoked when there is opposition between the urging cathexis and the restricting anticathexis.

There are three types of anxiety which are considered within psychoanalytic principles. Reality anxiety is a reaction related to the real dangers in the world. Neurotic anxiety is related to the fear that the instincts will get out of control and cause a person to do something for which he will be punished. Moral anxiety is related to conforming to the standards and values of the superego, that is, the fear of conscience. Anxiety is a warning signal that unless some measures are taken the ego will be overthrown. If the ego is unable to mediate effectively between the forces of the id and reality, the ego resorts to defense mechanisms as a means of self-preservation. These mechanisms operate unconsciously to delay, falsify, or distort reality.

The individual's personality develops in response to four major sources of tension: (1) physiological growth processes, (2) frustrations, (3) conflicts, and (4) threats. The individual must learn methods of reducing the tension. This learning is the process of personality development which may be accomplished by identification and displacement. Identification is the taking over of another person's value system and making it part of one's own. The individual learns to reduce tension by modeling his behavior after that of someone else. The people chosen are those who are experienced or seem to be better able to gratify their needs. The child may identify with his parents because they seem omnipotent to him.

As the child continues to grow he finds others whose ways are more closely linked with his current wishes. Thus he may adopt their value system as well as emulate their way of thinking and behaving. Displacement, on the other hand, occurs when a cathexis is blocked by internal or external forces and a new object must be found that will reduce the tension. The tension-reducing ability of this displacement depends upon its resemblance to the original object and whether or not it is sanctioned by society. The ability to form substitutes is the most powerful mechanism in the development of personality.

As already described, Freud's concept of human development is deterministic. He believed that everyone progresses through a predetermined series of developmental stages. The first few years are the most decisive in the development of character structure. The first four to six years, referred to as the preoedipal period, are divided into the oral, anal, and phallic stages. Following the oedipal phase there is a period of latency until pubescence (age thirteen), which is the beginning of adolescence.

The oral stage extends from birth until the child is approximately one-and-one-half years of age. The child's major gratification is derived from stimulation within and around the mouth. The development of many character traits has been attributed to sucking, biting, and swallowing. Pleasures originally experienced from these activities may lead to future pleasures related to acquiring knowledge and possessions. A person who has failed to progress successfully through this stage may be gullible— he will swallow almost anything he is told. Unresolved biting and oral aggression may later be displaced by sarcasm and argumenta- tiveness. Obviously the infant is totally dependent upon the mothering figure during this stage. The feelings of dependency are reinforced by the nursing and protectiveness received during this stage of development. These feelings remain throughout life and may be released when the person feels insecure. Thus the seeking of warmth from physical contact or gratification from food, preferably sweet, is common when a person is emotionally distressed or disturbed.

The anal stage occurs during the second and third years of life. The primary source of erotic gratification is in the anal area. The child receives pleasure from releasing accumulated waste through the sphincter muscles. Toilet training is the self- regulation of an instinct. Postponing the pleasure that is derived from releasing this tension, the child learns that he is able to control his own body. The parental attitude toward toilet training and specific methods used also affect the formation of traits and values within the child. For example, if the parent is overly demanding the child may retaliate by holding back his feces and thus become constipated. If this reaction is generalized the person may develop a retentive character and become stubborn and stingy. Under the strain of oppressive measures the child may expel his feces at the most inopportune times. This pattern may result in the individual developing explosive traits such as cruelty, destructiveness, and temper tantrums. As can be demonstrated in societies and nations, continued oppression of one's basic needs or natural human inclinations ultimately and inevitably leads to rage and violence. On the other hand, if the parent rewards and praises the child for successes in self-regulation, the child may develop the feeling that his efforts in this activity are important. Creativity and productivity may develop as a result of these feelings.

The phallic stage extends from the end of the anal period until the child is approximately four to six years of age. During this period the major erotic sensations are experienced in the genital area. The child develops sexual and aggressive feelings in relation to the functions of the genital organs. In conjunction with plea-surable sensations and experience from masturbatory activity and fantasy life, the oedipus complex appears. The child develops a sexual cathexis, that is, an attachment to the parent of the opposite sex. The child has a strong desire to possess this parent and to remove the parent of his own sex. Hostile feelings develop in reaction to the threat of competition. These feelings may be expressed in the child's fantasies during masturbatory activities and dreams. They may also be expressed in alternating acts of love and rebelliousness towards the parents. The oedipus complex is brought to a halt in usual psychological development by the repression of sex drives. This repression serves as a means of avoiding anticipated, irreversible injury such as castration or even annihilation by the parent of the same sex with whom the child is competing in fantasy. In an effort to avoid this most undesirable end the child identifies with the threatening parental figure and represses sexual drives.

The repression of sexual drives ushers in a latency period. During this stage of development the child's energies are directed toward intellectual and physical growth. It is a period during which the child learns to master his environment in terms of acquiring academic skills, learning to relate to peers, and establishing sexual identification. This latency period is later interrupted by the upsurge of pubescence. Those individuals who have successfully resolved the conflicts arising in the earlier stages of development will enter into the genital stage of development. This final stage may be viewed as the open road to emotional, social, sexual, and intellectual maturity. For those individuals who have retained unresolved needs related to the earlier stages of development, pubescence may provoke conflicts leading to the individual's developing self-restricting and self-limiting defense mechanisms.

Freud believed that pathological conflicts arose when there was a battle between two forces which were on different levels. For example, one force may have reached the level of the preconscious or the conscious part of the mind while the other force was still confined to the unconscious level. As long as the forces remain on different levels the conflicts never have a final outcome. Thus Freud considered the sole task of psychotherapy as aiding the patient to bring the unconscious force into the consciousness so that the conflicting forces might confront one another on the same ground. This process of raising the repression is accomplished by extending the unconscious into consciousness. First the existence of the repression is discovered and then the resistance which maintains this repression is removed. By eliminating the conditions which provoke symptom formation, the neurotic conflict may be exchanged for a healthy one and the individual is then in a position to resolve it. There are many factors and techniques which may be used in the analytic process.

A unique process recognized by Freud and utilized in the psychoanalytic process is that of transference. In the transference relationship the patient endows the therapist with feelings, character traits, and other attributes which were originally possessed by a significant figure in the patient's past. The endowed set of characteristics and attributes is not necessarily restricted to one significant person, but may vary from one person to another. For example, at one time the patient may experience the analyst as his mother and at another the analyst may be experienced as his father. The transferential process reveals information regarding the early experiences of the patient with varying significant figures in his life which may not be transmitted in any other way. Free association and dream analysis and interpretation are also methods which are used for the discovery and removal of repression. They serve to fill in the individual's memory gaps and enable the patient to exchange neurotic conflicts for normal ones.

The disciples and followers of Freud varied widely in their loyalty to the Freudian theory. Some maintained Freud's basic ideas and sought further clarity for them. Some made efforts towards expanding Freud's concepts into other areas of thinking. For example, Erik Erikson translated Freud's psychosexual developmental stages into eight social-developmental ages of man. Erikson believed that there are critical periods of development in which an individual demonstrates his particular ego strength at the given stage. This is indicated by the individual's ability to integrate the structure of the social, forces around him. For example, the first phase is the oral-sensory in which the conflict is basic trust versus mistrust. The development of trust results from the infant's first social achievement derived from his willingness to allow the mother out of sight without undue anxiety or rage. The child is able to do this because of an inner certainty as well as an outer predictability of the mother's return. The other phases of development include the following: muscular-anal-autonomy versus shame and doubt; loco motor-genital-initiative versus guilt; latency-industry versus inferiority; puberty and adolescence; identity versus role confusion; young adulthood-intimacy versus isolation; adulthood-generativity versus stagnation; maturity-ego integrity versus despair.

Some of Freud's disciples left the fold because of differences over the concepts related to personality development and the development of neurotic conflict. Alfred Adler was the first to develop a theory of personality, pathology, and treatment which was an alternative to Freud's. Although revolutionary for his day, Freud was scientifically conservative in that he firmly believed that the patient's inner psychological world was ultimately determined by objective causes that rested in his past. Adler proclaimed that the inner psychological world of the individual was not objectively caused, but was ultimately the individual's own creation. The individual's course of life received its directions from highly subjective goals and values. Adler's concept might be understood in terms of man's need to feel adequate. His strivings are oriented within the social context to make himself look better to others. The manner in which he does this is unique. Each person has a unique method of doing things, his own lifestyle. According to Adler the need for adequacy is the sole driving force in man. This drive is based on the biology of the individual. The outward appearance of the drive reflects modification by the particular experiences of the individual. Therefore man makes himself what he is. He is goal directed. The goal may be healthy or unhealthy. The individual's lifestyle can be either adaptive or maladaptive.

Adler believed that maladjustment resulted from the increased feelings of inferiority and related needs for compensation. The individual may be described as having underdeveloped social interests. He is likely to have an exaggerated and uncooperative goal of superiority. Usually he is a person with a mistaken lifestyle. Also he is an individual who leans upon rather than contributes to society. Following the Adlerian concept, the first phase of psychotherapy is discovering the lifestyle of the individual. This is done by analyzing the child in the family, old memories, unusual interests and strivings, and the goal of superiority. Essential in the therapeutic process is the establishment of a meaningful interpersonal relationship which will decrease inferiority feelings, develop stronger social interests, and establish healthier goals.

Carl Jung differed from Freud in that he saw man as primarily a racial creature. Each person is born with a unique predisposition obtained from his racial past to act in certain ways. All knowledge, feelings, superstitions, and so forth are accumulated by each individual and passed down from one generation to the next forming the collective unconscious. Jung also believed that whatever exists must also have an opposite. Opposites bring about conflicts which in turn generate progress. For example, motivation or action may be the result of a wish to alleviate the stress of conflict. Thus the maturational process is enhanced when the individual eliminates a conflict situation by seeking a suitable goal equally attractive as was the originally desired inappropriate goal. The therapeutic process proposes to aid the individual in his maturational process. The traditional indirect psychoanalytic procedures and techniques are utilized.

Karen Horney also broke away from the orthodox Freudian psychoanalysis. An independent school was established which had considerable influence on the American scene during the 1940s and 1950s. Although her ideas remain within the framework of Freudian psychology, she believed that man was not an "instinct ridden creature," but was capable of responsibility and choice. She emphasized that if an individual grew up under favorable conditions, the resultant effects would be the development of inherent constructive forces and the realization of the person's potentials. Under inner stress the individual tends to become alienated from the real self and throws up a false idealized self which, although based on pride, is harassed by doubts, self-contempt, and self-hate. Anxiety is the primary determinant of neurotic character trends. A neurotic need may be seen as an irrational solution to a problem of disturbed human relationships. From these neurotic needs inner conflicts develop. According to Horney's theory, neurotic dependency begins in the infant. When the mother is anxiety-ridden and insecure, she tends to provide the infant with attitudes of anxiety, patterns of contradiction, lack of interest, neglect, and lack of sensitivity to his own individual needs. The attitudes induce in varying degrees a process which Horney refers to as "basic anxiety." Basic anxiety is the result of anything that disturbs the security of a child in his original relationship to his parents and later to society. It is the feeling of helplessness towards a potentially hostile world.

Horney's earliest published work concerned her evolving theory of feminine psychology which she supported with data from her clinical observations. She believed that Freud's ideas concerning the female were derived from his nineteenth century male oriented philosophy and traditional Victorian upbringing. She differed specifically with Freud's belief that female conflicts grew out of the woman's feeling of inferiority and jealousy towards the male because of his possession of a penis. Offering as support the evidence from clinical work with men, she suggested that the notion of penis envy might have its roots in a male envy of the female. This evidence included the male's envy of women's experiences of pregnancy, childbirth, and motherhood, as well as the possession of breasts and the ability to suckle a child. Horney also referred to the male's attempt to deal with his historic fear and dread of the female by denial and defense. Males tend to deny their dread by love and adoration and attempt to defend themselves by conquering, debasing, and diminishing the self-respect of women. Horney differed from Freud regarding the concept of woman's wish for a child. Freud believed that this wish came into existence only secondarily because of the disappointment over the lack of a penis and therefore was not a primary instinct. Horney proposes that the wish for a child is a primary one and is instinctually anchored deeply in the biological sphere. This instinctual drive within the woman further illustrated the "psychic representation of a continuously flowing inner somatic stimulus." That is, the continuous physiological cycle functioning within the female reproductive system creates the maternal desires and drives.

The most important element in the psychotherapeutic process according to Horney is the patient-therapist relationship. She stressed that her psychoanalytic interpretations, although somewhat Adlerian in flavor, are fundamentally Freudian. Horney has emphasized that,

> the recognition of unconscious forces, of dreams being meaningful, the belief in the importance for therapy of the patient-analyst relationship, of recognizing and dealing with the patient's defenses, and the value of "free association" are all part of a common heritage which forms the groundwork of psychoanalytic theory and method . . . I believe that deference for Freud's gigantic achievements should show itself in building on the foundation that he has laid and that in this way we can help fulfill the possibilities which psychoanalysis has for the future, as a theory as well as a therapy.

Erich Fromm has refuted any idea that he is a neo-Freudian. He has described his goals as broadening rather than changing Freud's discoveries. His efforts have been directed towards interpreting Freud's work in terms of contemporary philosophical and sociological concepts. While Freud might be labeled a biological determinist because of his view that motivated behavior arises from the individual's innate biological equipment, Fromm could be labeled a cultural determinist because of his belief that man's motivation is determined by cultural influences.

The word *freedom* has a special significance in Fromm's theory. The child gains freedom by breaking away from the primary parental ties. Once the individual is free from the primary ties, whereby complete individuation has been reached, he is confronted with a new task—to orient himself in the world and to find security in ways differing from his preindividualistic existence. Where once he was a part of a family entity he must now stand alone to face the world. Fromm believes that the mechanism used by most normal individuals in modern society is automaton conformity. In this process the individual ceases to be himself. He adopts the personality offered to him by cultural patterns. He becomes exactly as all others are and just as they expect him to be. The self disappears and with it the conscious fear of aloneness and powerlessness. Feelings of insecurity make the individual ready to submit to new authority which offers him security and relief from doubt. It may be interesting to note that the concept of adjustment usually has been associated with the normal. The normal, in turn, traditionally has been connected with what is healthy. Fromm pointed out that large numbers of neurotics are commonly the best adjusted. The neurotic personality in its constriction and anxiety is more likely to conform and rigidly follow the rules to a fault. Such behavior leaves little room for productive and innovative responses or space for change and growth. The healthy personality is more flexible and can either conform or rebel when appropriate. Indeed, not everything in our world is acceptable. On the other hand, each step away from the security of a regressive and dependent relationship is accompanied by anxiety.

Fromm has proposed that the goal of psychotherapy is to help a person realize his human and individual potentialities for productive relatedness to the world, for self-awareness, reason, and love. Like Freud he believes the curative effect is based on bringing unconscious forces into awareness. Fromm differs from Freud as to the main area of repression. For Freud repression was found to operate mainly in the area of sexual instincts. Later he also expressed the importance of repressed aggression. Fromm, contrary to Freud, has given no single role to the repression of sexual drives. He believes that anxiety, aloneness, alienation, and narcissism are among the most significant areas of repression. Being an outstanding advocate of the humanistic approach in psychoanalysis, Fromm emphasizes the patient-therapist interaction as the primary tool that enhances the psychotherapeutic process. The patient must feel the need to relate to the world if productive change is to take place. The therapist, unlike the traditional Freudian, takes an active role in relating to the patient.

Theories of learning

People are capable of changing their way of behaving, their interpersonal relationships, and their attitudes. The proponents of learning theory believe that some of these changes result from learning new approaches to the problems of living. Other learning procedures involve modification or relearning of attitudes or approaches. When the person's methods of coping do not allow for adaptive functioning with the rest of the world, he may need assistance in modifying his attitudes and behavior. Thus the task of psychotherapy for the learning theorist is to help the person to attain a better "fit" with his particular environment or change what is undesirable. Regardless of the particular theoretical orientation preferred by the psychologist, there is evidence that the personal relationship established between the therapist and the patient is a major factor in influencing changes in the behavior of the patient.

The psychologist of today has seen the development of many theories of learning. In a sense these theories are present-day versions of behaviorism. In recent years psychologists have amassed a considerable amount of measured information concerning the various human processes, particularly in the field of learning. The word "learning" is used in the broadest sense to include any aspect of behavior acquired as a result of experience. This excludes changes of behavior which result from normal growth, development, and maturation or direct intervention in the functioning of the nervous system.

Basically the learning process in man is the ability to acquire the skills necessary for interacting and surviving in his complex society. In the context of the behavioral theory of psychotherapy, learned behavior is generally explained by relating it to two techniques—classical conditioning and operant conditioning.

Classical conditioning (sometimes called respondent conditioning or reflexive conditioning), which was first demonstrated by the Russian psychologist Ivan Pavlov, involves reflexive behavior. The reflex is an involuntary response that is elicited by a specific stimulus. For example, the prick of a pen causes reflexive withdrawal of a hand or a puff of air blown on the eye causes the eyelid to blink. In classical conditioning a new stimulus (conditioned) becomes associated with the original stimulus (unconditioned) and is able to produce a response on its own. If on several occasions a chime or bell is sounded just before a puff of air is blown at the eyelid, the individual will eventually blink his eye when the chime or bell is sounded, whether or not the puff follows.

In the experiment Pavlov conducted to condition the salivary reflexes in dogs, the unconditioned stimulus was food in the dog's mouth. The conditioned stimulus was the sounding of the bell or the flashing of a light. A hungry dog was exposed to the sound of a bell which was immediately followed by placing food in the dog's mouth. The repetition of this procedure produced a response pattern in which the sound of the bell (conditioned stimulus) eventually elicited salivation (reflexive response) without the use of food (unconditioned stimulus). Thus Pavlov demonstrated that if a previously neutral stimulus regularly occurs just before food is placed in the hungry dog's mouth, the neutral stimulus (bell) generally comes to elicit the salivation. The terms *unconditioned stimulus* and *unconditioned response* are used because the response (salivation) to the unconditioned stimulus (food) is innate and not learned. That is, the response does not depend on the organism's (dog) previous experience with the stimulus (food). The new stimulus (bell) that eventually elicits the response (salivation) is called conditioned because it is conditional upon the organism's previous experience, and is therefore learned behavior.

A contemporary psychologist, B. F. Skinner, has defined and demonstrated in the laboratory a different kind of learned behavior called "operant conditioning." The basic difference in procedure between classical conditioning and operant conditioning is that in classical conditioning the conditioned response is elicited as reflexive, while in operant conditioning the conditioned response is first performed voluntarily and then reinforced. In other words the subject, human or otherwise, in operant conditioning plays an active role in the learning process, whereas the subject in classical conditioning is relatively passive.

In everyday situations outside of the laboratory, human beings as well as animals perform many acts as a result of a conditioning process. The gambler who spends his money in slot machines is an example of this. But behavior learned as a result of conditioning processes may also be terminated. In classical conditioning, extinction, or cessation of response, takes place if the conditioned stimulus is repeated without the unconditioned stimulus. Likewise the learned response in operant conditioning may be extinguished by withholding reinforcement. An example of the latter is the child seeking attention who always gets his way by throwing a tantrum. The tantrum (reinforced behavior) will tend to cease if it no longer brings the desired result.

Emotional, intellectual, and physical behavior patterns may be established by means of conditioning procedures. For example, the young child learns to portray the role assigned by the parents as a result of positive reinforcement received when acquiescing to their desires. The young child also learns to avoid running into the street because of aversive reinforcement (punishment) rather than as a result of understanding that he may be hit and injured by an automobile.

John Watson initiated the behaviorist movement in America. He expanded the Pavlovian concept and developed laboratory procedures demonstrating the conditioning of emotional reactions. Using the sight and sound of a loved person (e.g., mother or girl friend) being molested a jealousy response was conditioned in human subjects. The conditioned jealousy response was measured by body stiffening, pronounced breathing, fighting, and reddening of the face. Phobias were also developed as a conditioned response. Using furry animals as conditioned stimuli and a loud gong as an unconditioned stimulus an eleven-year-old child was conditioned with phobias to animals and all furry objects. Later the phobias were relieved by an extinction or desensitization process. Furry objects, including animals, were presented at a distance without reinforcement of the sound. As the child became acclimated the furry object was slowly moved closer until the child was able to touch the object without fear.

A frequent objection has been made that behavioral therapy deals only with symptoms and leaves the basic cause of emotional disturbances untouched. Effective intervention and relief, however, may be obtained without knowledge or understanding of basic causes. Thus, behavioral therapy may aid individuals in coping with bed-wetting, stuttering, phobic states, and intense anxiety of long standing.

There are many aspects to the process called learning. John Dollard and Neil Miller believed that reinforcement of behavior is only one of four major areas in the learning process. The others include drives, cues, and responses. The cue serves as a catalyst to put the drives into motion toward a goal. This motion is the response, and responses are ranged in a hierarchy. If a response is followed by reinforcement, the connection between the stimulus pattern and the response is strengthened, so that the next time the same drive and other cues are present this response is more likely to occur. Dollard and Miller took the ideas and concepts of psychoanalytic theories and redefined them in the terms and language of learning theory. To these principles they added information collected from social anthropology so that an account could be given of the actual conditions leading to the development and maintenance of an individual's personality. They also tended to agree with the analytic concept that underlying all neurotic behavior is an unconscious emotional conflict. That is, adult disorders generally result from a conflict which originated in childhood and which is related to the way the child was trained to fulfill the expectations of his culture. The major areas of conflict are feeding, cleanliness, sex, and aggression. The maladaptive person is one who is unable or unwilling to understand the emotional basis of his behavior and thus unable to capitalize on his problem-solving abilities to find a resolution of his difficulties. In order to achieve a better adaptation to the demands of his environment, the individual requires new conditions of learning. The psychotherapeutic process offers a situation in which the maladaptive responses are extinguished while more effective responses are learned.

The attainment or restoration of higher mental processes is accomplished by means of therapeutic learning. This process includes the development and utilization of the *transference relationship, removal of repression,* learning to make *adaptive discriminations,* and learning to *label.* As in the psychoanalytic process, the transference reactions such as fear, hate, and love provide information which the patient is unable to provide directly. *Repression* is removed by means of extinguishing or counterconditioning the fear or anxiety associated with repressed material. This is accomplished by the utilization of free association on the part of the patient concurrent with the creation of a social situation within the therapeutic setting that is the opposite of the one responsible for learning repression. As the repression is removed, the individual begins to experience feelings which were previously unconscious. These feelings may be dealt with verbally by identifying and labeling the events going on within and from without the individual. Having a label, the person can represent his response in reasoning.

The new emotional experiences with the therapist lead to learning which may be more effectively utilized in other situations when adequately labeled. An example of this may be the clarification of typical transference reactions of the individual to authority figures. The individual may unrealistically experience any authority as threatening rather than as a possible source of assistance. The therapeutic process also offers the individual an opportunity to see that the conflicts experienced are not warranted by the current conditions of reward and punishment. The individual has the opportunity of learning that past conditions which created these conflicts are quite different from the current situation. When able to discriminate the present from past conditions, the patient has the strength to attempt new responses. These, when reinforced by positive responses, can break the neurotic impasse.

Gestalt concepts

The development of Gestalt therapy primarily evolved from the initiative of Frederick Perls. He viewed the Gestalt theory of psychology as the study of creative adjustments of the human organism and environment within the function of their interaction. All contact is viewed as creative and dynamic. Thus he believed abnormal psychology is the exploration of interruptions, inhibitions, or other deterrents in the course of creative adjustment. Perls considered anxiety as the "pervasive factor in neurosis," the result of interruptions in the excitement of creative growth. Gestalt therapy thus consists of analyzing the effects of the internal structure of the individual's experiences. The Gestalt therapist evaluates the unity and disunity of this structure in the "here and now," the person's current experiences. This process allows for the reshaping of the dynamic relations of the organism-environment boundaries until the contact is heightened. The awareness is sharpened and the behavior intensified. Perls contends that, "The achievement of a strong Gestalt is itself the cure, for the figure of contact is not a sign of, but is itself the creative integration of experience." The therapists who adhere to the Gestalt therapeutic approach maintain the primary pieces of Gestalt psychology—unitary wholes must be expected in regard to their "wholeness," and can be analytically separated into parts only at the cost of destroying the intended object of study.

Perls and his coauthors stress that neither the understanding of the functions of the individual nor his environment cover the total situation for the therapist. The neurotic feels his survival depends upon his continuing to repress, to censor, and to defeat the therapist's efforts to penetrate his defenses to reorganize the ego structure. The "unfinished" neurotic part of the patient is in the "obvious" functions of his being—the way he moves, talks, breathes, and so forth. In their approach to therapy Perls and his coauthors stress the need for a nondogmatic experimental situation. They suggest that any implicit or explicit demands on the patient are not only likely to be futile, but may possibly be damaging.

The types of experiments conducted by Perls and his associates are centered about leading their patients to make a creative adjustment to the current situation. To complete the wholeness in the present situation the patient must destroy and assimilate the unawareness as an obstacle. The therapeutic experiments allegedly bring out sharp delineation and precise verbal description of the disrupting block or void and open up ways to overcome it. According to this therapeutic technique, the "neurotic" has lost contact with reality. He has extreme difficulty in regaining touch with himself. He persists in a course that further removes him from actuality and those around him.

The patient upon entering into Gestalt therapy becomes an active partner in the process, "a trainee in psychotherapy." As an active participant within the therapeutic process the patient begins to transfer similar attitudes into other situations. The lifting of repression is brought about by encouraging the patient to become aware of the manner in which he inhibits or prohibits himself in various situations. This enlightenment includes attending to the methods utilized as well as the process involved in carrying out these maladaptive responses. For example, the patient learns to recognize the methods of withdrawal, symbolic images, muscles, and other methods he has utilized. The patient is also provided with opportunities to realize his methods of resistance as well as the knowledge of what he is resisting. Through experimental processes, there is the opportunity for resolution of these resistant forces. The experimental process also provides the individual an opportunity to experience his difficulties in areas where his abilities and creative images are being felt and productively utilized.

Holistic approach

Holism, a concept first developed by the Gestaltists, also maintains the view that the whole is greater than the sum of its parts. That is, one cannot understand the whole through the examination of the parts. Among the pioneers of the holistic approach are Gen. J. C. Smuts, who originated the term, Karen Horney, Kurt Lewin, and Abraham Maslow. Holism can only be understood in terms of the direction of movement. The individual's goal-directed behavior tends to reflect all past experiences and training as they are being expressed in and modified by his view of present circumstances, by his concept of the future, and by his intentions. In this perspective, behavior appears as purposive and is directed towards a goal which the individual has set for himself. The person decides the kind of conditions to which he will respond rather than allowing himself to be the subject of conditioning. He may select from the reservoir of all past experiences and from the multitude of stimulations to which he has been exposed, those influences which best suit his purposes. The individual may be considered to have a biased apperception in that he responds only to what he wants to respond, seeing only what fits his frame of reference. Thus, the individual directs his own activities. Those who espouse the holistic approach view the human being as an organized unity. They seek to understand various phenomena of human behavior in terms of underlying organization. This basic quality of organization or integration distinguishes a whole from an aggregate of its parts. It is only within a given whole that the partial phenomena and processes derive their meaning.

The fusion of organic, psychological, and sociological viewpoints to a holistic approach was not accepted readily. Adolph Meyer promoted holism through his broad eclectic approach to mental illness which he termed psychobiology. His approach was formulated basically on the holistic assumption that the study of the total personality of the patient is the only way to understand his behavior. He also believed that the determinants of the patient's behavior are pluralistic and interactional. He emphasized that all relevant biological, psychological, and sociological factors must be investigated and coordinated into the understanding of the developmental pattern of mental illness.

A holistic treatment program is primarily directed towards obtaining optimal gain in the treatment sessions through the utilization of a discrete set of concepts. There is equal concern for the utilization of the patient's life span outside the treatment room as a means of achieving therapeutic gains. This process includes helping the patient to become actively involved in making planned use of his living environment, his interpersonal relationships, and his vocational setting in order to achieve growth. The implications for the holistic therapist are to help his patient discover and make maximum use of his potentialities. At the same time, the patient works with and works through his emotional conflicts and debilities. This seeking out and unfolding of an individual's possibilities cannot be separated from the process of achieving personal authenticity, that is, a feeling of wholeness and personal freedom. The identification, utilization, and development of individual strengths and potentialities constitutes the basic and underlying premise in the interpersonal exchange. By working with as many facets of man's being as feasible, patient and therapist together strive towards recognizing the interrelatedness of these wholes and how they can contribute to bringing wholeness to man. The methods of treatment focus on improvement of the self-image and self-concept, and are essentially ego supportive.

Nondirective psychotherapeutic techniques

The nondirective approach to psychotherapy has been epitomized in Carl Rogers' approach, labeled client-centered therapy. Rogers' major concern regarding an individual is the self. The self-as-object includes the attitudes, feelings, and perceptions of one's self. The self-as-process includes the group of psychological processes which govern behavior, such as thinking and remembering. Rogers believed that the self developed out of the organism's interaction with the environment and that it strives for consistency. Experiences which are not consistent with the self-structure are perceived as threats. The self may incorporate by introjection the values of other people and perceive them in a distorted fashion. Also the self may change as a result of maturation and learning.

In client-centered therapy, the responsibility for the course and direction is left to the client. Thus the client or patient chooses the topic and finds methods of moving ahead, resting, and other aspects of the therapeutic process. Rogers sees a healthy person as acting on his own perceptions, incorporating experiences without distortion to himself and others. The therapeutic process relies on the fact that within the individual reside the constructive forces whose strength and uniformity have been either entirely unrecognized or grossly underestimated. The more deeply the constructive forces in the individual are relied upon, the more deeply they are released. The technique may give the illusion of simplicity because it is the natural inclination of the counselor to aid or assist. The effective counselor is described as having a coherent and developing set of attitudes deeply imbedded in his personal organization which is implemented by techniques and methods consistent with it. He has respect for the human individual to achieve reorganization. He must be able to assume the client's internal frame of reference. The therapist's techniques will be an implementation of his attitude.

Rational-emotive therapy

Albert Ellis has theorized that neurotic behavior results from irrational thinking which is expressed in overt behavior in the form of emotion. He believes that if the individual structures his thinking rationally, this will be followed by rational behavior patterns. Ellis describes man as organized so that he is in harmony with society and others. Alienation from one's self as well as destructiveness are a result of irrational thinking. He has developed a psychotherapeutic approach which he believes helps the individual to live a more creative, self-fulfilling and emotionally satisfying life by learning to organize and discipline his thinking. Therefore, "disordered emotions" may be ameliorated by changing the person's thinking. Rational-emotive therapy directs a "concerted attack" on the individual's illogical positions. Ellis proposes that the therapist is a "counterpropagandist who directly contradicts and denies the self-defeating propaganda and superstitions which the patient has originally learned and which he is now self-instilling." The therapist also persuades, sometimes even coercing, the patient to engage in activities which will "serve as a forceful counterpropaganda agency against nonsense he believes." The goal of therapy and the activity on the part of the therapist is to induce the patient to internalize a rational philosophy of life.

Cognitive therapy

Cognitive therapy developed out of the idea that emotional disturbances result from idiosyncratic thinking. That is, the individual's disturbance results from a constellation of negative perceptions of the self, the world, and the future. Aaron Beck, in his work with depression, describes a cognitive therapist as being actively involved with the patient in order to formulate the problem and goals as well as devise specific techniques to cope with each problem area. The cognitive therapist is primarily concerned with the overt behavior rather than the origin of the symptoms in unconscious conflicts or early experiences. The formulation of the symptoms presented by the patient is in terms of basic misconceptions and thought patterns which become evident as the individual reports spontaneous thoughts and experiences. The patient is trained to be attuned to "automatic thoughts" and to utilize selective therapeutic techniques to alter the maladaptive cognitions. The individual is encouraged to subject his perceptions to reality testing, that is, to determine whether the thought and concept are realistic or justified. Thus conditioned expectations tend to decrease and the individual is able to institute the old truism that "thinking does not make it so." Other cognitive therapeutic techniques include the exposure and evaluation of superstitions, prejudices, and misconceptions. Exposure of conditioned or automatic thoughts often reveals stereotyped themes that pervade an individual's thinking. The recognition and understanding of these stereotypical themes aid the individual in eliminating identical reactions in diverse situations.

Logotherapy

Logotherapy was developed by Viktor Frankl as a means of overcoming what he referred to as an "existential vacuum," which makes its appearance in an individual experiencing no worthwhile meaning to his life. Although considering the individual's despair over the worth of life as a spiritual distress, Frankl does not place this in the realm of a mental disease. Frankl has stated that philosophical conflicts regarding a person's perception of the world are influenced but not caused by biological, psychological, and sociological factors. In a personal discussion Frankl emphasized that man's search for meaning may tend to create tension rather than equilibrium. Such tension however is related to and fosters mental health rather than pathology. He believes that every neurosis has an existential aspect and may be considered as being grounded in the four basically different dimensions of man's being: physical, psychological, societal, and spiritual.

Logotherapy is concerned with and directed towards the existential and spiritual nature of man. The primary aim is to enable the individual to consciously accept responsibility for himself. The therapist's efforts are to aid the patient to realize latent values and to bring out the ultimate possibilities of the individual. Thus logotherapy may be considered specifically for existential frustration and conflicts.

The major therapeutic instrument in logotherapy is the relationship between therapist and patient. Within this relationship the patient's responsibility for himself is uppermost. The therapist restricts his role to bringing the patient to the point of experiencing this responsibility.

A personal experience which took place as a workshop demonstration offers an unedited view of the logotherapeutic procedure.

A middle-aged white male complained of having reached a state of development where life had little meaning. The patient had experienced a rather satisfying and enjoyable life. He held a position of associate professor in a small college. His professional achievement had been recognized by publications in professional journals, books, and election to office in national, state, and local organizations. He had already been actively involved in professional as well as civic activities. His work in these areas had been effective and recognized. His familial life had been relatively smooth and happy. His wife of twenty-five years was described as a most enjoyable person and the marriage most compatible. Both he and his wife worked and had independent activities as well as many common interests and collaborative efforts. His two sons had left the fold. The older had recently graduated from an outstanding engineering college while the younger son was a senior in the same college.

As a therapeutic relationship evolved, the patient began to describe his present feeling of emptiness. While in the past he possessed a driving force of vitality, he currently experienced sluggishness and a lack of zeal in any of his undertakings. Frankl's gentle probing led the patient to reveal that the intellectual stimulation, emotional fervor, and creative drive experienced in the interaction with students of the past no longer existed. Student interest, which had been an important stimulant, had been replaced by student lethargy. Continued interactional discussion led to a description of the patient's feelings and a conceptualization of the process involved. During a life span of fifty years, the patient had an active existence. The adult years especially had been composed of creative adventures, explorations, and productivity. He had constantly and continually been involved in mutually stimulating activities with his wife, sons, friends, students, and colleagues. He had always been a "doer." The diminishing physical energy level created what Frankl termed "lag."

The patient, with Frankl's assistance, reviewed his life experiences. The occasions of self-fulfillment and the contributions to others were recalled and illuminated. The events and situations which might have been but were never used for self-fulfillment were also recalled. The discussion began to take a new direction emphasizing a change in the patient's philosophy. The modification to be achieved was a change from being a "doer" to being a "receiver." The patient was to review his philosophy and initiate a direction towards allowing others to do for him. That is, to enjoy a good play, a concert, a beautiful sunset, and other wonders of nature and man. The drive behind the need to *do* might be diminished by considering what has already been offered and how the patient's productivity is being used successfully by others, for example, his family and his students.

Transactional therapy

During the latter part of the 1940s, Drs. John Dew and A. M. Bentley reported on their concepts of transactional relationships. In 1959, Dr. John P. Spiegel of Michael Reese Hospital began to explore this transactional theory as it might apply to the psychiatric functions of the social worker. Later Dr. Roy R. Granker, Sr., and his associates followed up this work. The transactional theory and analysis were later popularized by Dr. Eric Berne in his book *Games People Play*. The transactional theory encompasses the relatedness of the individuals with each other within a well-defined setting. That is, each person has a reciprocal effect on the other person and the processes of action and reaction are cyclical. The interpersonal relationship is influenced by the life pattern of the individuals as well as the therapeutic setting. In the therapeutic situation, the transactional approach reveals and provokes old repetitive maladaptive patterns. Implicit roles may be brought into awareness of the patient by making them explicit. These may then be modified and controlled by the individual. Behavioral changes in the transactions are then translated and transferred into changes in relationship with people in other environments.

Berne, in developing his concept of transactional analysis (TA), postulated that each individual has three *ego states*. These ego states respectively are *Parent, Adult,* and *Child.* He defines an ego state as "a coherent system of feelings, and operationally as a set of coherent behavior patterns." The Parent essentially is a replica of the authority figure who operates on information assumed to be true because of its origin. The *parent ego* has both nurturing and prejudicial components. The *adult ego* may be considered to be objective, with behavior based upon estimation of probabilities as to results. The *child ego* state is considered to have originated in its entirety from childhood. The reactions of the Child manifest a retention of the perception and feelings of early childhood. Berne describes the Child as being exhibited in two phases: "the adapted Child, who is acting under the Parental influence, as evidenced by such adaptations as compliance or withdrawal; and the expressive

Child who acts autonomously in expressing creative, angry, or affectionate tendencies." These postulates are only a few examples of a well-defined terminology developed by Berne.

The methodology of transactional analysis is not quite as clear as its terminology. In fact, marriage between its terminology and an alternative methodology may be frequently observed. For example many individuals have combined transactional analysis vocabulary with Gestalt techniques.

Transactional analysis most often is conducted in a group setting. Using the group as a laboratory situation, the therapist directs his efforts towards analyzing the various transactions among the patients as well as between patient and therapist. The TA therapist may engage in reeducation. For example, if an individual finds that he has an insufficient parent ego, more appropriate behavior may be taught in a process called reparenting. The therapist also may help the patient to make a redecision. If the child ego of the patient was instrumental in making an original decision that dictated too much of his behavior, a new decision based on more accurate information may be instrumental in changing that behavior.

Claude Steiner has outlined three tools of the transactional analysis therapist: *permission, protection,* and *potency.* Permission is a transaction from the therapist's Parent ego to the patient's Child ego. This transaction counteracts the *injunction* (prohibition) given by the original parents. Thus, the patient receives permission and is able to allow himself to engage in other behavior. *Protection* may be considered as consequent to *permission.* The therapist has given the patient permission to disobey a powerful force. Therefore, protection and support must also be offered. This process is also a parent-child transaction. *Potency* is the process whereby the therapist undertakes the transactions of *permission* and *protection* and thus becomes fully involved with the patient.

Treatment modality

Different psychotherapy theories are neither unique unto themselves or to their use by therapists. Psychotherapists with different theoretical orientations may function similarly in their practice. There are also many occasions when therapists with the same theoretical orientation function differently.

The various theories of personality as they are translated into treatment procedures have been a part of different modalities. For example, all of the theories described above have been applied in the dyadic, or the one-to-one relationship. In fact, most of the traditional psychotherapeutic procedures occurred in the one-to-one relationship. In the traditional psychoanalytic approach the patient reclined on a couch in order to allow himself greater relaxation and greater freedom to free associate. Going to the other extreme regarding the directiveness of the therapeutic approach, the conditioning processes were also utilized on a one-to-one basis. Later however, the many therapeutic concepts were applied to the psychotherapeutic group approach. Generally when group psychotherapy is considered one thinks of four, six, eight, or even ten or more patients in the therapeutic setting. However a triad which may be composed of a married, engaged, or other related couple and a therapist might also be considered a group. A therapist meeting with parents and children of the same family is also a group setting. However the latter two situations are referred to as couples therapy and family therapy, respectively, rather than group psychotherapy. In these modalities, any theoretical orientation may be applied. The modalities and the respective techniques utilized are further elaborated later in Chapters five and six.

Goals of psychotherapy

The goals of various psychotherapeutic approaches may vary. For example, as stated in the discussion of logotherapy, the primary aim in this approach is to cope with the individual's spiritual philosophy. This idea, however, does not restrict the theoretical orientation to any specific goal which may be selected by the therapist and the patient. In essence the theoretical orientation connotes and often denotes the philosophy of the therapist and may be evinced in any of several therapeutic endeavors. The goals of psychotherapy are more extensively discussed later. A short description of levels of therapeutic intervention may be of value at this time. In a *guidance* situation the patient or client is seeking someone to show him the ropes, that is, someone to help him see a direction. Often this includes the attainment of specialized information and learning how to obtain knowledge required to develop skills.

Counseling requires more efforts and expenditure of energy on the part of the counselee. The goals of counseling usually include the individual's desire and attainment of understanding of himself and his interpersonal relationships. The therapeutic modality is utilized in the individual developing better methods of coping with his own drives and goals and with others in interpersonal relationships.

Psychotherapy usually has as a goal the patient's understanding himself in terms of his drives and motivations. The therapeutic relationship is used to develop better self-directed action and interpersonal relationships. The psychotherapeutic process also includes working through anxiety-provoking conflicts, developing better levels of frustration tolerance, increasing ego strength, and promoting greater development of potential.

Psychoanalysis is a method of psychotherapy usually referred to as depth therapy because of the intensity of the therapeutic effort and the personality level at which the therapist and patient relate. The ultimate goal of psychoanalysis is character reconstruction, that is, to modify basic attitudes and character traits which were initiated in the early years of the individual's life. This therapeutic process is directed towards the resolution of intrapsychic conflicts and personality dysfunction.

The innate drive to stay alive makes every newborn child vulnerable to the value judgments of the mothering figure who is the needed source of life-sustaining nutrients and care. This influence is readily observed in the infant's response to muscular tension and fondling by the mothering person. The great majority of children learn well, adopting the unconsciously assigned role and value judgments of parental and surrogate figures. Although some parental figures allow and enhance the development of natural potentials, most grown people use the young child as an object to be shaped. Innate feelings become fused with behavior and take on the value judgments of the individual's subculture. Feelings become "good" or "bad," "right" or "wrong," "evil" or "virtuous," "natural" or "alien." Where the molding process and rigid value judgments are strenuously imposed, the individual becomes a victim of others' manipulation, possessed by alien, unacceptable feelings.

An example of the latter is "fear." Fear is a feeling which is essential for self-preservation, an alarm system which is set off by a threat of danger, immediate or anticipated, actual or imagined. However, people usually learn from early childhood that to experience fear is a sign of "weakness," being a "baby," or a "sissy," and other demeaning attributes. Thus the feeling of fear is to be negated. Rather than accepting this feeling the person denies or seeks other means of battling against experiencing the fear. The battle is an anxiety-producing conflict. Experiencing and accepting the fear allows for recognition of the threatening situation, an opportunity to evaluate the degree and extent of danger, and to establish priorities of appropriate optional actions.

Effective psychotherapy allows and encourages the individual to experience and to accept his feeling as part of himself. Recognition of the situation which stimulates the feelings provides an opportunity to evaluate the appropriateness as well as the intensity of the activated feeling response. The origin and evaluation of the merits of the value judgments fused to the stimulus situation are explored. The individual is then in a position to differentiate the merits of the stimulus situation in light of the individual's present status as compared to the past. For example, the infant can remain alive only if someone else feeds him, while the adult can feed himself. The patient is also allowed and encouraged to initiate both ideas and overt behavior. He is thus able to recognize and accept himself as influencing things and people, rather than merely being a victim of his environment. As these processes progress the individual develops his potentials optimally. He accepts accountability for his actions and is better able to adapt effectively. He is able to enjoy the people and situations which comprise his world, as well as to enjoy his own being.

In essence, psychotherapy may be viewed as a relationship which offers the patient an opportunity to reevaluate and restructure basic attitudes, value systems, and modes of adaptation to life situations.

The psychotherapeutic approach—the personality theory orientation as well as the goals sought—might be accomplished in one or more of the psychotherapeutic modalities available. This might be a good time to describe and discuss the various psychotherapeutic modalities, that is, the treatment settings which exist.

5
The Forms
(Modalities)
of Psychotherapy

Now a discussion of the nature of the psychotherapeutic environment and the forms or modalities of psychotherapy is in order. The environment is divided into three primary areas. These include the physical setting, the personal versus the public climate, and the human environment. Within this total environment is found the experience of psychotherapy. Psychotherapy may take many forms which usually are referred to as modalities. A modality refers to the basic structure which is used in psychotherapy and should be differentiated from a theory or technique. Theory involves the concept or philosophy of the therapist that guides him in his working with the patient. Techniques are specific methods or procedures that may be used within the theoretical framework or with a particular modality in the therapeutic setting.

Modalities may be used alone or in combination with each other. These are individual psychotherapy, group therapy, family therapy, couples therapy, co-therapy, and multiple therapy. There are also allied or related experiences that may be therapeutically beneficial when used in conjunction with ongoing psychotherapy. They include the encounter group, the sensitivity group, and the marathon.

The physical setting is less important than the human climate but it still requires some consideration. Therapists try to achieve a reasonable sense of privacy and minimal distraction from external sources. In private practice the decor and ambience are a personal choice of the therapist and generally a reflection of his tastes. This is understandable since he spends a large part of his week in the office. Thus most therapists provide an atmosphere that is conducive to their comfort and ability to concentrate, in order to facilitate their effectiveness. In institutional and clinic settings there may not be much choice. Such facilities will vary in their physical arrangements depending upon the finances and attitudes of the administrators.

In individual psychotherapy, which is a one-to-one relationship between therapist and patient, there should be two comfortable chairs and possibly an ottoman or hassock that can enhance physical relaxation. For the other modalities which involve more than two people there are additional seating arrangements. A couch or recliner is commonly used to facilitate not only the ability to relax but also the ability to remember and experience fantasies. It may be helpful if the room is soft in mood and quiet in tone. Curtains and carpeting contribute to this effect. Still there is no universal rule or physical setting that is perfect or the most desirable. As part of the comfort and hospitality some therapists may have beverages or snacks available. Many other therapists feel that this is a form of feeding and should not be done. For those who see such offerings as an expression of warmth there may be coffee, pretzels, cookies, or the like available. This kind of giving by the therapist has usually been regarded as more acceptable with children than with adults. However, times and theories have been changing. At one time any type of physical contact such as hand holding or a reassuring arm on the shoulder was considered minimally tolerable with children or psychotic patients but not with the less disturbed adults. Today, in the flow of the humanistic movement, physical contact is becoming an acceptable form of human communication.

As indicated before, one should not overemphasize the physical environment. The physical characteristics can make for more comfort but the real therapy is a function of the human scene and the kinds of interactions that occur. Let us look, then, at the personal versus the public climate and the human environment.

The personal climate is usually regarded by the therapist literally and with respect. Psychotherapy involves a person-to-person relationship and recognizes the specialness and uniqueness of each individual. Each person is treated as important regardless of his public image, social status, educational achievement, or occupational position. Seeing the real person behind the social mask or public veneer is necessary to the process of therapy if help is to be rendered so that the patient can become more creative and grow.

Needless to say, psychotherapy is a personal and private matter. The person and his privacy are privileged and confidential in the eyes of the therapist. In some states there is legislation that protects confidentiality. In public institutions the degree of privacy and confidentiality will vary with the nature of the staff and administration.

The human environment is a composite of all those conditions that contribute to creating an optimally productive atmosphere on behalf of the patient. It is a result of the kinds of human relationships that are based on caring, sensitivity, openness, and willingness to change. Change in this sense means becoming more of what you are and more of what you can be.

In the environment described, various modalities may be used.

Individual psychotherapy is a singular relationship between two people, therapist and patient, who agree to work together towards shared goals of change. The one-to-one relationship is a basic social unit in all forms of psychotherapy and all aspects of society. It is the most irreducible interpersonal interaction or microcosm in the world as seen in the parent-child, husband-wife, or friend-friend relationship. It is a primary means of learning about oneself and others. Our concept of people begins with the one-to-one relationship in our earlier years. This early concept and the associated attitudes and feelings are initially generalized to the rest of the world. As we grow and increase our relationships, changes occur for better or worse.

In individual therapy the therapist comes to know the patient through the nature of the therapeutic interactions and communications. We can only know each other through what happens between us and by a willingness to hear what is really being said and felt. The therapist tries to tune in and listen with his "third ear" because knowing the patient matters to him. The "third ear" is the expression frequently used to denote being tuned in and hearing what is not obviously or consciously communicated by the person seeking help. It involves listening to more than the words. Whatever the theory or techniques of the therapist, he communicates his perceptions and interpretations of what's happening so that the patient can come to see that he has difficulties that interfere with his living. Whatever means of communication are used—words, nonverbal or body language, intellect, feelings—the therapeutic experience is an emotional one. This is where people live and where real change occurs.

As children grow up, they go through a period of socialization where they learn to deal with more than one individual relationship at a time. The basic one-to-one social unit expands to a larger microcosm of the world to include more people. This brings in the concept of the group. Just as any one-to-one relationship is not regarded as psychotherapy, any group is not defined as a therapy group. Psychotherapy is specific in its definition and arrangement. It involves a professional and theoretical framework where one person provides his professional skills in the service of a human being who, in need of help, comes with both his health and his emotional problems. It should be mentioned that the fee the therapist receives is for his professional services and skills. The feelings of the therapist may be given but not sold, whether they occur in individual or group therapy.

A group may be defined as consisting of three or more people meeting at the same place for a common purpose. Therapy groups vary in size but usually consist of between five and ten people and the therapists. Group size is determined by several factors. If the room is exceptionally small more than five or six people may not fit in without each one doubling up on another's lap. Of course while this may possibly be therapeutic it would be somewhat uncomfortable for an extended period of time.

Group psychotherapy is an ongoing experience. After the group has been formed and established people may leave at different times depending on when they have been sufficiently helped. New people will come in at different times. Actually, individual therapy is similar in that there are the experiences of meeting and separating between two people, patient and therapist. The group involves similar experiences with more people. It is similar to the life experience itself. When we grow, we form new relationships as we enter into the lives of others or others enter into our lives. Separation does not necessarily mean losing a relationship. It could mean giving up an old and less satisfactory way of relating, as when one gives up a neurotic interaction for a healthier way of living. When a child gets older, he gives up the childlike way of relating to his parents in the process of finding his separateness as a person and his own sense of being. Although this separation may be felt with a sense of loss and anxiety, it opens the way for a new and more productive level of relatedness to his parents and others.

Sometimes patients leave therapy as a defense against the fear of separation and the fear of growing up. This is the kind of separation that is a real loss. It is a loss of both the relationship and of oneself. It is a way of holding onto the old, familiar life. Change is resisted by unconsciously acting out the fantasy of security and therefore not finding it in reality.

As you can see there are similar dynamics in all forms of psychotherapy. The modalities are primarily differentiated by the number of people involved, the constellation of people who are brought together, and the specific goals that are worked towards. The goals particularly emphasize the person in relation to social and family dynamics.

As already indicated, three or more people together may form a group but are not necessarily a therapy group. Members of a group can be nonrelating or even destructive to each other as well as creative. Groups can be social, economic, political, religious, and so forth. Such groups may have therapeutic value but are still not regarded as forms of psychotherapy. Similarly, as Jules Barron has stressed:

> Society should not be confused with community.
> Society is, conceptually, any kind of organizational
> structure. It may be contractual, practical,
> rational, impersonal, or personal. Community, as
> described by the sociologist, implies the presence
> of a sense of kinship in the social sphere and an
> emotional, personal connectedness to each other.
> Society may exist on the basis of a primary individ-
> ualism where competitiveness is the rule and
> where one's gain is another's loss. Or it may occur

on a communal foundation where winning is
dependent on a joint or cooperative philosophy.
The value of the *one* is enhanced rather than
diminished by the value of the *other*. . . . In group
therapy a patient enters the community of others
hopefully to find that being part of the whole,
which is necessary for his existence, does not have
to threaten his sense of self but may even add to it.
It can be found that selfness and otherness, one-
ness and groupness, do not have to be antithetical
to each other.

A sense of kinship with another person which enables personal growth can be achieved by working through one's own
emotional conflicts. If this process can be accomplished with one
person in individual psychotherapy, the process may be enhanced
in a group setting. Group therapy provides an additional dimension that is pertinent to the socialization process. It is an opportunity to work out problems connected to the ability to have more
than a single one-to-one relationship at the same time. The
selection of individual, group, or a combination of the two therapeutic approaches depends on the condition of the patient, the
kinds of difficulties he is having, and where he is in his life
experience. Frequently people begin with individual therapy or a
combination of individual and group. For others it may work best
by beginning with group and later adding individual therapy, or
just using the group modality.

In the earlier history of psychotherapy it was considered
inappropriate by many therapists to see more than one person at
the same time. To quote Barron, "The doctor treats the patient
within the confines of the one-to-one relationship and is not to be
contaminated by esoteric social realities." We have learned that
extending the single "I and thou" relationship to the mixture of I
and thou relationships that is possible in group therapy facilitates the process of positive change. For example, feelings of
jealousy, competitiveness, loyalty, and so forth are more vividly
evidenced in the group and facilitate working out related
problems.

Therefore, since the individual is a social being who is a

product of environmental as well as of intrapsychic forces and biological drives, the group appears to be a natural setting for experiencing and working through interpersonal as well as intrapersonal conflicts. Within the group the person is able to establish and communicate on a one-to-one basis. As a group member, he may reexperience a familial constellation, whether it be his nuclear family or some other group or groups. As the individual communicates in the group, the therapist is able to observe his patterns of behavior towards others and how they are influenced by the varying stimuli provided by the group. The therapeutic process almost always results in the development of the special kind of relationship called transference. Within the group setting the relationship may develop not only with the therapist but with other group members.

Group therapy is used in government and private mental hospitals, general hospitals, outpatient clinics, social agencies, schools, as well as in private practice settings. The way in which group therapy is used may vary in the same setting. It is dependent upon the aim and goals of both therapist and patients. One of the important outgrowths of group therapy is a tendency to organize mental hospitals on the basis of group participation. T. P. Rees and M. M. Glatt, two exponents of this procedure, state: "We believe that the most satisfactory, as well as the most practical, way of organizing the mental hospital as a therapeutic community is one based on group therapy, including occupational and recreational therapy." They indicated that the patient's conflicts are produced by his relationships with others in society. A meaningful way of clarifying such relationships is through group participation. Many mental institutions have developed treatment programs which include group psychotherapy for psychotic patients, group counseling with patients' relatives, and group treatment of the patient together with his family in the same therapy group. Parents and children have an opportunity to work through their individual inner conflicts as well as the family's interpersonal difficulties. Sometimes treating two to four families (maximum of twelve persons) in one group increases effectiveness.

Group psychotherapy has also become a means of preventive mental health in many settings. Group treatment of alcoholics, drug addicts, and parents of handicapped children has been reported. Community and social agencies have developed group programs to treat juvenile delinquents. Modified forms of group therapy are now used to treat emotionally disturbed children in camp settings. Guidance groups are used in child guidance clinics as well as in the treatment of adults. Many other settings have used different kinds of group psychotherapy.

Probably the first person to apply psychoanalytic theory to group psychotherapy was Trigant Burrow. His method was based on the theory that people live in and are part of a society, and that isolation of the individual may destroy his relationship to his group or society.

Burrow felt that the greatest value of the group was its potential for helping the patient to be more responsive to the treatment process. As the person becomes more aware that his problem is not unique, he is more readily able to give up his secrecy and isolation. The loss of this need helps to resolve the patient's resistance. Burrow emphasized that man is not an individual but a societal organism and should be treated as such. "In my interpretation, the group method of analysis is but the application in the phylogenetic sphere of the individual analysis as first applied by Freud without the ontogenetic sphere." He placed the need for greater emphasis on *immediate material* with a proportionate disregard for reminiscences.

In psychotherapy groups with psychoanalytic orientation the working through of conflicts on a deeper level is the goal. Utilization of the multiple transference relationships explores id impulses, ego strengths, and superego restrictions. In these forms of group treatment, free association, dreams, and fantasies are used as material for discussion and exploration.

Groups also have been used for guidance purposes. Such groups are problem-centered. The goal is to make it possible for each individual to function better in his life situation. The group stimulates discussion and also tends to increase patients' self-esteem through acceptance by other members, as well as by identification with their problems. Guidance groups of college students who function poorly in their academic work despite their high potential are an example of this form of help. Although each member of the group may present different neurotic problems and symptomatology, the focus of the sessions is on the members' common difficulty in applying themselves and attaining their academic goals.

The group leader encourages open discussion of universal, common, and individual problems which lend themselves to the creation of cohesiveness among the members. As the members become involved in the discussion, they begin to express conflicts which have created the anxiety that interfered with their studies. As the sessions continue the members begin to find some community in their problems and so are able to identify with one another. Childhood experiences with parents and siblings are discussed. The leader focuses all discussions on their relevance to the problem of the academic difficulties. The discussions during the sessions provide each member with an opportunity to understand and accept each other as well as themselves. As their self-esteem improves they can begin to formulate and carry through corrective measures.

Counseling in groups is another way in which the group approach has been effective. Although the major focus in counseling is problem solving, changes in personality may occur. The therapist focuses on the group members' overt reactions, interactional patterns, and the underlying value system which determines their perception, either realistic or distorted, of their environments. Feelings of support and acceptance from other group members enhance the patient's ability to expose guilt-related feelings, thoughts, and activities. This support emanating from the group leads to the further development of personal strength. As a consequence frustration tolerance is increased and the person is able to seek more satisfying solutions to life problems. As in all modalities of psychotherapy, transferential relationships among members develop in counseling groups. The intensity of these relationships, however, is kept at a minimum by interpretation of the reality of the situation. Dreams may be discussed in the group, but analysis of them is limited to the here and now.

In each member of the group we can find a piece of ourselves which brings out more feelings through the multiple interactions. Also, as already indicated, such interactions tend to unconsciously reenact the patterns of the family. Historically, the family unit has been the nuclear social group from which other social experiences evolve. Therefore it would seem natural that the modality of family psychotherapy would have come about as a form of treatment in its own right. It does seem a little curious that a group of strangers meeting for therapy as a treatment form should have antedated the family group. However, this was consistent with the original orientation that forbade a therapist from seeing more than one member of a family.

As is apparent, family therapy is when the family unit is the therapy group. In a sense the whole family is the patient. Typically this includes parents and children. Sometimes it includes all those who live together on a continuing basis, such as a grandparent, an in-law, an aunt, or an uncle.

Although people can live together as strangers for many years, the family group is unique in its ongoing presence of the same people interacting with each other. On some level family members have come to know each other and form certain alliances and defenses. This interrelationship differs from group therapy, which begins with strangers and where such dynamics are yet to be reexperienced. The kind of defenses that interfere with closeness, openness, or satisfying relationships are explored, evaluated, and worked out in family therapy. This modality is valuable when most or all of the family is involved in the kind of relatedness that produces friction, strife, and unhappiness. For example, arguing itself is not necessarily an indication of a family in stress or at an impasse. Arguing can be a form of communication or it can be a means of creating smoke to cover the real problems. In the latter case many small issues take on undue importance and become the focus of attention. During the therapeutic process the therapist enters into the family arrangement, interacting in a way that helps the family members to see how their styles are self-defeating rather than self-enhancing.

Couples therapy, as the term implies, is treating or working with one or more married pairs of people. A couple may work with a therapist in a kind of mini-group or threesome, in a mixed therapy group, or in a couples group where all the people are there with their mates. The modality of choice, of course, varies with each couple. Whatever form is used, each couple member is regarded as a separate person. Before a couple can be helped in the same therapeutic arena and with reference to their marriage, there must be some sense of commitment, not only to change, but to change in relation to each other. Each person must be at such a level of development as to be ready and willing to form a marital bond. The readiness and willingness, however, may vary widely between the partners when entering therapy. If there is a lack of readiness for this interaction it may be best for each mate to be helped separately at first.

Some therapists work with couples who have less formal or socially sanctioned arrangements. Such arrangements are noninstitutional or nonlegal. This would include premarital, postmarital, extramarital, or homosexual couples. The problems in these cases often are similar to those found in the more typical marriage. The underlying dynamics however may be somewhat different, particularly as related to their social and cultural status.

Co-therapy is a modality where two therapists work together with one or more patients. They may work with an individual, a group, a family, or a couple. Co-therapists may continue through a complete therapeutic experience or just come together for one or more co-therapy sessions. For example, two therapists who have been treating a wife and husband separately may come together for a couple session. This may be a single or a repeated experience. Sometimes a child is in therapy with one person and a parent with another. It may be determined and agreed that having a family session with both therapists can be of value. The two therapists share the responsibility and interact with each other as well as with the patient(s). On a deeper level they usually represent two parents in the experience. At one time two therapists working together in this way was probably considered as heretical as one therapist seeing two members of the same family concurrently.

Just as there must develop a feeling of trust and respect between therapist and patient, so must this relationship exist between the co-therapists if they are to be of help to the patients. This does not mean that they must agree with each other. Rather it is important that, where necessary, they are able to constructively disagree in a way that contributes to the therapeutic experience. It is important that their differences as persons or as theorists do not interfere with their ability to help those who come to them for resolution of their difficulties.

Most often co-therapy arrangements are limited experiences and may be used to move through impasses or, at the appropriate time, accelerate the therapeutic process. Co-therapy may also serve as a living consultation, as when one therapist calls in another, or as a form of supervision. However used, the co-therapy should be presented for what it is and the purpose known to the patients.

Another form of therapy which is used less frequently is multiple therapy. Multiple therapy may be defined as a modality where there are three or more therapists. These therapists may work with an individual, a couple, a group, or a family. The multiple therapy approach would not be economically feasible for most people since each therapist would receive a fee for the time. Outside of a residential institutional setting multiple therapy is not practical because of the problem of arranging a convenient time for three, four, or five therapists to get together at the same time. Rarely is multiple therapy continued for a long period of time. It has been used in hospital and clinic settings for experimental and learning purposes.

A group exists whether there are several patients and one therapist or several therapists and one patient. The participants vary in what they have to offer to the therapeutic process through their knowledge and the nature of their interactions. The symbolic family pattern becomes evident as members of the group move into roles of parent and child. Of course those roles may shift around. Yesterday's child may become today's parent and vice versa.

On a short term basis the impact of many therapists can be dramatic in stirring up more feelings and more anxiety in the patient. However, it is the continuing process of working with the feelings and the anxiety that facilitates changes and growth. On a long term basis there is little or no evidence to conclude that four or five therapists are more or less effective than one or two. For example, would it help to have four or five good parents rather than one or two good parents? There is probably more empirical evidence to demonstrate that the multiple therapy experience provides a unique opportunity for the therapists to learn from each other and further develop their skills.

Multiple therapy can be of value in the following ways: (1) as a catalytic agent to increase or accelerate the reactions of the patient, (2) as a way to break through an impasse, (3) as a form of consultation, (4) as a method of teaching or supervising new therapists, (5) as a way of enhancing the knowledge and skills of experienced therapists. It should also be clarified that multiple therapy is only one way of accomplishing any one or more of the five purposes mentioned. Furthermore, the number of therapists is undoubtedly less important than the quality of the therapists and the therapeutic interaction that occurs in the process.

Sometimes the concepts of modality and technique overlap. Psychodrama is an example of this. Psychodrama was innovated and developed by Dr. Jacob Moreno, one of the earliest innovators and contributors to the field of group psychotherapy. Psychodrama has been used in its own right as a form of crisis intervention as well as a continuing therapy and a process of treating people in. trouble. The therapist usually plays the role of the director and the patients are members of the cast. Significant roles of self and others are acted out as a means of experiencing part of the self to enable the patient to open up the doors to his unconscious, to remove obstacles to his living, and to find more of the self and its resources. More frequently, psychodrama will be found as a technique rather than an ongoing modality.

In other forms of psychotherapy patients and therapists may deliberately assume different roles and act them out in order to regain contact with parts of the self that are lost or hidden. Role playing can help to make the experience more real and therefore more useful to the patient and therapist in working out the persisting conflicts. It helps to take the person beyond the intellectual level into the emotional area of living.

People can talk about their problems, seem to know what they are, and even have knowledge of the causes without resultant change or improvement. This is known as intellectual understanding or pseudo-insight. The question sometimes asked is "How can I know the answers and still be suffering or unable to eliminate my symptoms?" The patient may, in fact, know all the necessary answers and still be debilitated. What has happened is that the person in trouble has protected himself through his intellect. The knowing has become a defense against real knowing, the kind of knowing that is meaningful and total, where the patient knows not with a part but with all of himself. In a sense we can have smart heads and "dumb" stomachs. A part of ourselves is cut off or alienated so that there can be no integration of what is learned. Therefore there is still a lack of integrity or wholeness.

Again it is important to emphasize that there are many modalities or techniques which can accomplish the same purpose. There is neither one way for all people nor one way for one person at different times. There is no substitute for good clinical judgment, intuition, and a flexibility on the part of the therapist that allows him to change his approach when it is beneficial to the patient.

It would be remiss not to include other processes which may or may not be forms of psychotherapy. Generally they may be referred to as encounter groups, sensitivity groups, T-groups (training), or marathon groups. Outside of the usual psychotherapeutic context, encounter groups are arranged to provide an intensive, face-to-face interaction in the here and now. The number of participants may vary from five or six to twenty or thirty. At the extreme there have been as many as a thousand or more at a single encounter. Encounter and sensitivity groups are frequently indistinguishable from one another. They may be relatively short in duration and limited in frequency and length of the total experience, or be an extended session that runs into many continuous hours. A long and continuous encounter group of anywhere from twelve to forty-eight hours or more is called a marathon.

The group movement, in contrast to its earlier history, spread rapidly into nonprofessional as well as professional areas. Particularly in the sixties people formed into groups and communes of every type and description for many different purposes and under a variety of labels. These groups mushroomed outside of the traditional establishment setting. There have been encounters for religious, political, social, marital, and most significantly, for human purposes of contact. A history of anxiety, competitiveness, and alienation helped provide the groundwork for such developments. The groups have come under such headings as sensory or body awareness, consciousness-raising, and meditation and growth experiences. They have been led by professionals, educators, paraprofessionals, religious leaders, and lay people from various walks of life. They have had therapeutic or social values and at other times have been antitherapeutic or harmful.

Honesty, openness, and authenticity are usually encouraged in these groups. Efforts are made to promote freedom of emotional expression and to achieve real human contact. Usually the emphasis is on the person being himself. In such situations there may be therapeutic value especially if the person is psychologically ready for this kind of experience. Unfortunately, sometimes a person may be unable to tolerate the emotional pressures brought to bear and have an adverse reaction or even a breakdown. The problem that often exists is that there may be inadequately trained leadership or lack of screening of the participants. Because encounter groups are largely conducted outside of the professional arena they have become attractions not only for the honest person but a hunting ground for exploiters and desperate people. Among the leaders of such groups there are those who genuinely seek to help others and believe in the meaningfulness of the humanistic and group movement in society. In contrast there are also those who use the group to exploit others financially and emotionally, act out personal needs in the name of genuine human interaction, or abuse the "sensitivity" concept. The participants may be a mixture of people who are either striving for real growth and human relationships or people who unconsciously try to experience reality in the form of illusion, as in the sensitive play *Glass Menagerie*, written by Tennessee Williams.

In the field of psychotherapy such groups, when used, are associated with some form of psychotherapeutic experience. In a sense, they become adjunctive modalities—experiences that are added to or combined with one of the modalities already discussed. Any form of psychotherapy may occasionally or periodically reach a psychological impasse. "Impasse" is used here as a seemingly insurmountable barrier. For example, it can be of value to combine two groups, each of which meets typically for one-and-a-half hour sessions, and hold a marathon session that lasts for twelve hours or more. This procedure can help break through the impasse and facilitate the ongoing process of each group. The intensive experience can be an opportunity to open up more of an area for each of the group members to see and be able to work through. The "more" that is opened up is the path to more of the person and his potentials for healthier living and an increased ability to enjoy living.

6

Techniques of Psychotherapy

A brief discussion of some of the techniques which may be common to many different modalities, or general approaches to psychotherapy will provide further clarity.

The techniques may be separated loosely into either verbal or nonverbal approaches. Verbal approaches range from the direct to the more nondirect techniques. The direct approach would include giving advice or specific information, and outlining specific directions about what to do or say in particular life experiences. You, as the patient, may be told when to leave the house and what to do at a particular time and under particular stress situations. You may be told when and where to do something and what to look for in terms of your own responses and relations to the situation. Most often what the therapist is attempting to accomplish is to enable you to behave in ways that are acceptable to society and to yourself. Another variation in the direct approach is John Rosen's Direct Analytic Interpretation. Here the meaning of the patient's behavior is explained to him in a positive, direct fashion. In the more traditional analytic approach, he is to explore and reach these interpretations for himself. This approach is used primarily with a disturbed individual, since this is when the patient would find it difficult to use his intelligence to grasp subtleties to work out the interpretations for himself. The therapist also hopes that the direct interpretation which touches a sensitive area will have shock value and establish contact.

The therapist may attempt to persuade the patient to change

his behavior and his responses to others. In Albert Ellis's "Rational-Emotive Approach" the patient receives an explanation of how his distorted thinking affects the way he responds. He is educated, and persuaded into both accepting the explanations and changing his behavior.

The therapist may be somewhat more nondirective or open-ended. He acts as a listener-participant in the relationship with the patient. Here he functions partly as a resource person and partly as a guide. The therapist tries to help the patient to understand, explore, and redirect his behavior, feelings, and ideas. The therapist offers neither specific advice nor specific interpretations except as these interpretations may arise out of the various aspects of the relationship. Part of the technique called "reflection" is one that is often used in these approaches. The therapist does not interpret the behavior, but reflects what he believes to be some of the underlying feelings involved in the behavior. He sums up what he sees as the patient's typical modes of behavior and the feelings which may motivate this behavior.

Many years ago Jacob Moreno developed the method he called psychodrama. While this is a modality in itself, some of the psychodramatic techniques are used in other modalities. For example, the patient and the therapist may switch roles during a therapy session. In a group setting the patient may be asked to act out a specific incident in his life and to explore it in a motor rather than verbal manner. The therapist may ask the patient to play the part of another person in his life who is important in the particular situation. The patient may be asked to maintain a soliloquy, or to "talk to himself" whether in the office with a therapist or in a group setting.

In the group approach there have been a number of changes in techniques over the years. The traditional time limits have been modified in many directions. Groups have met for single sessions which may last from an hour to an hour-and-a-half, double sessions which last upwards of three hours, or for marathons. The marathon may last for as long as two or three days including sleeping, eating, and absences only for taking care of bodily needs. The therapist believes that the extended period of contact helps break down resistance and increases the pressure level on the individual. The people who take part in the marathon are selected rather carefully by the therapist. Often other therapists will refer a patient to a marathon group in the expectation that this will help "open up" the patient in the therapy.

The earlier psychotherapy approaches specified quite strongly that there was to be no physical contact between therapist and patient and that the patient must be immobilized during the session itself. Recently there have been some interesting changes in these ideas. For example, there is an increasing use of sensory and body techniques either as a separate form of therapy or in combination with other techniques in various modalities of therapy. For example, rather than just talking about being angry, the patient is told to stand up and scream the anger out as loudly as possible. One of the more prominent recent methods is the "primal scream" development in which the therapist tries to help the patient express the anger and frustrations that have been bottled up for so long. There are times when a patient is unable to express himself in words. This may happen either in a hospital setting, a clinic, or an office.

Years ago, several innovative therapists developed the idea of letting the patient express himself through the use of art, poetry, or dance. While this developed initially in the hospital setting it has been expanded and used in many other settings. The body techniques, then, are another development in this general direction. The patient is helped to express, in any way possible, the feelings, frustrations, angers, tenderness, that he is unable to verbalize. Some therapists feel that a combination of verbal and body techniques is the most effective. The patient may both talk about and live out what is happening.

Another approach which may bridge both verbal and nonverbal methods is the use of hypnosis as an aid in therapy. At times the patient may reach an impasse in attempting to explore certain aspects of relationships, experiences, or memories. There are other times when the patient is so anxious that he cannot respond to the psychotherapeutic process. In both of these instances, hypnosis may be used either to relax the patient or to help him explore, in the hypnotic state, areas that would be too painful otherwise.

Typically the therapist's office, whether in private practice, a hospital, or clinic, has been the setting for the meeting of therapist and patient. The office provides an environment which enhances the development of the psychotherapy relationship. Therapists working with young children have developed techniques that involve being out of the office. For example, the therapist and a young patient or patients can take a walk, go for a ride, or share a soda or bite to eat. They may go outside and play games and wander around the neighborhood of the clinic or hospital area rather freely, limited only by the reality situations of weather and time. The therapist has understood that the child tends to communicate in ways which would be difficult on a verbal level when confined to an office. The youngster may consider himself hemmed in by the office walls. He or she has a need to explore and expand his or her physical horizons. This approach has been extended into therapy with adolescents. As an example, the therapist and the individual adolescent or group will go out and become involved in sports. With older adolescents the automobile may be both a topic of discussion and used physically as a means of exploration or communication. Important in the development of any human relationship is the sharing of food. This may be either in the office or in a local shop or cafeteria. The therapist and the patient both recognize that this is more than a social relationship. There are overtones in the sharing of food which go beyond the immediate situation.

There are therapists who feel uncomfortable leaving the office setting when working with adult patients. Some therapists consider that it may become important for the adult to use motor activity during the therapy session. The therapist may use various techniques in working with adults. For example, one therapist meets with a female patient on the back deck of his home where the patient can sit surrounded by trees, flowers, and open garden areas. For the patient this is extremely important since she comes from a circumscribed, restricted life. This setting aids her to open up and to relate herself more reflectively than would sitting in a chair or lying on a couch within the four walls of an office. At times a patient may be seriously ill or incapacitated as the result of an accident. A visit to the patient's home and meeting in the living room while sharing a cup of coffee or tea has been effective in many instances. Similarly if the patient is hospitalized for either emotional reasons or physical illness a visit to the hospital might well be indicated. The therapist's visit in this setting might do as much or more to enhance the therapeutic relationship than a series of meetings within the confines of an office.

With some adults the sharing of food becomes very important. Again this may be done in the office or in a local restaurant or cafeteria. A question that might arise is who pays? Sharing of the expense or "dutch treat" is usually effective and acceptable to both. A question which sometimes arises relates to the use of alcoholic beverages by either or both. As discussed elsewhere, there are times when the patient and the therapist meet at a party and exchange conversation over an alcoholic beverage. Alcohol at times is a solvent and may result in a mutual "loosening up." Both the therapist and the patient have to evaluate carefully the possible long-term effects before alcohol is intro-duced into the therapeutic relationship.

Changes and modifications in the more traditional techniques are open to critical evaluation and discussion. Therapists have pointed out that progress is often made when changes and modifications are developed within a particular theoretical thera-peutic framework. Change or technique for the sake of tech-nique, modification for its own purpose, and being different for the sake of being different may prove to be both ineffective to therapy as well as untenable in a long-term relationship. Modifica-tions, innovations, or changes are considered as part of a total therapy program. The use of any technique must be evaluated before application. This does not limit flexibility, but it does raise questions about the "by the seat of one's pants" approach and the "it feels right" justification. There is also the legal implication of some of the activities. This may include sexual or affectionate contact, aggressive outbursts, or physical confrontation. For example, if therapist and patient go out to lunch as part of the therapy and the patient becomes ill, is the therapist responsible? If a patient and therapist or a group of patients and a therapist go for a ride as part of the therapeutic procedure and an accident occurs, who is legally responsible for the accident and for the possible ensuing problems? Legal considerations are not viewed as reason for not undertaking an activity where it is therapeutically indi-cated. Prior to a serious consideration of some of the activities the therapist might best check with an attorney for legal advice.

The therapist may on occasion find the approach undertaken is not as effective as expected and a change in technique is indicated. The possible reasons for the change are many. The therapist or patient may have encountered snags in the original technique of choice. Change may be considered as a means of exploring other procedures which may free the process and enable progress to continue. The therapist may consider that therapy has achieved as much as might be expected with a particular approach, and further progress may be achieved through a different approach. The decision to change and the changes themselves are more effective and meaningful if done jointly. The patient and the therapist become involved in a mutual exploration of the reasons for making the change and talk about the changes that might be indicated. These changes may include going from a verbal to a nonverbal approach, from a group to individual therapy, or from individual to group therapy. Choices also include continuing to use a single therapist or changing to multiple therapists, and changing from one therapist to another.

Major changes would best be broached, rather than "sprung" on the patient. The therapist may raise the question of a change or modification of approach and find that the patient has also been considering changes but has been reluctant to bring them up because of possible fear of offending the therapist. The selection of a particular technique at the beginning of therapy does not preclude changes and modifications which may be more beneficial in the ongoing process. Patients rarely view the idea of a change as an error on the part of the therapist or as an indication that he has been shortchanged in therapy. A mutual exploration of the reasons for the decision frequently will remove the necessity for the change. At other times a new direction develops which had not been under consideration prior to the discussion itself.

7

Purposes, Goals, and Values in Psychotherapy

People enter into psychotherapy for different reasons. Their purposes and goals may vary markedly and sometimes their goals will determine the therapists they choose. However because therapists also differ in their theories or orientations they too may have different purposes or goals. This may be a matter that has to be worked out between patient and therapist. Therefore purposes and goals can vary with the theory followed, the therapist who applies the techniques relating to the theory, and the person seeking help. Again we can see the importance of flexibility on the part of the therapist. He should have a broad perspective and an openness that enables him to change, shift, and adapt himself in ways that are the most beneficial to the health and growth of the patient. As the patient changes the therapist must be particularly capable of changing his role in the relationship. As a patient grows or heals, he will relate differently. For example, a patient who functions in more childlike ways and then matures requires that the therapist now accept him at a different level and be able to act and work differently with him. Goals are determined in relation to the problems, symptoms, attitudes, and needs of the patient. There must develop a rapport and an understanding between the patient and the therapist that allows them to work together in a common cause. Frequently part of the process involves helping the patient to change unhealthy goals and to find new and creative ways of living. Goals involve changes in attitudes, feelings, and behavior. The distinction between immediate and long-term goals and the concepts of management, adjustment, and adaptation will come up later. We will also consider the question and criteria of success and failure in psychotherapy.

The concept of values is inseparable from purposes and goals in psychotherapy. Every person grows up with a developing system of values and philosophy of life which may be either conscious, unconscious, or both. The individual's values as represented by his philosophy or orientation to the world, nature and people, determine in good part how he thinks, feels, behaves, and relates to others. His values are intimately connected to whether he is creative or destructive in his goals and human relationships. Values are at the base of each person's ethical and moral system. Values and orientations to life determine the nature of the therapist and his theories. They underlie his style and the way in which he works. Equally, values weave through the life of the patient to profoundly affect his whole personality and the quality of his existence. Thus, let's try to bring together purposes, goals, and values so that they are meaningful and understandable.

In practical terms we can differentiate between purposes, goals, and values. When the patient enters into psychotherapy, he comes with some conscious statement of his purpose, whether vague or defined. The purpose is his reason for being there. Usually it is related to some problem in his life or a troubling symptom. The problem in living could have to do with interpersonal difficulty or another kind of stress. Complaints in this area take a variety of forms. Several years ago a woman spent the entire first session talking, complaining, and being highly critical of her husband. When asked why she was here instead of her husband since so much was apparently wrong with him, she replied, "Well, he couldn't make it so I came." In another first interview a man spoke of how much he's invested himself in his marriage and how hard he tries to make it work without being properly treated and rewarded by his wife. Each of these people came with two questions. The first question was "What can I do to make my husband—or wife—treat me differently?" The second question of deeper concern was "What's wrong with me?" The questions are the patient's expression of his purpose in seeking help. One woman uncomfortably spoke of her feelings of loneliness. "Even when I am with people I feel alone." A man of about thirty-five years said, "I need someone to talk to . . . I have friends, I date, but there is no one to whom I can talk about my real personal feelings." An attractive and apparently successful executive expressed anxiety about his job even though he received continual reassurances regarding his competence. "I often feel that I'm not doing well enough. I feel like a fraud and am afraid that I'll be found out." These are only a few examples of the themes that indicate the person's purpose in coming for help.

The purpose is usually expressed in the reason for seeking professional assistance. "I want to straighten out my marriage." "I wish you could tell me how to change my wife (or husband)." "I need to understand why I am unable to get close to anyone." "I know that I am competent and still I feel inadequate and live with so much anxiety." Some people are overly critical of others and other people are too critical of themselves. Thus far I have talked about anxieties that are stimulated by specific life situations. The purpose involved is to find a way to change the situation that produces the anxiety. As indicated elsewhere, the method could involve working with the individual alone, in combination with another significant person, or in a group.

There are other areas of difficulties that are not primarily presented as reactions to external conditions or people, such as a job, spouse, or friends. People can experience a variety of symptoms.

Jean goes through a great part of her days and weeks with anxious and uncomfortable feelings that seem relatively vague and unexplainable. Even though she can occasionally attribute her discomfort to something or someone, in reality she is aware that the pattern of her problem largely has to do with herself.

Harry often feels depressed. He feels down and lives much of the time with the feeling that neither he nor life has much to offer. Over the past few years he's noticed that he gets tired too easily. He has lost the motivation to do many of the things that were once important to him despite moments of feeling good. At such times the world looks good to him but it never lasts.

John periodically suffers from an acute flare-up of an ulcer that worries him. He is bright, sharp, and intellectual, with a need to have his life run in a orderly fashion. In his intense need for logical explanations he reads whatever he can. His readings include literature on psychosomatic disorders. When he found out that his ulcer attacks could be related to a psychological problem he sought help. His purpose was to remove the ulcer problem and for him it was a logical step to take when he decided to find a psychotherapist.

There are many Johns and Jeans who come for help with the purpose of getting rid of a disturbing or discomforting physical symptom. Colitis, asthma, and severe attacks of eczema are only a few of the symptoms that precipitate people into psychotherapy.

Max is forty-nine years of age. He had been going through an increasing number of periods of sexual impotence. More and more he had become preoccupied with concerns about his virility and feelings of masculinity, particularly since he was thoroughly checked through physically with no resulting medical explanation. Finally his family physician suggested that he obtain a psychological consultation.

Most often when people have physical symptoms of an emotional problem they take a long path of physical examinations before going for a psychotherapeutic consultation. It makes good sense to be checked physically. Some people, however, wait an unduly long time with the hope that the symptom will someday go away or that they will eventually find a physical explanation that can be cured by pills. People come for help with different levels of awareness, understanding, and insight. Many have a clear intellectual understanding of the problem but are still unable to resolve their difficulty, as in the case of the man with the ulcer.

Another person who goes into therapy is one who experiences a lack of satisfaction in living. He may have all the things he once believed he wanted and thought would make him happy. His relationships with people appear adequate. Marriage, work experience, and financial status are all good, but "Something is missing; something is wrong." There is an absence of clear-cut symptoms. There is no depression or strong anxiety. His physical health is good and he is without overt complaints. His purpose in asking for help is to find out what's wrong or what is missing that produces an inner sense of dissatisfaction that slowly gnaws away at him.

In short, the purpose of the patient is expressed in his reason for coming to the therapist. It is usually to find relief from some kind of anxiety or discomfort. The goal is closely connected to the purpose. For some people the purpose and goal may be the same. For example, one person may come only for relief from his anxiety or the discomfort of a physical symptom. Others may want relief to enable them to function more effectively, experience life more fully, increase their productivity, improve their creativity, or find higher levels of growth. Here is not primarily a matter of coping better or maintaining things as they are but rather of changing in some meaningful way.

At the beginning of therapy the goal is rarely clear. The person knows that he needs or wants something but is not sure of what it is other than relief. The goal is not necessarily determined at the beginning. The goal is part of a dynamic process which may change with developments in the therapeutic relationship. Goals may be immediate, short-, or long-term. The available resources of the patient and his current condition help the therapist to decide what to do. If the patient initially is sufficiently disturbed or if he is in personal danger it behooves the therapist to be more responsible in the area of decision-making until a minimal state of equilibrium is achieved. This would be the immediate goal. As soon as possible when progress is made, the therapist encourages an increasing sharing of responsibility and the working out of additional goals. The ability of the patient to assume more responsibility for his choices and his existence is an indication of growth and healthy change. Such change is usually a long-term goal.

Of course people have varying degrees of health and disorder and therefore start off in therapy at different places. It could take one person six months or a year to reach a point where another person began. This is not said in any competitive or negative sense but rather to emphasize that people cannot be placed in a mold. They neither look alike nor are alike. Each person is regarded as a unique human being who must be helped in a way and at a pace that is consistent with his strengths and difficulties at any particular time. The therapist's goal is not to recreate the patient in his image. The therapist must not impose his personal needs or wishes on the patient. To do so would likely defeat the patient in his struggle to find his sense of meaning and autonomy as a person.

Wherever possible the short-term goal is to alleviate painful or distressing symptoms. It is therapeutically desirable to do this

when the symptoms interfere with the patient's ability to productively participate in the therapy. Long-term goals are a function of
the cooperative arrangement between patient and therapist.
Immediate or early relief is not always possible and thus the
patient requires patience and a feeling of hope. The therapist
requires an ability to stay with the patient, to sustain his efforts,
and to care.

After the purpose of entering into therapy has been
translated into a goal by the patient, choices are made. These are
not always to the patient's benefit. After a number of sessions
Joanne began to feel more comfortable and felt grateful to her
therapist. It wasn't too long before her gratitude turned into anger
towards him. She resented the gratitude she felt because it made
her feel obligated and therefore controlled. Being seduced and
controlled by men was an important part of her history. With
strong convictions she expressed the wish that all she wanted out
of therapy now was to achieve the ability to be powerful enough to
seduce and control men. She warned her therapist that unless he
agreed to help her achieve this goal she would not continue her
therapy. It was evident that she was starting her course of action
by an attempt to control the therapist. The therapist did not
counterattack but rather understood the fear that prompted the
choice of her therapeutic goal. Through his support and acceptance of her feelings it was ultimately possible to help her see that
her behavior would actually result in self-defeating and unsatisfy-
ing relationships. The working through of this phase of therapy
wasn't easy for either person. There were ups and downs along
the way and more and more it became apparent to Joanne that her
victories would be hollow ones. As she recognized that her goal
was really a defensive rather than a creative one she gradually
changed it in favor of finding a relationship with a man that would
be based on loving and sharing rather than a power struggle
where no one could win.

George went into therapy because of feelings of inadequacy
that interfered with his success in business. His purpose was to
resolve the problem of inadequacy on behalf of his goal to make a
lot of money. He felt that if he were rich he would have everything
he wanted or needed. For him money represented the kind of
power that could buy things and people. The therapist saw this

goal as part of George's inner anxieties and conflicts. They worked together to explore what was going on inside of George. George eventually came to his own admission that money alone would not bring him the fulfillment he wanted. He saw that there were goals in life that were either as important or more meaningful to him than money. As with Joanne, George changed his goal from one that was unhealthy for him to one that was more personally fulfilling and meaningful.

Goals vary and change with each person in terms of his therapeutic process but also with geography, setting, circumstances, and conditions. This is often unfortunate because there may be limitations of type and quality of professional service that are related to external factors, not to the patient. Frequently, ideal treatment situations are not obtained. Although the ideal is not always necessary in order to help people, limited or substandard conditions do affect the nature and quality of the treatment program or therapy. Therefore the goals are limited and determined by such conditions. For example, there are geographical areas where few or no qualified psychotherapists are available. As in the case of most professionals such as dentists, physicians, and lawyers, psychotherapists are largely concentrated in metropolitan areas. Community mental health clinics are too far away to make regular visits feasible or practical for most people in more isolated places.

The setting where mental health services are rendered will affect the kind of therapy that is provided or even whether any psychotherapy is available. Institutional settings such as state mental hospitals are often primarily custodial places. The main purpose of custodial care is to use management procedures as a means of maintaining the patient. Restoration towards health, personal renewal, and growth are not intentional goals. The patient exists within the confines of a relatively secluded environment. He is removed from the mainstream of society. This serves a number of purposes which can be a mixed bag of the right and the wrong reasons. The confinement may be in a place of protective custody for those who would injure themselves or others. It may provide a place of temporary security that is relatively free of the stresses and pressures of the outside world. If the conditions of the institution are poor or substandard one set of stresses may merely be substituted for another. At best, custodial institutions provide a haven for those who have been unable to adequately survive in the real world. At worst, they can be stressful, unpleasant places that intensify the problems of the already disturbed person. Generally, in such places with custody as the major purpose and goal, the people become demoralized and eventually deteriorate. Lack of stimulation to create and grow in an atmosphere that is staid and colorless leads to psychological and physical death.

In the better places efforts are made at some kind of therapeutic endeavor. The hope is that the patient will return to the community in a healthier state than the one in which he entered. What is commonly referred to as the "revolving door" experience refers to people going in and out of institutions. They go into the hospital, achieve a minimal degree of stabilization and equilibrium through management procedures, and return to the community. They function for variable periods of time until the stress again becomes too great. They have relapses and go back through the institutional door.

The current management approach involves chemotherapy or the use of drugs to control behavior. Resolution of the basic problems is neither sought nor achieved. Thus the recidivism rate increases. Recidivism is the repetition of breakdowns. The concept of *cure,* however vague or defined, is not an important part of the orientation. There are severe personality disturbances that do not seem to respond adequately to any of the current available therapeutic procedures. This is not a legitimate basis for giving up and justifying many of the unfortunate and even horrid conditions that exist today. Often the quality of care is a problem of public or private funds. The value of human life is frequently measured in monetary terms. This, significantly, reflects a value attitude and leads us into the concept of values in psychotherapy.

The very nature of psychotherapy and its historical development implicitly and explicitly emphasizes human values as the highest and most essential orientation to our existence. As long as money and statistics are regarded as more important than people in practice, regardless of lip service given to human values, we will be faced with a problem of inadequate professional psychotherapeutic services. It is much easier, more convenient, and less time-consuming to medicate or shock people than to invest time and energy in helping them. This is not to negate the value of pills or other management procedures whenever necessary. Indeed in the light of current knowledge they are sometimes necessary and helpful. However, these shortcut methods are overused, misused, and at times substituted for a program that would be oriented towards conflict resolution and human growth.

Each person carries his own biases because of different values. The question is in terms of the direction of the biases. In or out of the scientific arena there is probably little or nothing that can be said without suggesting an underlying value system.

Values are at the heart of the matter of all human behavior. This includes the patient and the psychotherapist. When either one speaks of purposes and goals, values are revealed in what is asked for or given. Let us focus a little more on psychotherapy itself and the meaning of values.

There has been some discussion of theoretical orientations and modalities. Based on his value system each psychotherapist selects what he regards as most important and beneficial in his *art* of helping others. The body of knowledge that the therapist draws from is born of the science. This includes theory, technique, and modality. How he applies the science and the skillfulness with which he uses his knowledge involves the art of psychotherapy. This would be comparable in the practice of medicine to the relationship between the knowledge of the body and the "bedside manner."

There are therapists who believe that the cognitive process or thinking is most valuable in determining mental health. There are others who regard feelings as basic to a person's emotional condition. Then there are psychotherapists who maintain that thinking and feeling are both of primary value in human behavior. The therapist whose value is thinking and who emphasizes rational experience contends that the way one thinks determines his feeling, and therefore his behavior. The therapist whose primary value is feeling holds that how one feels determines his thinking and his behavior. The psychotherapist who gives major value to both thinking and feeling regards each in mutual interaction. This may be an oversimplification of the matter for there are varying degrees of attitudes that can probably be placed on a continuum between thinking as the highest value or feeling as the most important one.

Of course what is probably most important with respect to the patient is the therapist's ability to tune in and to understand the values of the patient and what he does with them. Underlying every thought is a feeling and with each feeling a thought can be elicited. To argue which is more important is like becoming trapped in the old and endless dispute of heredity versus environment. It seems that without the soil a tomato plant would never germinate and without the seed nothing would be produced. To diminish the value of either thinking or feeling is to diminish a part of the person.

The therapist should not impose values on the patient. He must be able and willing to recognize and accept that all people cannot properly be pressed into a single mold. People bring their values into therapy. Where there is a personality disturbance there is also a disturbance and imbalance in the value system. People who emphasize either thinking or feeling at the expense of the other are in a state of imbalance which distorts their perceptions. A person cannot discuss psychotherapy and deny the presence of a value system.

John, the young man with an ulcer who was discussed earlier, used his intellectual ability as a way of denying feelings that were frightening and painful to him. His reasoning ability was impeccable. He could use facts and logic with great skill. He made undeniable "sense." He valued thinking and rational behavior as the highest form of human interaction. Yet his lack of emotionality, except in the form of occasional expressions of anger or even rage, interfered with his ability to form any intimate or sustained relationship. There was no real joy in his life. Yes, John had the facts straight but he used his facts in ways that divorced him from the reality of his human self and from relationships with others. The excessive focus on rationality as a way of life kept him a fragmented person. The problem was not his facts but how he used them. Logic was used as a denial of truth and reality by selecting those aspects of reality that comfortably fitted into his system. His value as a total person was diminished. Indeed, the abilities to think and to reason are characteristics that are specifically human and of inestimable value when used for creation rather than primarily defensive purposes.

Then there is Charles, who is all feelings. Whereas the rationality of John had an irrational base, the total emphasis of Charles on his emotionality was irrational in its quality. For John, truth was a function of his logic. If his thinking made sense then he must be right. For Charles, truth was simply determined by his feelings. If he felt something, then he must be right. John and Charles represent the either-or division between thinking and feeling as the primary source of strength and the basis of human existence and behavior. Charles was not better off than John. He couldn't seem to maintain adequate relationships. He was so caught in a web of his own feelings that he could no more establish a connection with others than John.

The fact that a person thinks logically does not necessarily make him healthier than one who feels strongly. Emotionality is more often associated with irrationality than is thinking. It is important to point out that the processes of thinking and the experiencing of feeling can either be rational or irrational. Either can be used in the service of health or illness. Each is a valuable and unique aspect of total human behavior and relatedness.

Every person has a value system just by virtue of having lived in the world. Values are at the very core of all human behavior and interaction. Literally, *value* means *strength* or *worth*. It represents what is most important to each person and what is meaningful in his life and is the essence of his "raison d'être," or reason for being. Values are at the bedrock of all human existence. They determine not only the nature of individual styles of living but the behavior of nations, cultures, and societies. Each political, religious, or economic point of view rests on a set of values. People value the old or the new, the old or the young, money, things or people, and so on. Premiums are placed on different aspects of life. Purposes and goals are expressions of these premiums. The danger lies in the fact that wherever a disproportionate or inappropriate emphasis is laid on a particular value it may be manifested towards destructive goals.

You have seen illustrations of how the rationalist may use thinking in unhealthy ways and how the emotionalist may do the same thing with his feelings. Thinking or feeling per se is not necessarily good or bad. What matters is how and for what purposes they are used. As T. S. Eliot indicated in *Murder in the Cathedral*, a person may do the right things for the wrong reasons. Invariably this ends up in calamity.

We have seen the example of George who valued money above all other things. In his desire for money as his source of strength or worth he could only be self-defeating and exploitative with others. While it would be unrealistic to deny the necessity of money in order to live, it is unhealthy when money means more than money and becomes an all-consuming drive. Any single and limited value that dominates a person consumes both the person himself and those he relates to. It is the difference between the value being in the service of the person or the person becoming énslaved by the value, whereby the value becomes valueless.

Each political system whether it be capitalism, socialism, communism, or any variations thereof reflects certain attitudes towards people and life. National Socialism in Germany focused on Aryanism as its highest value. On investing itself in the development of the pure race Nazi Germany justified the destruction of millions of people and produced a holocaust of terrifying dimensions. Every nation engaging in war justifies its actions in terms of virtuous values. To properly understand Aryanism or the value system of any nation requires a study of the pertinent history of the country's development as a nation and a people which is beyond our scope right now. Suffice it to say that Germany stressed an authoritarian and patriarchal structure with deference for authority. Japan held to the myth of the emperor's divinity and a patriarchal system which, as in Germany, came under the domination of the military. America has emphasized individualism and competitiveness as a means of achieving success. In contrast the Hopi Indians, a member of the Shoshonean Pueblo Indian people of northern Arizona, had a well-organized tribe based on a cooperative economic structure. The Mundugumor, a Papuan people of New Guinea, have a history of head-hunting, cannibalism, much conflict, and no cooperation. The Mountain Arapesh, also a Papuan people of New Guinea, stress docility rather than aggression. On the other hand the Manus of the Admiralty

Islands encourage aggression which becomes expressed in intense competition and rage at frustration.

These are all examples of attitudes or behavior that reflect underlying values. The examples are endless and involve all individual, group, and institutional structures. Political, religious, economic, and cultural attitudes are based on values that give rise to them. What is crucial is that the primary values determine our ways of living and relating to each other. If the real values are regarded as unacceptable they are likely to be hidden and disguised. Individuals do the same thing by some form of deception which either disguises their real motives from others, themselves, or both. As long as a person continues to deceive himself by a process of rationalization he can go on repeating behavior that is hurtful to others or self-defeating. When he is able to gain insight into what he is doing he is more likely to change such behavior by finding more productive ways of achieving satisfaction for his personal needs.

Finally, something should be said about the concept of success and failure in psychotherapy. Generally one may consider that a person has had a successful psychotherapeutic experience to the degree that he gets well, improves, gives up disturbing symptoms or self-defeating behavior, and is more successful in his human relationships and work experiences. Yet it is not really as simple as it sounds. People, both therapists and patients, have different values and therefore may have different criteria of success and failure. What may be success for one person can be failure for another. We are now in a complex area that can become difficult and that penetrates the matrix of value systems. For example, in the case of various physical illnesses treatment may be considered successful if the patient's life has been extended a year or two, or more. Is the same approach applicable to emotional problems? If a person's sanity is extended for a similar period or his life lengthened by temporarily preventing suicide would this be considered successful psychotherapy? Perhaps this is not so absurd. As a matter of fact there are people whose attitude may be "he's better off dead." Others believe that life is to be cherished however painful. Attitudes about euthanasia or mercy killing also involve the question of one's values.

The critical issue involves the criteria of success or failure. Is treatment successful when a person behaves properly, conventionally, or rebelliously? Has therapy been successful when a person fits into the norm or deviates from it? Or, does it depend on what we believe *normal* means? Is all deviant, crazy, or rebellious behavior necessarily abnormal or insane? Is all conforming or conventional behavior necessarily sane or healthy? A sick person living in a sick social milieu is normal in a statistical sense but may be psychologically unhealthy. A healthy person in the same environment would appear abnormal because he deviates from the norm. Some people may have a successful psychotherapy experience when they can behave more conventionally. Others may be successful and return to a healthier state when they become less conventional or even rebellious. Any behavior that is destructive to oneself or others—and they cannot be separated—is unhealthy.

Perhaps an appropriate criterion for emotional health is the state when the person is able to develop and use his potentials. He functions on the basis of personal prerogative. With an armamentarium of skills, knowledge of his limitations, and a true sense of self, the person is able to function as a result of choice rather than by unwarranted pressures from within and without. With a value system that is congruent with creative living he can experience enjoyment. Thus emotional health is based on a humanistic value system, the ability to fulfill one's potentials and achieve fulfillment, and the ability to enjoy living.

8

Who Is
a Psychotherapist?

Many people may wonder whether there are any essential differences between a psychotherapist and other people who might help someone in emotional trouble. For example, are there differences between counselors and psychotherapists as well as between family physicians, clergy, friends, and members of the family? The answer, of course, is yes. A critical feature of the psychotherapist is that he remains neutral and sufficiently uninvolved emotionally that his decision-making, judgment, and interpretation are neither judgmental, biased, nor swayed by the emotional factors. Also the psychotherapist, while he may be an adherent of a specific school or format of therapy, does not have a particular "axe to grind." A clergyman is bound by the doctrines of the particular faith as to what he may or may not morally and ethically accept in his parishioners' behavior. He is thus limited in ways that a psychotherapist is not. When the clergyman is also a pastoral counselor, one would hope that he would not permit his religious orientation to adversely affect his helping an individual with emotional conflicts. However, under those conditions, he may still be bound by the tenets of his faith.

One might expect the family physician to be knowledgeable in the area of human relations and human behavior. Regrettably this is most often not so. The medical training of the physician includes a minimum of psychiatric and psychological training and does not lend the type of knowledge and training necessary for the physician to be a good listener and a nonjudgmental therapist. The physician also is sharply limited as to the amount of time he can spend with any given patient. The dictates of a busy family practice preclude the opportunity for psychotherapeutic work. Probably the members of one's family plus friends are people one would most often turn to in times of stress and need. Here too the question of emotional involvement, freedom from bias and prejudice, the lack of training and ability to refrain from giving advice, and the intense emotional involvement all mitigate against an objective and helpful relationship. Close friends and family members are certainly most important in helping one over immediate stress situations. Their support and reassurance are both necessary and desirable under these conditions. However, when the stress is over and the situation is not as imminent, the problem of rehabilitation, analysis, and synthesis becomes a most important one. It is in these instances that the friends and family members are less constructive in their attempts. Emotional involvement, bias, the inability to see past certain immediate situations, and one's own unconscious fears and hope for someone else all interfere with the most rewarding and effective helping relationship.

Counselors are also members of the helping professions and these individuals have a specific function. It is just this last aspect that precludes involvement in psychotherapeutic work with these helping individuals. A vocational counselor focuses on the problems of work and career. A guidance counselor in a school system will function well in the area of school problems, both academic and interpersonal, involving teacher and student and administrator and student. The marital counselor may well help a couple clarify specific aspects of their relationship. Once the individual goes beyond this, the counselor is no longer in the position to be most effective and helpful. The counselor is usually trained to focus on specific problems and remain within specific limits of these problem areas. The psychotherapist goes beyond these limits and beyond the immediacy of the problems themselves to other involvements and other aspects of the person's life. For all of the above reasons the psychotherapist, by virtue of his training, supervision, and experience, is in the most advantageous position to be of long-term help rather than the others who, while they would be effective in certain areas, might be less effective in the overall.

We have looked at what differentiates the psychotherapist from others. Let us look at some of the specific disciplines involving psychotherapists. There are specific subspecialties within each of the major helping professions where the individual specializes in psychotherapy. Among psychologists, the clinical psychologist is the individual who devotes a major portion of his work to helping individuals with emotional problems. The psychiatrist is the specialist in the general area of medicine who has the training background and experience to do psychotherapeutic work. In recent years social workers have developed a subspecialty known as psychiatric social work. While at the onset these individuals were primarily assistants to the psychiatrist, in recent years they have developed their own practices and techniques and have extended their work to include independent functioning in the area of psychotherapy, particularly with families and children. As mentioned earlier, pastoral counselors are individuals who have the training and background to work primarily with the emotionally disturbed in religious settings. They may be members of the clergy, professed brothers and sisters, or selected laypeople. Some pastoral counselors receive advance training in psychotherapeutic theory and technique. Their orientation includes a religious moral value system and a goal of enhancing the individual's ability to experience his innate "lovability." One should bear in mind that being a clergyman or a professed member of a religious community does not automatically make one a pastoral counselor. A guide which may be used as a general criterion for pastoral counseling is the general philosophy of The Graduate Division of Pastoral Counseling, Iona College, New Rochelle, New York. In addition to required specialty training encompassing didactic courses and supervised experience, this philosophy includes:

(1) Men and women have psychological needs to fulfill and emotional conflicts to resolve before they can freely develop and value their innate spiritual being.

(2) The pastoral counselor has a moral value system recognizing the inherent worthiness and lovability of the human individual.

A person must remember that whether one is a psychologist, physician, social worker, or pastoral counselor, the training and education received in any of these areas is not sufficient to enable a person to work as a psychotherapist. The individual should

receive specialized and intensive training in the area of psychotherapy no matter what his profession is and what areas he will
work in as a psychotherapist. A look at the background and
preliminary training of each of these subspecialties will provide a
clear picture of what goes into the selection, education, and
training of each psychotherapist.

The psychologist usually goes for the doctorate degree in
psychology. This may be most often in clinical psychology, but
may also be in counseling psychology, or in marriage and family
living. While studying for the degree itself the psychologist must
take work in various areas of psychology as well as more specifically in the area of psychotherapy. During this time he is observed
and supervised by a number of trained psychotherapists. One of
the functions that the psychotherapist's supervisors have is to
evaluate his individual emotional maturity and ability to work
with people as well as his ability to acquire the more formal
knowledge and training. Part of the doctoral degree is a minimum
of one year supervised internship. This may be in a hospital,
community clinic, outpatient setting, or under the supervision of a
licensed psychotherapist who is practicing in the community.
After the successful completion of both the degree and the
internship the psychologist may consider himself a clinician and
begin his work as a psychotherapist. As will be indicated later the
learning process never ceases. There are many opportunities for
further development and growth as a psychotherapist, clinical
psychologist, and human being.

The psychiatrist first must complete the necessary requirements for the medical degree. At the completion of the degree he
serves a general medical internship for a year in a hospital. At that
time he may spend a brief period with a psychiatric service, after
which he may decide to undertake psychiatric residency. At the
completion of this he may decide to go into the practice of
psychiatry either in a hospital, a guidance center, clinic, or in
private practice. The psychiatrist may prescribe medication and
may utilize electroconvulsive shock therapy. Frequently he practices chemotherapy or drug therapies. He may also do psychotherapy in his work.

The psychiatric social worker, after the completion of the
undergraduate degree usually in either psychology or sociology,

then goes for a master's degree in social work. This is a two-year program which also requires a minimum of a one-year supervised field experience prior to graduation. At the completion of the master's degree he is then qualified to consider himself a psychiatric social worker. As has been indicated earlier one of the major functions of the psychiatric social worker has been in assisting the psychiatrist in the hospital setting by interviewing families, marital partners, and working with them in conjunction with the program outlined by the psychiatrist. More recently psychiatric social workers have moved into the community in direct patient contact as independent practitioners without the training and/or supervision of the psychiatrist.

The individual choosing to go into pastoral counseling usually has completed the requirements for a bachelor's degree or the equivalent before entering this specialized training. The variety as well as the intensity of training varies depending on the particular pastoral counseling program selected. An example of a competent master's degree program is that offered by the Graduate Division of Pastoral Counseling at Iona College, New Rochelle, New York. This program is designed to accomplish several goals including 1) the development of the "participant's awareness of the dynamics of human behavior underlying the problems encountered by the pastoral counselor . . . ; 2) enlarge the participant's insight into the forces affecting the counseling process; 3) augment the sensitivity and understanding required of the pastoral counselor in counseling situations; 4) to accord participants a practical opportunity to develop or increase those skills that make for greater efficiency in counseling." As indicated, the training programs include didactic courses, seminars and interacting experiential group workshops. A major emphasis is placed upon supervised counseling practicum experience which continues over the three-year training program. Some pastoral counselors further their formal training to the doctoral degree.

A look at the formal aspects of the training and certain other aspects of specific training in the area of psychotherapy may be of value. An important part of any psychotherapist's training involves an understanding of normal human growth and physical and emotional development in our society. The psychotherapist must also understand what other societies and cultures consider normal and abnormal behavior. However the focus is on those aspects which are found most typically in the society in which the psychotherapist will function. The psychotherapist must understand what social pressures mitigate against a person's maintaining an emotional stability and balance, as well as what internal psychic and physical factors may tip the balance against emotional stability. Therefore the psychotherapist must understand both what it is to be normal and abnormal, what are society's demands and pressures, what are the typical modes of coping with internal and external pressures, and what it means to be different and/or abnormal. The psychotherapist also receives instruction in the whole question of problems of living in current society. The psychotherapist has to understand how one goes about meeting the demands made upon the man, the woman, and the child in our society. The psychotherapist also has to know what effect changing social pressures have on a given individual and/or family structure.

An additional part of the training of the psychotherapist involves techniques of interviewing and assessment. The psychotherapist uses the initial interview as both a diagnostic and prognostic instrument. While it depends upon the particular orientation of the psychotherapist as to what other techniques of assessment are used, the interview is common to all. The psychotherapist therefore receives intensive training in interviewing and the use of the interview in assessment and prediction. The psychotherapist must also understand the dynamics of behavior. He has to develop the ability to evaluate and assess what is taking place within the patient and the meaning of the patient's behavior as well as what is involved in the impact of this behavior on others in the patient's world. The psychotherapist has to understand that behavior which may seem to be random or inexplicable to others has its own meaning and its own value. Part of the training of the psychotherapist, then, also involves how to work with this understanding of the behavior and verbalizations of the individual. This has to do with techniques and procedures which will be explained at some length later.

There are a number of aspects of psychotherapy training which are important. Careful supervision of everything the beginning psychotherapy student and also the beginning psychotherapist does has already been mentioned. An experienced psychotherapy supervisor carefully reviews what the student psychotherapist does and explores with the individual the pros and cons of specific approaches, the understanding of what is happening, and the formulation of prediction and process. Supervision is intense and on a regular ongoing basis. This is considered one of the most important aspects of psychotherapy training no matter what the discipline might be. Regularly every patient is presented at a case conference. The psychotherapist in training learns how to organize his material and how to develop methods of understanding and presenting this material to his peers and colleagues. The case is attended by representatives of many disciplines who all work together for the best interests of the patient involved. The case conference also serves as a supervisory vehicle for the beginning psychotherapist. This is an additional aspect of the overall training and helps focus on areas in both the personal approach of the psychotherapist as well as the theoretical orientation that the psychotherapist may follow.

Some of the training institutes require their candidate to undergo personal psychotherapy. The psychotherapist in training selects his own psychotherapist, usually from a roster maintained by the training institute. The psychotherapist then must complete a course in personal psychotherapy which may be of one or more times a week over a period of a year or more. Often the psychotherapist is asked to present to the training institute some evidence that the psychotherapist in training has satisfactorily completed the program in personal psychotherapy. The major purpose of a psychotherapist's psychotherapy is to enable him to understand himself and his relationships with his patients with more clarity and with less bias and prejudice. Psychotherapy is not expected to remove all problems from the psychotherapist, but to enable him to function most effectively with the understanding of his limitations and personality attributes.

One might raise the question of where the beginning psychotherapist obtains the specialty training, depending upon his interests and particular bent. Most of the larger cities in this and other countries have a number of institutes or training schools where specialty training is available. These programs include formal class work, supervision, and practice as required before the diploma or certificate is granted. The requirement is usually the doctorate degree in either psychology or medicine, or the master's degree in social work or ordination as a clergyman. There is an ongoing process of review during the time the psychotherapist attends the institute. There are training institutes that focus on Freudian and non-Freudian psychoanalytic approaches. There are also training institutes that emphasize the group processes, either as group psychotherapy or psychodrama. There are also training institutes that travel around the country. They usually present a three to five day training institute that runs for ten to twelve hours a day. This is not a replacement for the longer training program but is usually a short-term intensive program for practitioners of that particular specialty or orientation. All of the major modalities and schools of psychotherapy have institutes that provide specialty training in their particular approach. At the completion of the training the psychotherapist receives a certificate. Often the psychotherapist/student must agree not to practice independently or utilize those procedures and techniques until he is certified by the faculty of the institute.

As indicated earlier, psychotherapists are not limited in what methods and techniques they might use with a particular patient. The differences among psychotherapists might well be more one of the explanation of what, why and how a particular method is selected and used, rather than what method or technique is actually selected and what the results are with a specific patient. We'll take a look at this question later on.

Learning and training are ongoing processes. The various disciplines require, or at least strongly encourage, continuing of training and education. These may be in the form of specific workshops, which may be of several orientations. Some focus on the patient and discuss methods and techniques of therapy. These may last a day to a week or even more. There are workshops given on the state and national level which require personal involvement of several psychotherapists working together. Workshops may also focus on the therapist. In these sessions therapists get together to explore themselves and their personal improvement as therapists and human beings. These sessions also may last from a day to a week or more. More common today is the general program of a workshop which involves both focus on techniques and working with patients as well as focus on therapists and their better understanding of themselves and of their patients.

Professional meetings are held throughout the world. A person could easily spend a week out of every month attending professional meetings somewhere in the country or somewhere in the world. These meetings involve formal presentations of papers on theoretical research material, symposia, and general discussions on topics of interest as well as personal exploration of patients and self for the psychotherapist. Every major organization has a professional meeting at least one or more times a year at which there is a program prepared for that particular group by its members. Here the individuals share with each other knowledge, information, and ideas. The professional meeting or workshop is also the area in which the psychotherapist may personally become involved in presenting and exploring his own ideas and theories. All professional organizations have their own journal which includes articles of general interest, theoretical material, and material on techniques and specific problems. While time is very limited, the psychotherapist expects at least to review as much of the material in his own subspecialty and his own orientation as time permits. This includes writing some of the articles for publication as well as reading them for the latest information and ideas in the field. The national organizations also present postdoctoral and postgraduate courses. The postdoctoral institutes are short-term intensive presentations in a specific area. These are on all levels—some for the beginning psychotherapist, some for the psychotherapist of some training and experience, and some for the experienced therapist who has been in the field for many years. All psychotherapists are encouraged to explore, innovate, and continue developing as psychotherapists for the best interests of the patients.

This information should provide you with a fair idea of what goes into the background and training of various therapists. We can continue from this point to get into more specific areas of psychotherapy.

9

What Is It Like
to Be a Therapist?

What is it like to be a therapist and live the life of a therapist? Books on psychotherapy most often include a discussion of the characteristics and attributes of the "good" therapist. This person is a unique individual—warm, empathetic, understanding, accepting, permissive, without flaw or taint, who represents all that is good and hopeful in the world today. What the books do not include is what it is like to be a therapist out of as well as in the office or clinic. There is rarely a discussion of what happens to a therapist in the nontherapeutic world. Little is mentioned of the human qualities of the therapist. Omitted also is what happens with and to the therapist as a human being in his relationship to the world and within himself. We might look at some of the things that go into the life and the world of the therapist. There are facets that one rarely finds written about except in the journal *Voices—The Art and Science of Psychotherapy* or in an occasional presentation at a meeting or convention when the therapists feel freer and less formal.

A person who has been a patient, a therapist, a psychotherapy training supervisor, and a human being has come across most of the problem areas and the aspects that trouble and befuddle the therapist, whether a beginner, journeyman, or master. Some of these are presented as problems without definitive statements and conclusions. Some are opinions and others are dicta to be slavishly followed. You might like to share and enjoy these experiences, views, and ideas.

How do others, professionals and nonprofessionals, look at the therapist? How does a member of a family look at father or mother, older brother or sister, who is also a psychotherapist? How do friends and relatives respond to this person? What may happen when this individual is introduced at a party or other social gatherings as a psychologist or a psychotherapist, or sometimes as a "shrink"?

Many people, whether friend, relative, or stranger, are somewhat concerned as to whether this person can "see through them." They wonder whether he is really able to understand everything that is hidden and everything they are trying so hard to keep from being evident. Often the therapist may float around being oblivious to the fact that other people are counting their words, selecting their responses carefully, or responding circumspectly. They are doing whatever they can to avoid the possible analysis they assume is being done of them by the therapist. It is interesting to watch how people sometimes will interact with a person in a rather relaxed social way until they find out that the individual is a professional therapist. Sometimes there is a sudden freezing up or a withdrawal, and a sharply decreased response with some evidence of discomfort. It is as if the individual suddenly touched a hot wire, or found his phone was being tapped, or learned that he was going to be summoned into court to account for whatever he says, does, and thinks. Another approach to the sudden discovery of being confronted by a therapist is the "my friend has a problem" ploy. At this point the individual launches into a long discussion about the details of the friend's problem. At times people do forget and begin to talk about themselves in the first person rather than as the friend. This change rapidly clarifies issues. Of course a problem may occur if the therapist responds to the individual as if he were a patient. This may become a real problem with members of the immediate family in that it provokes anxiety. It is questionable whether complete objectivity is ever possible even in the most scientific or professional person. What is important is that the therapist be in touch with his own subjective self and not get it mixed up with that of the patient. Some people may want the therapist to listen or want a professional opinion. At the same time they may not want the therapist to know too much about them. If the therapist is a relative, they may not have sufficient faith in his opinions. They can remember the therapist when he was in diapers, dribbling food, acting as an arrogant adolescent, and beginning to take himself seriously as a budding psychotherapist. At times relatives may approach the therapist with an interesting request. They would like him to divorce himself from the reality of being a relative and view them in an objective dispassionate way. As recognized in other aspects of the healing arts this can be extremely difficult, if it is possible at all. Most therapists would rather not become professionally involved with a close member of the family.

What are the possible personal benefits of being a psychotherapist? The therapist, if he has exposed himself to his own therapeutic process, is able to understand himself, as well as others, more clearly. This does not mean that the therapist is completely free of personal difficulties. He may have problems with a member of the family or he may have some specific hangups. However it is hoped that these problems do not interfere in his daily functioning and the therapist is able to be more open with himself as well as with others. He should be motivated to be sensitive out of conscious choice rather than by undue anxiety or fear. Therefore one would expect that the effect on his family—parents, siblings, spouse, or offspring—would be a positive one. When therapists meet the inevitable difficulties of living there should be a more positive attempt to clarify the issues and to modify the feelings and behavior so as to reflect the increased rapport.

There is another positive aspect to being a therapist. As Eric Berne has pointed out, everyone has something of the parent within himself. Everyone wants to take care of someone and has the need to be needed by others. Being a therapist provides an outlet for this need. Not only do strangers with emotional problems need a therapist but family members and friends directly affected by the therapist also have a need for him. Everyone also has a child within himself. The therapist can experience his own child through the patient. Another important plus is the ability to share one's own growth, fears, hopes, and desires with other people. Sullivan, Berne, and Freud have pointed out the need to share with others those aspects of oneself that people tend to hold secret. All too frequently this is not possible in our world. The therapist is able to share with others on a give-and-take basis those parts of himself that express his uniqueness as a person and as a member of a group.

There are, however, negative aspects to being a psychotherapist. The task of sitting in a chair, hour after hour after hour,
provides little opportunity to express oneself in motor behavior or
exercise. The lack of exercise is conducive to the development of
circulatory difficulties, overweight, and other typical physical ills.
People need physically and emotionally satisfying activities. An
important aspect of living is that there must be varying sources of
satisfaction and gratification for everyone. With the therapist this
might be even more important psychologically than for some
others. The psychological demand made on the therapist to be
emotionally responsive to people in trouble, people with troubles,
and people who are troubled is extremely wearing. Responsibility
literally is being responsive or responsible. The therapist who has
the profession as his sole life function often finds there may be
difficulties in other areas. He may begin to lose perspective and his
personal life begins to suffer. Conflict can develop with a loved
one, with siblings, with offspring, and with colleagues. There is a
need "to turn off" at times, or to stop being a therapist. The
concern some people have when meeting a therapist socially was
discussed earlier. A comforting thought is that the therapist can be
a person. Therapists often like to indicate to friends, relatives, and
to patients that after a certain time of day, during the weekend, or
on holidays they are "turned off" and out of business "professionally." This does not mean that they are unresponsive or insensitive
as human beings, or that they are in a shell. It does mean that they
regard some parts of their lives as private for themselves where
they can rest from the pressure and struggle, pain and interaction
often characteristic of the therapeutic process. They are available
for an emergency but not for the routine of a therapeutic process.

There are a few psychotherapists who involve other members
of the family either as co-therapists or ancillaries in the therapeutic process. One of the problems in this approach is that there may
be a blurring of the distinction between one's life as a therapist and
one's personal world. This approach is limited to a relatively small
number of therapists who recognize the problems and confusions
that may exist and are exploring it as an innovation in a therapeutic approach.

A problem common to the beginning therapist as well as to
more experienced therapists throughout their professional career

is the feeling of being an all-powerful omnipotent God to everyone. Therapists, as other human beings, face the choice of taking
themselves too seriously or being able to see and laugh at their
own foibles and hangups. At times a patient will seduce the
therapist into the feeling that he is so necessary to the patient's life
that his very word controls fate and destiny. Sometimes the
therapist's own need for power will drive him to play the role of
God. The therapist may experience great difficulty in avoiding the
feeling that what he says and does so strongly affects another
person's life. The psychotherapist also has the responsibility to
recognize that this is so at times whether these words are spoken
by himself or someone else the patient considers important.
Possibly all psychotherapists have some drive toward power and
the control of others. As long as this remains within bounds few if
any adverse results will occur. However when the need for power
and omnipotence gets out of control, then damage may occur.
Sometimes the need for power is so great that the therapist sees
himself as omnipotent and all-knowing in reference to anyone and
everyone, even colleagues. A corollary to this is the need to have
everyone, particularly patients, like him. If the psychotherapist
finds it necessary that everyone think well of him, this can make it
very difficult for him to function adequately as a human being as
well as a psychotherapist.

The reverse may also be questioned. Does the therapist have
to like everyone with whom he works? Is it possible to work
effectively with and have respect for someone without liking him
in a personal way? This area of thought has been debated for
many years and has become an issue in the dynamic and humanistic approaches to therapy. For those who base their therapy on a
specific learning approach the relationship between therapist and
patient is not regarded as important. The question of liking or
disliking is not considered relevant to the therapeutic procedure.
In these approaches the technique and procedures are the important variables. Sometimes a therapist has difficulty in admitting
that he does not like everyone and does not respond to each
patient with the same degree of liking. As in a family there are
some who are liked more and some less. In every therapist's
practice it is quite frequent to have one or more patients who pose
extremely difficult problems. Presenting a difficult problem in

psychotherapy does not necessarily indicate that the patient is being demanding or personally difficult. It may or may not be a problem of technique, or of outcome, or of problems in the relationship between the individuals involved. At times a patient may be extremely demanding, frustrating, irritating, and simply unlikeable. There is the question as to how much of this dislike is communicated by the therapist directly to the patient. It has become more professionally accepted to express and discuss one's own personal feelings with patients. The honesty that the therapist asks of the patient extends also to the therapist himself.

A patient may be upset when the therapist expresses negative feelings about being a therapist. This may occur when the therapist is extremely tired, worn out, or looks at what others do with a feeling that it would be easier to work hard physically or intellectually rather than to take responsibility for the emotional lives of others. There are moments when honest and introspective therapists will admit that they would just as soon not have become a psychotherapist. However, this is said not with the conviction that it should be so, but with the cathartic effect of expressing one's feelings. A therapist may speak negatively about himself when he feels that he has not been effective. Sometimes it is fun as well as a way of escape for the therapist, when out socially, to pretend that he is a plumber, electrician, or generally in some type of work that involves more working with objects than with people. This is not a negative view but a recognition that at times a therapist does feel a need for change. He should be free to express this even where patients, colleagues, or family may hear.

Another difficulty may involve feelings of competition when working with colleagues. There are those professions where there is constant competition for patients, for status, and for power. There are other professions where a strong collaborative approach is emphasized. Psychologists, particularly psychotherapists, are becoming more aware of the need for and importance of collaboration and cooperation. In the approaches involving multiple therapists, co-therapists, and joint therapists, there is a definite need for collaboration and a feeling of trust in one's colleagues and in oneself.

The question might be raised whether the therapist needs to present a certain image. If so, what image does a therapist want to forward to the viewing public? The question might be more effectively asked, present to whom? This would include the therapist, society, patients, colleagues, or relatives and friends. Psychotherapists, like all other people, react differently to different people. It is unreasonable to expect the therapist to be the same way at all times and with all people. Some therapists would not express doubts or questions directly to a patient, or to society, but might express them clearly to colleagues, or to themselves. There are others who would share doubts and concerns with patients and colleagues. The therapist is not a neutral individual who responds to all situations in the same way nor expects others to respond to him in the same way. Frequently there is some intent to project an image or picture of the person one would like to be. As with all humans the closer the image is to the reality the less difficulty the individual encounters in living. Generally the therapist is expected to have more understanding of these factors and to have a closer relationship between his image and the reality.

The therapist has a world both as a person and as a professional. He learns either early in life or through training and experience to become a freer person. The therapist is able to relate, respond, and interact with others in an open honest manner and learns to tolerate frustration and anxiety. Theoretically the earlier a person learns to be free and to be able to enter into honest and open relationships the more effective he is as a human being. This openness may be acquired later in life, but it does necessitate greater concentration and greater effort and struggle at that time. The therapist may, then, distinguish between his world as a professional/human and as a human/professional. Some therapists feel there is no clear difference and that to concern themselves with limitations and strictures is an artifice. There are those, however, who feel that one must keep some distance between the two.

We might consider some of the aspects of being a human being. For a considerable time there were specific distinctions made in the area of touch. As a human it is quite acceptable for the therapist to touch another person in certain ways and under prescribed conditions. However, in the early field of psychotherapy, the whole area of human touch and physical contact was considered taboo and the therapist was taught that he was not to touch a patient. Experimental evidence as well as pragmatic experience have demonstrated that human touch—the touch of hands or a touch on the shoulder—can be important to another person.

All humans become involved in sexual or sexualized relationships. These may be on a verbal, symbolic, physical or emotional level. Any type of sexual contact with patients, either heterosexual or homosexual, has been another very strong taboo, probably the strongest taboo in the entire area of psychotherapy. Sex for the gratification of the therapist is considered destructive to the patient and should not be entered into. There are therapists today who feel that this taboo is artificial and unrealistic. There are therapists who feel that sexual relationships between therapist and patient may be therapeutically relevant. This is an extremely difficult and troubled area, since the eventual possible benefit or consequences of the sexual behavior are difficult to ascertain at the onset. In the past the sexual activity may have been for the benefit of the therapist, not for the passive patient. The therapist may be sexually stimulated by or attracted to the patient. Barriers to the therapeutic process may well arise when the therapist denies or puts into action his feelings, rather than exploring them.

Another consideration refers to the mutual sharing of affection with a patient. This activity might well include holding hands, putting an arm around someone, or using terms of affection and mild endearment. There is a distinction between affectionate behavior and sexual behavior. In the past any indication of affection, as well as sexual or physical contact, was strongly inhibited. It has become difficult to continue these taboos with the development of the encounter group approach and with the experimental evidence demonstrating the need for physical contact in the growth of personality. There is a need for the therapist to innovate and change as he continues growing within himself and in the profession.

A therapist may be employed by many different private and government agencies. A question often arises concerning the therapist's responsibility. For example, if a therapist is employed by a prison or hospital, is he responsible to the prison authority, the hospital administrators, to society, or does he represent the patient? If a patient indicates some type of misbehavior, punishable either morally or legally by the authorities, does the therapist then report this? There may be a conflict between the demands of the agencies and the therapist's own feelings and philosophies. In most instances a therapist does feel himself to be the agent of the society or the specific authorities. In the behavior modification methods the therapist represents the world of reality and social controls. The patient's behavior is modified to meet the needs of society, the authorities, and the external world of reality. The approach is to have the individual conform to the needs of the outside world. Of course if the behavior is destructive to either self or outside world, the choice is simplified. In general, however, the answers are not that simple. Often it is an extremely difficult choice to be considered by both patient and therapist. Decisions are sometimes less complicated in private practice. The decision may be made without regard to the needs or demands of an external agency.

Another aspect of the earlier question regarding personal contact with patients involves the area of social relationships. For many decades it was considered unacceptable to have any social contact with a patient outside the office setting. However, what is the therapist to do if while at a party he finds that a patient is a guest at the same party? What happens when a group is organized to travel and the therapist finds his patient is a member of the group? At the turn of the century and again more recently therapists and patients have gone to the same general resort areas and have become interwoven into a social matrix. Among the problems often created is the possible loss of the psychotherapeutic relationship which is replaced by a social situation.

Beginning with some of the earlier experiences of a therapist in training, further exploration of the personal aspects of being a therapist might be enlightening. The therapist may find interpersonal difficulties in his supervisory experiences. These may be disagreements of fact or personality. They may occur with a therapist's own supervisor or with a trainee when the therapist is the supervisor. The therapist may also experience problems in his personal therapy. He may discover things about himself which are extremely discomforting and which may pose problems to him. This has to do with what happens when one encounters one's "real self." The general hope is that the therapist work out these problems to the mutual benefit of himself and his future patients. However each therapist has limitations. These may be limitations of knowledge, ability, emotional tolerance, or the ability to relate to certain types of people. The therapist has to accept, understand, and learn to cope effectively with these limitations to his own therapy. There is no single therapist who is the therapist of choice for all people under all conditions. This fact is often recognized more by the patients than by the therapist himself. The more accepting of his real limitations the more effective will the therapist be with his patient.

Most humans in our Western culture develop the need for success. This may involve the fear of failure, or the need to succeed and improve on the success itself. The therapist has comparable needs. These may be expressed as an inability to accept the possibility of failure, or a realization that there is a realistic limit to his ability to help others. A result of this need for success may be the seduction of the patient to continue unsuccessful therapy, and to be "the good patient" for the therapist rather than for the patient's self.

Most therapists recognize that there are certain realistic aspects in the relationship with a patient and that these should be honored. A patient may or may not benefit in a relationship with a particular therapist. The beneficial aspects may depend on the therapist rather than on the patient. The therapist's need for success should be tempered with the recognition that success has many faces and is encountered under many guises. Another aspect in a therapeutic relationship is the effect of the therapist's value system. Traditionally, therapists are to avoid imposing their values on the patient. The idea is easier to accomplish than the task. The patient looks upon the therapist as a model, an expert, and as the one to whom he comes for help. Therefore the value system shown by the therapist is one often adopted by the patient. Research has indicated that the patient often responds to what he perceives the therapist wants him to respond to and to behave in a similar manner. A patient has extreme difficulty in maintaining his own values in the face of those demonstrated by his therapist. The therapist refrains insofar as possible from imposing his values on the patient. Explorations and discussion of contradictory value systems will sometimes counter the patient's uncritical acceptance of the therapist's values.

Many therapists use techniques of innovation balanced with traditional approaches. Therapeutic techniques seen as radical departures at the onset may gradually become institutionalized and later become traditional. The therapist is usually on the alert for productive innovations and change in his field. A change might well be a positive one if it enhances the therapeutic relationship and furthers the therapeutic goals. A change may be questioned as problematic or even damaging if it is for the aggrandizement or the personal benefit of the therapist. Change without rationale and without goal orientation may be suspect and open to question. However, a refusal to change and blind adherence to tradition may be just as dangerous as fads and random change.

A therapist grows and changes. However, the change may be either in a negative or in a positive direction. Experiences between the therapist and another human being in a therapeutic relationship provide a climate for reassessment of his goals, life's expectations, and professional commitments. The therapist continues in his efforts to expand his personal horizons, learning, and experience. Just as there are innovations in therapeutic technique and modalities, there are innovations and change within the therapist himself. There are continuing explorations to assess life and goals. There are of course attendant risks to this process. It is often less painful to maintain one's status quo rather than explore and face the changes that might be necessary in one's life for further growth. Anyone who is the same over a ten year span has not grown and developed. However, continued growth and development is more important for the therapist than for most other individuals. The therapist directly influences other people's lives. A continuing exploration for the purpose of change is important for the therapist. This is in order to enhance his effectiveness to those involved on a personal basis and those with whom he will work in a professional capacity as psychotherapist. While the risks are great, so are the rewards. There is a feeling of growth and the experience of expanding that allows for greater fulfillment and enjoyment in living.

The therapist like anyone else encounters mundane

experiences. While these may be viewed as humorous, they are real. For example, what happens if the therapist has a mild gastrointestinal upset that results in a sudden need to go to the bathroom in the middle of a therapy session? This is further complicated if an intense and emotionally charged dialogue is occurring at that particular moment. The upset and related need may be assumed erroneously to be related to an emotional process rather than to the infectious process. What happens if a therapist has taken a fair amount of fluid during the day and finds, possibly as a matter of misjudgment and mistiming, the need to visit the toilet for relief? This is something that is never taught as part of a therapeutic relationship. The ability simply to excuse oneself and leave without embarrassment and without the feeling of "doing something wrong" is developed through the therapist's own experience and security.

The therapist may become ill during a therapeutic session. The illness may be transitory or may involve a sudden spasm of coughing, nausea, or the need to leave and lie down for a short period of time. The therapist is human and these things do occur. The therapist may find himself hungry shortly before mealtime and discover that he is focusing more on food than the patient involved in a session. Can a therapist be effective while eating a sandwich or sharing a cup of coffee or tea with a patient?

There are some patients and some relationships that may be boring. Sometimes patients will ramble on about trivia and incidentals that are boring and tiresome. The therapist might explore the reasons for the boredom and analyze the feelings of boredom within himself. However there are times when the therapist or the patient is simply bored. Does the therapist indicate the boredom either directly or indirectly to the patient? Honesty and openness require that the therapist explore this with the patient.

The therapist may find himself exhausted to the point of physical or emotional emptiness at the end of a long day. This is particularly so if there have been a number of difficult and draining emotional relationships. It may be unfair to either the patient or the therapist to insist that the session continue. Many of these questions are not discussed in the usual courses in psychotherapy and at times not in the supervisory process. Some of the important specifics of the day-to-day aspects of the human interrelationship are at times overlooked.

Sometimes there may be a patient who through his behavior, manner of dress, odor, or whatever it might be, evokes a feeling of nausea in the therapist. On the other hand the therapist may engender the same feeling in the patient. Good social creatures tend to overlook these factors and to accept the individual despite them. The therapy relationship might well be improved and go forward in a more positive direction if either or both bring their feelings out into the open and discuss them in a mutually honest way. The therapist is human, as human as the person who comes to him for help.

10

Finding a
Psychotherapist

Psychotherapy is practiced in a variety of physical settings by persons of different theoretical orientation and training. In addition to psychotherapy for the inpatient population within a hospital, psychotherapy is available in a practitioner's private office, a social agency, community or private mental health center, and the outpatient department of diverse hospitals. The specific procedures of the psychotherapeutic process are determined by the emotional status and the goals sought by the respective patient as well as the orientation and training of the psychotherapist. The search for and selection of a psychotherapist *might* be simplified if he could be displayed as an automobile or a suit of clothes. Then the prospective patient might look over each model, evaluate how the attributes of the different therapists might best serve his needs and then take a test drive or try one on for size. A psychotherapist, however, is a human being with whom the patient is to form an ongoing therapeutic relationship. He is not a mechanical instrument or a piece of fabric that can be altered for varying occasions.

The search for and selection of a psychotherapist is often the second or third, rather than the first step in a progressive process. The initial consideration regarding psychotherapy might be the best reason for undertaking such a venture. Motivation for entering psychotherapy may originate from internal or external pressures. Internal pressures may include experiences of intensive anxiety-provoking frustration, feelings of depression, and an inability to utilize one's potentials effectively. External pressures

may include an inability to develop satisfying interpersonal relationships, rejection resulting from nonadaptive responses to
school or work situations, or coercive threats from family
members, friends, or superiors in the individual's work situation.
The choice and the direction of psychotherapy should also be in
terms of the goals sought. For example, the immediate symptomatic relief of anxiety may be effectively achieved by taking a
tranquilizer. The development of effective means of coping with
or resolving the conflict causing the anxiety would require
psychotherapy.

Once a person has determined that he is going to explore the
need for or the desirability of undertaking psychotherapy the
question arises as to where to go. As previously indicated, psychotherapists make their services available in a variety of physical
settings that include private offices, mental health clinics, general
and mental hospitals, churches, and even storefront establish-
ments. The most readily available source of names would be the
local telephone directory. The Yellow Pages of telephone books
generally provide listings of practitioners or places offering psychological services. For example, the directory may contain major
headings such as "Psychologist," or "Physicians and Surgeons,"
with a subheading listing "Psychological and Mental Health Services," "Marriage Counselors," and "Hypnotist." This method of
finding a name or place requires the least amount of expended
energy. There are however several drawbacks to this method. The
psychologist listed may not offer the services specifically desired
by the individual. For example, the psychologist may limit his
practice to behavior modification, adolescents, or posthypnotic
suggestions; the mental health clinic may offer family counseling
when the individual desires individual psychotherapy.

Other more reliable sources of securing names of mental
health practitioners include: (1) local mental health associations,
(2) local and state psychological associations, (3) local or state
medical societies, (4) social work organizations, (5) local hospitals,
and (6) other professionals. The prospective patient may learn
where and how to communicate with any of these sources by
either referring to the local telephone directory or seeking assistance from the telephone information operator. Each of these
sources will have advantages as well as disadvantages in securing

psychotherapeutic services. The therapist(s) recommended by the respective professional association will be limited to their own members. For example, the medical society will supply the names of physicians who are practicing psychiatry. The qualifications or specific types of services offered may not be known by the person representing the medical society. The names offered by the psychological association will be limited to psychologists who are members. Although the membership directories of the American Psychological Association and the American Psychiatric Association usually contain the education, specialty training, and types of services offered by their respective members, the person answering the telephone may not have this information available. Also the association may or may not be willing to exert the energy required to supply this information. The national and local social worker organization may be in a like position. It may be able to supply the names of social workers who are offering psychotherapeutic services and may or may not have information regarding training background of their members. The referral rosters of local hospitals vary. Some carry all the names of those on the hospital and clinic staffs while others may restrict the referral roster to a few or possibly even to the head of the service. Mental health associations may vary in their referral procedures. Some limit their referral list to specific professionals while others may go to the other extreme, listing any and every one who wishes his or her name supplied.

A prospective patient may acquire a therapist's name through individuals who have had contact with psychotherapists. These may include the family physician, clergyman, school personnel such as school psychologist, teacher or counselor, and relatives and friends who have been in psychotherapeutic treatment. If there is a past or present interprofessional relationship, the referral source is in a position to supply the prospective patient with relevant and important information. This information may include the prospective psychotherapist's educational and training background, his psychotherapeutic orientation, and perhaps even a personality description. However, well-meaning persons may have no direct knowledge or experience with the psychotherapist but may have themselves obtained the name from a directory or professional roster. Relatives or friends who have been in psychotherapy are in a relatively good position to describe many aspects of the therapist with whom they have been in treatment. Although the information may be slanted by their personal experience, they can describe the psychotherapist's personality, the fee requirements, and other facets of their experiences. However, the needs and desires of one person may not be identical with those of another. Thus the prospective patient might best reserve final evaluation and decision until experiencing the interaction with the psychotherapist.

Formal qualifications are the initial criteria which may be considered for evaluating a psychotherapist. As described earlier, a psychotherapist may come from one or more of many disciplines, for example, psychology, psychiatry, social work, pastoral counseling, or nursing. Academic or professional degree(s) will indicate the formal education and discipline of the psychotherapist. The lack of the latter, however, does not mean the absence of such training or experience. Publications, both professional articles and books, may also offer an indication of the psychotherapist's professional philosophy and abilities.

Clinical qualifications are additional important criteria for evaluating the psychotherapist. The setting, philosophical orientation, and goals of the institute(s) in which the psychotherapist has trained are usually indicative of his clinical practice. For example, an individual who has trained exclusively in a large state mental hospital usually has been exposed to a limited supervised experience. The goals of such institutions are primarily directed towards returning the patient to the community as soon as possible. Thus the typical treatment might be psychotropic drugs with a minimum of psychotherapy or guidance. Training in a community mental health center would likely expose the beginning therapist to a variety of different experiences. In the latter setting, the psychotherapist in training is very likely to undertake intensively supervised short-term and long-term psychotherapy experience with patients having a variety of emotional, personality, marital, and family problems. Specialty training in various techniques of psychotherapy for different emotional problems is an important criterion. A person seeking psychotherapy because of persistent family turmoil may derive more benefit from a psychotherapist training in family therapy than from an individual whose training experience has been limited to individual therapy. A variety of experiences and continued training also reflect the psychotherapist's attitude and efforts towards his own professional growth and development. The greater the variety the larger the fund of knowledge and skill from which the therapist may draw to meet the psychotherapeutic needs of his patients. Another important, although sometimes overemphasized criterion, is the professional post held by a psychotherapist. A clinical *training and supervising psychotherapist* usually atttains this position based on his psychotherapeutic knowledge and skills. However there are occasions when lecturers or department heads receive these titles as a result of teaching skills and administrative ability.

The formal education and clinical qualifications of the psychotherapist are extremely important but have relatively little value for the particular person unless effectively applied. The prospective patient might well ask himself how effective this psychotherapist has been with others who have experienced similar situations. The answer to this may be derived from relatives or friends who have been in treatment with that particular psychotherapist. The family physician, clergyman, or school personnel may be able to supply this information. Their knowledge may be derived from direct interprofessional relationships or indirectly from observations of other patients who have been in treatment with the particular psychotherapist.

Informative knowledge of a psychotherapist is not limited to outside sources. The prospective patient may obtain the desired information by means of personal observations. There may be opportunity for a variety of nonprofessional contacts' with psychotherapists. These contacts may be made at meetings or lectures where interactions between the psychotherapist and the individual as well as with others may be experienced and evaluated. There are also occasions when direct or indirect contacts may be made with a psychotherapist in social situations. Although these latter settings may not be conducive for a display of professional knowledge and skills, there is an opportunity to observe the psychotherapist's ability to relate and interact as a human being. Establishing professional contact on a limited or extended basis is a more direct method of obtaining information. The individual may make an appointment for a consultation. The appointed time may be used to describe and discuss the individual life situation and to obtain information regarding the treatment and therapist. Although the patient's questions may be considered and discussed in relationship to the patient's life situation, the psychotherapist who is secure in his professional effectiveness will readily supply the requested information regarding himself.

After examining the educational and clinical qualifications of the psychotherapist the patient may evaluate how the two of them will function in a collaborative relationship. Although first impressions are not always valid, the first session offers the patient an opportunity to assess the therapist as a person. The patient may experience vague notions which he is unable to formulate and entertain relevant questions which are difficult to express. For example, is the therapist sensitive to my fears and anxiety? Is he able to hear what I mean or does he merely listen to the words I say? Is he able to sense and understand my emotional need or is his interest directed towards getting me to do what he wants? Is he able to reformulate and clarify my feelings and thoughts or does he get lost in the tangle of my confused thoughts? Does he communicate in such a way as to help me dissipate my fogginess or does he add to my uncertainty and anxiety? Is he firm yet gentle in his manner, does he assume a rigid dogmatic position, or is he wishy-washy in trying to appease me?

The patient's reactions to the therapist essentially will determine the establishment of an effective relationship. In addition to observing and evaluating the therapist's sensitivity, response pattern, and method of communication, it may be wise for the patient to evaluate himself in this setting. The therapeutic relationship is not a social situation in which the therapist and patient are to be entertained, nor is the patient there to provide an audience for the therapist to lecture. For the psychotherapeutic process to be effective, interaction between the patient and therapist is essential. Anxiety and fear are experienced by almost every patient. If these emotions rise to a level which immobilizes the patient verbally, the therapeutic process will be blunted. The patient also must eventually feel secure enough in the presence of the psychotherapist to be willing to undertake revealing information which may be experienced as painful, shameful, and otherwise unacceptable. Although at times frightened of the possible outcome, the patient must be willing to attempt open communication with the psychotherapist. The conviction that the therapist can actually help is also very important. The absence of this latter feeling, however, should not be used to deter a patient from entering psychotherapy with a particular therapist. Some people initially have the mistaken belief that their life situation is of such a nature that no one could possibly be of help to them. The important element here is the willingness to take the risk and commit themselves to a process which may be beneficial.

A particular therapist is not automatically the therapist of choice for all patients despite the possession of an excellent formal education, psychotherapeutic training, and experience, as well as a proven treatment effectiveness. As in all relationships, psychotherapy entails the meshing of two individual personalities—therapist and patient. Initial impressions are very influential in determining a patient's decision. However, initial impressions are not always valid. Therefore, a continuing evaluation by the patient of the therapist as well as of the therapeutic relationship is suggested. This ongoing assessment usually takes place with the knowledge of and collaboration of the therapist. A recognition of how the patient and therapist mesh or fail to do so tends to enhance rather than hinder the therapeutic process. The inability of the patient and therapist to enter a psychotherapeutic relationship should be recognized if it exists. An early referral might then be made to a therapist with whom the patient is more apt to develop a desirable therapeutic relationship. There is no rule regarding the time it takes to know whether a therapeutic relationship will work out. The decision is based on the patient-therapist discussion rather than as a unilateral decision by either. The patient's feelings towards the therapist can be valuable in the therapeutic process. A patient may not like the therapist because he is unlikeable. Or a patient may not like the therapist because of a transference response that is connected to special areas of difficulty.

There are serious problems which a patient might experience when selecting a psychotherapist. These might be quite apparent or very subtle. For example, the patient-therapist interaction throughout the session may be one of continued bickering which generates anxiety-provoking frustration and resentment. Neither patient nor therapist can be open or spontaneous with the other. The nonproductiveness of the relationship is overshadowed by each person's need to prove the other accountable for what is happening. There are some people who readily select any negative element in order to justify terminating the relationship. This often results in "psychotherapy shopping" where the patient continues an unsuccessful search for the "right" psychotherapist. The danger of psychotherapy shopping is two-fold. First, the patient's feeling of hopelessness is reinforced by the experience of rejection by the therapist during the last consultation. Secondly, the individual sharpens his critical evaluation in the direction of seeing more and more limitations on the part of the therapist. The dangers involved in shopping around should not be used as a prohibition against an individual changing his mind about continuing in treatment with a particular therapist. Reevaluation of what the patient experiences as an unproductive relationship is warranted and advisable. This appraisal is best done with the therapist's participation. Thus, the opportunity to examine how and why the relationship has been stymied allows both the patient and therapist to expose themselves to critical observation. Negative feelings towards or conflicts with the therapist are not indications of a nontherapeutic relationship. The relationship which is suggestive of a nontherapeutic relationship is one in which there is no movement in any direction. If the opportunity is made available, a critical evaluation of the nonproductive therapeutic relationship usually leads to a better understanding between the people involved which in turn enhances progress of therapy. If, however, the patient and therapist conclude that they are unable or unwilling to expend the energy required in overcoming a static relationship, the patient should consider getting into treatment with another psychotherapist. Therapists whose emotional security has allowed them to accept their own limitations will often aid the patient in securing a psychotherapist who is more apt to be effective with this particular individual. If the therapist reneges on this responsibility, the patient is on his own to repeat the process of seeking a new psychotherapist, but with a more discriminating ability.

11

What It Means
to Be a Patient

Being a patient in psychotherapy engenders both positive and negative feelings and attitudes. The patient is seen and felt in many ways which depend upon the attitudes and feelings of the viewer and on his relationship to the patient. While there may be overlapping and similarity, I will attempt to clarify how the patient is regarded from the many possible positions of the viewer. This includes the concept of the patient and how he sees himself and feels about being a patient. I will also discuss the patient as seen through the eyes of the world he lives in, how he appears in the eyes of the family or significant others, and the ways that he is perceived and experienced by the psychotherapist.

Origins of words are often of interest because they provide clues to the history and meaning of the terms used. People in psychotherapy have commonly been referred to as *patients*. However they are sometimes referred to as *clients* and in many situations as *analysands*. As is frequently the case, English words can usually be traced back to their Latin origins. *Patient* came from the Latin base *pati* which literally means "to suffer," "endure," or "to be patient." It is related to the word *passion* which has a similar meaning, as in the passion plays or sufferings of Christ. Of course, words change in their meanings with usage and applications. And so, *patient* took on other meanings such as "one who is acted upon," or "passive," or "someone who is under treatment or care." These meanings were associated largely with the medical concept of the patient.

There are important differences between medicine and psychotherapy which the dictionary doesn't include. In most psychotherapies the patient is not merely acted upon nor is he a passive recipient of treatment. Instead he is regarded as a partner in an *interactive* relationship. He is not anaesthetized or operated upon but is rather a conscious participant.

In an effort to dissociate the earlier and still prevalent concept of the patient, some therapists have preferred the word *client*. Whether this is a more desirable term or really makes any difference in the attitudes engendered is not clear.

Client is derived from the Latin word *cliens* which means a "dependent," or "one under the protection of another." It also refers to "one who employs the service of a professional man, as a lawyer," or loosely, "a patron of any shop." *Analysand* has simply been used to indicate any person who is in analysis or the recipient of psychoanalytic treatment. It too carries the implication of a more passive role in that one is being analyzed. This sometimes causes confusion as when people say "Here I am, analyze me" with the expectation of sitting back and being acted upon.

The label or title used is less important than the attitude towards the person seeking help and what happens between the person and the therapist. What is primary is that two people can eventually relate to each other and work together in a common cause. All of this takes much patience on the part of both patient and therapist. It often takes a long time before the person becomes aware that he has emotional problems or a psychological disturbance and longer before he acknowledges the need for professional help. And the next step is even more difficult. To enter into a psychotherapeutic relationship requires courage, a sense of commitment and patience. Working through or resolving difficulties and conflicts that have taken years to develop takes time. For even as the patient struggles to remove the interferences in his living he tends to resist change. Unfortunately, people sometimes keep delaying until they reach a point of despair or desperation before seeking help.

Not everyone requires long-term therapy. Some people experience problems that have recent origins and are not deep-seated. As a matter of fact a consultation or a few sessions can be of value in providing a sense of direction, a reorientation, or change in perspective that can be invaluable in helping the person to go on more effectively.

As with every person, the patient comes into therapy with a particular background of experiences, human needs, a system of values, and some kind of philosophy of life, however incomplete or unorganized. He becomes a patient because, in some degree, his ability to live adequately or fully has been interfered with by undue anxiety or confusion. He has been unable to grow sufficiently to permit a way of living that is either bearable, satisfying, or simply fulfilling. As indicated elsewhere in this book, expressions of the person's difficulty are often in the form of symptoms. These symptoms may include overt anxiety, physical complaints, somatic or actual body illness, depression, tiredness, and so forth.

Since each person has a unique history it is expected that different patients will feel differently about being a patient. However, there are some basic similarities, particularly regarding expectations. Patients usually come into therapy hoping for help with their difficulties with or without conviction that they will receive help. A person may feel that no one can really help him with his particular problem, and there are occasions when a person feels undeserving of help. There are also times when the individual anticipates that he once again will be deprived rather than helped. The kinds of problems people enter therapy with will strongly affect how they feel and the kind of help they want. It is natural to feel anxious or apprehensive in new or unfamiliar situations. This is especially so in psychotherapy because the patient is expected to reveal himself. Self-revelation, or exposure to another or even to oneself, is probably one of the hardest things for anyone to do. It is interesting that people will often engage in daredevil activities at great risk to their physical lives more easily than they will show their emotional insides. Commonly, people will expose their naked bodies before they will show their naked feelings. People come to therapy needing emotional support, human contact, and someone to care, even though they may deny this or fight against it. They need to feel special and important. Indeed if they are not seen as important by the therapist a real question may be raised as to whether he can be very helpful.

People see themselves in a variety of ways before they become patients. Once one becomes a patient, which is an admission of a need for help, additional feelings may come into consciousness or focus. The patient may see himself as crazy or overly dependent, as weak or inadequate, as a child or immature. On the other hand, he may regard himself as courageous, and anticipate an adventure in self-exploration. Often the patient has mixed feelings about entering therapy. Sometimes becoming the patient is experienced with a feeling of shame at needing help. Other times it may be felt with a sense of pride or accomplishment at taking the step. People may enter into psychotherapy out of courage or out of desperation, in search of growth or self-actualization, or in an effort to find relief from anxiety or fear.

How a person sees himself in psychotherapy is a direct or indirect reflection of how he sees himself as a person.

Of course the patient is affected by the world in which he lives. Although we all are part of the same larger world, all of us come from smaller worlds that profoundly influence our feelings. Whether we are black, white, red, or yellow, male or female, Jewish, Christian, Moslem or Buddhist, each characteristic is part of what we are. It makes a difference in our attitudes whether we have lived in a ghetto, in the city, or in the country, or how big or small our world was when we entered psychotherapy. How the therapy patient is viewed by the outside world, in turn, depends upon which part of that world we are talking about. For example, historically it has been more comfortable for women to seek help than it has been for men. The roles of men and women have been markedly dichotomized. It has been acceptable for women to cry, to be needful, emotional, and dependent. These were regarded as feminine characteristics. Therefore, if the man were truly masculine he would have to maintain an image of "strength" which meant he could not lean or cry or reach out for help. The problem of *machismo* may be greater if you are from such countries as Mexico or Spain and probably less if you are white or Jewish. Machismo is an exaggerated, distorted or unrealistic concern about one's masculinity.

Generally the world at large has come to accept and recognize the value of psychotherapy in relation to mental health. Still, as with the patient's view of himself, there is no one answer as to how the world sees him. It is always a personal matter.

What are some of these personal reactions that express attitudes towards the patient? Here are presented some contrasting reactions.

"Joan must be crazy. She's seeing a shrink."

"Joan must be courageous. She's in psychotherapy. I wish I could do it."

"You are intelligent and should be able to solve your own problems."

"I think you were smart to get help with your problems."

"A strong person doesn't need anyone to help him. He can do it himself."

"He had the strength to go to a psychotherapist."

"Control yourself and you won't have to see that therapist."

"You ought to see a therapist. You're too uptight."

When a member of a family becomes a patient, any of the above attitudes may be shown. However, the family members have a special emotional investment in the patient-member and may feel especially pleased or especially threatened. He may be viewed with a sense of relief, despair, or with a feeling of hope.

If a child needs help, psychotherapy has been used as a reward or a promise, or misused as a threat or form of punishment. Getting a child therapeutic help may give the parent a sense of support and allow him to feel less alone or helpless with the problem. On the other hand the child's therapy could be scary for the parent because of anxiety about being revealed through the child. The parent may be worried about guilt and being blamed. The blamegame is an unfortunate but usual experience in our society. "Who is wrong?" "Who is at fault?" These are typical questions asked, and the fear of the answers may cause much resistance to going for psychotherapy. Blame is often confused with responsibility. Blaming another or oneself is not being responsible. Rather it is a way of scapegoating. Accusing or punishing for mistakes or problems is at best nonproductive and at its worst destructive. To be responsible is to be responsive to another person, his needs, and his difficulties. It is being sensitive and accepting in a way that allows for growth and creative action that leads towards resolution of problems. Blaming only helps to perpetuate the problems.

Blaming may occur between parent and child, brother and sister, or husband and wife. The parents may pass accusations back and forth until the interaction seems like an endless ping-pong match. Such behavior only serves to screen the real problems. The fear of blame causes the passing of the blame to another. Such smoke screening behavior also intensifies the fear of exposure and anxiety about changing the relationship. A husband or wife may be afraid of therapy for the other because it may upset the neurotic balance in their relationship. The fear is that any change in this interaction will result in a loss of the partner. This fear is usually unconscious and distorts the perception of the patient, therapist and therapeutic process.

Some of the specific attitudes found in the family may be expressed in the following and varied ways:

Parent to Child: "If you continue with this behavior I am going to take you to a nut-doctor."

Parents to Child: "We know that you have been unhappy, Billy, and we would like to help. We would like to take you to someone who helps people with their problems."

Child to Parent: "Mommy, my friend Joey told me that he had worries and his parents took him to a doctor he talks and plays with. Can I go too? I've been worried."

Husband to Wife: "If you don't stop getting so emotional I'll send you to a shrink."

Husband to Wife: "What do you need a therapist for. Why don't you talk to *me!*"

Husband to Wife: "I don't know whether it's you, me, or both of us but I think we ought to get some help."

Wife to Husband: "You're so cold and rational about everything. You're such a cold fish in bed, maybe one of those professionals can warm you up on the couch."

Wife to Husband: "If you go into therapy I just know you will change and not love me any more."

Wife to Husband: "You've been getting depressed a lot. Do you think it would be worthwhile seeing someone who can help you?"

In 1967 an interesting symposium was published in a professional journal of psychotherapy which presented different therapists' views of "good" patients. "Good" is not used here in a moral sense. Generally, it refers to the person's motivation to help himself towards health and growth. We have borrowed a few parts of the symposium to illustrate some ways in which psychotherapists see patients.

Becoming a good person

Categorization of this matter is not desirable for me. If necessary I would say that a successful or "good" patient cannot be defined in static terms but is seen in the process of "becoming." There is little difference between a "good" patient and a good person. Technically, one becomes a patient when he clearly asks for help. Therapeutically one becomes a patient when he begins to accept the help and shares in the therapeutic experience. He becomes a "good" or successful patient as he takes responsibility for his part in the relationship, as he comes to regard therapy as a growth experience. Having become a truly good patient, he no longer *must* be one. —by Jules Barron, Ph.D.

Both get better

In thinking about my definition of what a successful patient is, I am reminded of a patient who said that I looked "sick." I told her that generally I get well as treatment progresses. It is now one year since we began collaborating in therapy together and on occasion she will remark to me, "You're looking much better." — by Alfred Berl, M.D.

Take me seriously

To qualify to be a successful patient, first you have to make every effort to be and become yourself. You can't be yourself if you don't respond to what I am saying to you and what I am. Further, you can't respond to me if you don't take me and my responses seriously enough to really get the central point of what I meant when I shared my impressions of your struggles and pain for me. Finally, don't let me get away with any unclear statements; have me clarify any statement I am making to you. —by Ivan Boszormenyi-Nagy, M.D.

Interested in experience

The naive patient who is intelligent and able to permit direct experience in the therapeutic situation is the one who seems to profit most. I believe that the patient who pretends to have much information about psychopathology and methods of treatment is the most resistant and difficult. I prefer patients to become sophisticated and interested in experience, rather than in techniques of therapy as such. —by Henry Guze, Ph.D.

A stubborn search

Stereotyped concepts sometimes keep people from getting the most out of psychotherapy. I find it helps to think of the process not as therapy or treatment, but as teaching and learning— learning in all four behavioral modes of feeling, thinking, perceiving, and acting. Optimal results are more apt to derive not from working with patients, but with *persons* who are experiencing frustration and confusion and who are blocked by self-defeating methods of dealing with their problems. The most will be gained by a person who is determined to develop a more effective and enjoyable way of life and who finds a therapist who will confidently join him in a stubborn search for such a way. —by Robert A. Harper, Ph.D.

To shed respectability

Into the mouth of Jack Tanner *(Man and Superman)*, G.B. Shaw put the words, "The more things a man is ashamed of the more respectable he is." Tanner continues: "For if I were ashamed of my real self, I should cut as stupid a figure as any of the rest of you. Cultivate a little impudence, Ramsdan; and you will become quite a remarkable man." —In my experience the patient who derives the deepest benefits from psychotherapy is the one who experiences the growing courage to shed his respectability. For optimum results the patient must respond to the therapist's adroit resistance analysis and/or permit a relationship so full of trust that he can risk exposing all that he has been, wishes to be, and is. —by Sol. S. Rosenberg, Ph.D.

Expressing all feelings

To get the most out of therapy, the patient must be motivated to do the "getting." This includes encouraging him to express all feelings, especially negative feelings regarding treatment and the therapist. It also includes encouraging his cooperation in attempting prescribed "homework," varying in relationship to the particular type of therapy such as perhaps self-hypnosis, self-conditioning, self-aversive conditioning, assertive conditioning, facing symptoms in vivo in increasing dosage, writing dreams, vocational and environmental changes, etc. Obviously these details vary with each patient. I consider a patient "successful" when he gratifies both of us by his growth, in and out of therapy, and succeeds in utilizing more of his potential in life. —by Irwin Rothman, D.O.

Plunging into fear

A young woman who was making excellent progress in her treatment once said to me, "Doctor, after that last session I was violently angry at you. You brought up a matter that hurt. I did not want to discuss it. Obviously, it is an important point in my problem. Let's start in talking about it today." This woman had learned one of the most significant secrets of achieving rapid progress in therapy—the willingness to confront that which we would most prefer to avoid. If one has the courage to approach each therapeutic hour by plunging boldly into those matters which threaten shame, aversion, hurt, humiliation, and fear, he has forged a powerful weapon for attacking the defensive maneuvers by which we delude ourselves into illness. —by John G. Watkins, Ph.D.

12

Psychotherapy
for Children

Psychotherapy for and with children requires an understanding of
the nature of the child and his world. How and why a child comes
for therapy is connected to how the child lives, how he sees the
world, and how he communicates his ideas and feelings. Thus
developmental and maturational changes must be considered.
When a child is brought for psychotherapy the therapist has to
determine who is really the "patient"—the child, the parent, or the
entire family? This is part of the problem of diagnosis or evaluation which will be clarified further. There are additional questions
to be raised and answered. How does the healthy child differ from
the unhealthy child? What is meant by deviance as different from
emotional disorder? What are the roles and attitudes of the family
members towards the child before and during psychotherapy?
What are the roles and attitudes of educators towards the child
who is a patient? (Educators include administrators, guidance
counselors, and teachers.) How are psychotherapy and the therapist seen and felt by the child? What are the ways in which the
therapist works with the child? How does the therapist work with
those people who are influential in the life of the child, such as the
family and school personnel?

Each child is a unique being with his own history of experience even amidst the apparent similarities of culture, environment, and family. It is not possible to talk about the child as a
person at any specific age as though he represented all others in
his age group. For the most part, and with all of the individual

differences, the young child's world is characterized by a large amount of fantasy and imagination. Play is an expression of this world. As the child grows, he develops a concept of himself, of others, and the world about him. His sense of time and space is felt as unbounded, for he hasn't yet come to understand his limitations or mortality. In the imagination anything is possible and he hasn't yet clearly separated fantasy from reality. If the young child can see the moon it is difficult for him to understand why he cannot reach up and touch it. Because separation of self has not yet developed the child responds more powerfully to the influence of others, particularly to those people who have been significant to his existence, to his satisfactions, and to his frustrations, such as parents and educators.

The child is an extension of those who strongly determine the nature of his existence. As he grows up and matures with an awareness of his own resources and possibilities, the nature of his attachment changes. Instead of being an extension or a function of others he becomes more independent, with an increased ability to relate in a way that involves more feeling of choice. Dependency is in balance with an attitude of self-determination. Dependency is no longer a primary style of relatedness but an aspect of being an autonomous person.

The child is an explorer in the truest sense of the word. The world is unlimited in its possibilities. He approaches it wide-eyed, open, and receptive. Literally his mouth, as a primary organ of satisfaction, is open to his environment. Notice how the young child will put almost anything he touches in his mouth. Similarly he will try to touch everything within his reach. Touching is the most basic form of human contact and is necessary for security. Harry Harlow's studies of monkeys demonstrated that touch is even more important than physical warmth or physical nourishment.

As with monkeys, children who lack experiences of human touch develop a problem of sensory deprivation which affects their later development. Even though the use of our eyes and ears increases with maturity, the need for the human touch is always present. The popular expression often used in jest—"Beat me but don't ignore me"—has a real basis in fact. However children who are beaten as a form of contact do not grow up to be healthy or happy people. To the contrary, the battered child grows up with a feeling of and need for violence that becomes destructive to himself and others. The abandoned or untouched child will likely become withdrawn, live in a world of fantasy, and slowly perish. There is no substitute for TLC—tender loving care—early in the person's growth.

Thinking, feeling, and overt behavior are not clearly defined in the child's mind, and often easily merge with each other. Wishfulness and reality may be confused. Additionally, imagination has a magical quality in which the child may feel a sense of power or omnipotence. If the child wishes someone dead and the person dies, the child can readily believe that it was he who caused the death. Omnipotence in children as in adults is a way of compensating for feelings of helplessness and extreme dependency. In the child such reactions are relatively normal. In the adult, excessive feelings of powerfulness are a form of grandiosity and may be indicative of emotional disturbance.

The child easily loses himself in time and space. Tomorrows feel like forever. Remember your own childhood. The summers seemed to be so much longer. Waiting for tomorrows for a special treat was an eternity. As an adult you may have a similar experience when anxious about the possibility of not getting what you want or fearful that tomorrow may not arrive. Difficulty in waiting for gratification is characteristic of the anxious child or adult. It is well established that the adult under stress is more likely to regress and react in a childlike manner. He will return to forms of behavior that were part of his earlier experiences. For example, people under stress will even revert to earlier speech patterns or the language of childhood. In extreme cases of regression the adult may develop a form of behavior or adaptive style that is called schizophrenic. Unable to tolerate the strains of reality, the person withdraws into his inner life to protect himself from a world that is too difficult or painful to handle. He lives in a framework of personal reference insulated from the effects of others. His thinking becomes autistic, that is, his thought processes are disconnected from the real world, and he escapes to the life of the child with his fantasies of magic. The child who becomes extremely threatened by the conditions of his life may become or remain infantile in his attempt to find a sense of security from those forces in his existence that threaten his survival.

Of course most children are neither schizophrenic nor autistic though there are larger numbers than we would like to see. Emotional disturbances can vary from the mild to the most severe. The disturbances can be reactions to an immediate situation or a long-term response to continuing anxiety. The reaction may be acute or chronic. As we grow, we are affected by everything that happens to us in smaller or greater degree. Rarely does a single incident or trauma result in a serious emotional problem. Children have great resiliency and can make a good recovery from severe anxiety. However, everyone has a tolerance level which when exceeded results in a breakdown of his normal functions. Often the breakdown is temporary. The episode passes because there is enough strength to allow spontaneous recovery. However, if the stress persists the recovery potential decreases and the child remains in a relative state of emotional disorder. In some way his emotional equilibrium is disturbed and may adversely affect his thinking ability, his affective or emotional responses, or both. Learning ability may be impaired. He may behave in ways that are disturbing to others as well as to himself. He may be disruptive or develop physical symptoms or complaints.

How do we determine whether a child requires psycho-therapeutic help? A child may be referred by another professional such as a school psychologist, a physician, educator, or by a friend. Frequently the parents seek help directly because of their concerns about the child's behavior or functioning. Most often, by the time a child reaches the office of a psychotherapist the difficulties have existed for some time.

The evaluative procedures may involve a family interview, an interview with the child, a historical and developmental study, a psychological examination, or a combination of these. The family session provides a crosssectional picture of the nature of the interactions among the family members, a view of their conflicts, concerns, and ways of relating to each other. The therapist is more able to see the family *in vivo* which is more accurate and real than the reporting of events and the problem as expressed by any one family member. Each person's role in the family shows up more clearly than would be evidenced in a one-to-one interview. The one-to-one interview with the child is valuable because it shows how the child interacts and behaves when he is without the influence of his parents. The therapist can note differences and similarities between the family interview and the interview with the child alone. The child also has an opportunity to express his personal and more subjective reactions to his life experiences. The therapist is not as much interested in "facts" as he is in the way the child perceives himself, his world, and his life. He can't really know a patient through another person. It is the patient's feelings and perceptions that count. That is, how does he see, react to, or live with the "facts"?

The historical and developmental background of the child provides the therapist with the perceptions of those reporting them, which may include parents, siblings, and educators. The therapist also obtains a picture of earlier experiences, maturational growth, and significant and critical events. Sometimes contact with the school psychologist, guidance counselor, or teacher is helpful as it adds another dimension to the picture of the child in the school situation. At times the child, depending upon his age and ability to communicate, does not reveal his personal self. In this case a psychological examination may help to present a picture of his more personal self and inner world. In addition to the personality picture, a kind of psychological "X-ray," the psychologist obtains information about his patient's intellectual functioning, perceptual reactions, and neurological state. Some psychological tests are especially sensitive to learning disability problems. "Differential diagnosis" is a term used when the examining psychologist tries to determine whether the problems endured by the child are primarily a result of neurological impairment, a psychological disturbance, or both.

Through the various evaluative procedures the psychotherapist can determine who the patient is or should be. That is, what would be the most beneficial therapeutic approach? It may be desirable to work with the child alone, with the parents individually or as a couple, or with all of them. When treating the child, it is always important to include the parents by arranging counseling sessions as necessary. Frequently it is also helpful for the therapist to have some communication with the teacher, guidance counselor, or school psychologist. It must be recognized that once the child reaches school age school people become significant and influential figures in his life. The child probably spends as much time with his teacher as he does with his parents. The teacher, like the parent, strongly affects the child with his attitudes and value system.

When the family itself is disturbed the therapist may recommend that the family unit be the patient by participating in family group therapy. He may suggest that each parent and the child participate separately in a therapeutic experience. It is not uncommon to have a child brought for professional help and not become the patient. This may occur because no one may truly require psychotherapy. A short series of consultations may be sufficient to help guide the family towards a more productive path in dealing with their difficulties. In such situations the problems involved are neither profound nor severely disturbing. Or the child may have served as the entrée, or ticket of admission, for the parents to obtain help for themselves. There may not be a clinically significant personality disturbance in the child. The symptoms evidenced may be reactions of the child to situational familial difficulties that are symptomatic of the parents' problems but have not yet had enough impact on the child to warrant treatment for him. There have been parents in therapy who later admitted that their child helped them to get help for themselves. The child was like a barometer of the parent in trouble and served as the justification for seeking personal therapy.

All human beings living in the real world will inevitably experience times of stress which may result in neurotic symptoms. In the healthy person such symptoms are transitory. However, a recurrence of the anxiety either without apparent cause, or if excessive in relation to the circumstances, warrants a consultation. The anxiety may be consciously experienced or somatized— that is, the anxiety may be expressed in recurring physical symptoms without organic cause. The child may experience stomach aches, nausea, or skin or respiratory reactions. Even where there is a constitutional or organic basis for the physical symptom, emotional disturbance may well lower the tolerance level of the child and trigger off an acute reaction. When we use the term *psychosomatic*, we refer to a physical ailment that is either the result of or intensified by emotional stress. The healthy child is not immune to stress and may show similar reactions to situational difficulties. However, such reactions are transitory and recovery is spontaneous upon removal of the source of trouble. The basic principle in differentiating a healthy from a disturbed child involves the appropriateness and reality of the response. Of course to the best of existing knowledge no one is perfect; any child is entitled to occasional inappropriateness, as are adults. Repetition of disturbed behavior or difficulty in living should always be considered as a warning signal.

Mental health is not an absolute concept and is therefore not definable in any static way. This is particularly true of the child who is changing rapidly and dynamically. More than at any other time, the child moves through many periods of transition requiring continuing adaptation. Life is generally characterized by stress, particularly after leaving the warmth and comparative safety of the womb. Changes always carry with them some degree of stress. The child experiences notable changes in his physical, mental, and emotional life, with dramatic alterations occurring right through adolescence. However, because of the uniqueness of adolescence, a separate discussion is required.

Since mental health is relative, it can only be understood individually in terms of the child's age, personal experiences, social and familial structures, and cultural and subcultural influences. We won't delve into specific concepts and theories of mental health but rather we will try to provide whatever information may be helpful in understanding more about psychotherapy with children—when it is required, how we determine the need for therapy, and the kinds of therapy that are used. Accordingly, something should be said briefly about the concept of deviance.

Deviance is oftentimes confused with mental or emotional disturbance. Literally, the deviant child is one who deviates or differs from the norm. In his deviation he may be regarded as *abnormal*—behaving in ways that are "away from the norm." The norm is the way the majority of the population behaves. This is actually a statistical concept. A deviant child may or may not be emotionally healthy. For example there are healthy rebels and unhealthy rebels. The child may engage in the same behavior or mode of adaptation for different reasons. One child may rebel against an authority figure because the authority is truly oppressive. Such rebellion may be a courageous action. Another child may rebel against an authority person primarily because of his position. This child would not be responding to the person as much as to his position. What is also important is the nature of the rebellion. Is the child being destructive or attempting to change a condition that is truly threatening or detrimental to his person? Among the deviant people of the world we have seen tyrants and destructive behavior, as well as productive leaders and creative human beings. While it is important that the child adapt to the world, he should never lose his spirit. Adaptation doesn't mean resignation and is not necessarily adjustment. There are many conditions that one should not accept or adjust to. As the child grows up, he learns that the world is not a fairyland. It is neither all beautiful nor all ugly, all good nor all bad. It is necessary to know and respond to the differences.

Attitudes of and towards the patient have already been discussed. We have seen that such attitudes will depend on the health of the viewer and his position in relation to the patient. Parents, siblings, educators, professionals, and others are all people with varying degrees of health, sensitivity, and concern. It should be emphasized that the parents, contrary to some popular beliefs, are not the only culprits. And besides, finding someone to blame resolves no problems and is antitherapeutic. Children blame parents or teachers. Parents blame children and teachers. Teachers blame parents and children, and on and on. Blaming someone, including oneself, is not being responsible. Responsibility is shown when a person evaluates the circumstances that are destructive or defeating and proceeds to change them. The blame game is a way of avoiding the process of constructive change. Each person involved with the child must look at his role and the nature of his reactions to the child and contribute to the process of change.

In addition to the parents, the other significant people in the life of the child must come to recognize their attitudes and behavior with a willingness to change. How often have you heard or felt the attitude that says, "If only you were different, I would have no problems." This reaction commonly occurs between parent and child or parent and parent. Parents and teachers may blame each other rather than attempting to confer and share in the resolution. When a child is brought for psychotherapy it is more possible to work therapeutically with the parents on an ongoing basis than with the educators or professionals who come into meaningful contact with the child. The psychotherapist may try to elicit the cooperation and assistance of others through conferences. If this doesn't work, it may be necessary to change the conditions of the child's daily experiences by recommending situational rearrangements. If the problem involves an unreceptive educator it may be necessary to change the child's class or even his school. The first effort is to work out the problem successfully within the current school situation. If a professional such as a physician, dentist, or psychologist is insufficiently sensitive to the needs and difficulties of the child, changing to another may be appropriate. This is particularly the case with children having learning disabilities, the so-called "special" children who require a unique understanding and sensitivity by family, friends, educators, and professionals of various kinds. Sensitivity does not mean treating children with problems as cripples but rather it means regarding them with respect and an attitude of caring.

Thus far much has been said about the nature of the child and the people and conditions of his life that must be considered. The topic of psychotherapy with children has been approached in this way deliberately to emphasize that working with disturbed children has many ramifications. There is no magic to psychotherapy. The child, by his natural level of development, is realistically a relatively dependent person and must be helped simultaneously in a variety of ways. The adult has the potential resources to independently work through his own problems, make his own choices, and take the kinds of autonomous actions that can result in personal, social, and economic changes. The immature nature of the child as compared with the adult requires a different orientation. With the child it is necessary to work with the external human environment. In therapy with the adult, the therapist can help the adult-patient work out changes in himself and the world he lives in. The child's ability to reason, solve problems, or understand the relationship between his feelings and fears is much less developed than in the adult. Treatment of any person, regardless of age, is geared to the emotional development of the person. Yet however disturbed the adult is he has the potential ability not yet developed in the child. Most often the child doesn't even understand why he is seeing a psychotherapist; the decision and choice are usually made by an adult.

As you can see, working with the child involves a whole network of relationships in which the therapist becomes involved either directly or tangentially. As a matter of fact, when the child is brought for therapy many wheels are set in motion which are as important as the therapy itself in effecting changes in the child-patient.

If the child enters into a psychotherapeutic relationship there are several forms that it may take. Once one understands the problems, the world, and the language of the child, what is the best course of action to follow? The choice made by the psychotherapist will depend upon his orientation and his concept of the maturational process and theory of personality development. There is not always necessarily one best procedure; more than one procedure may work with a child. As discussed before, therapy may be primarily supportive or reconstructive. In the former the purpose is to help the child maintain himself in his daily functioning. In the latter form the goal is towards personality change. The therapeutic approach may be based on any one of a number of psychoanalytic theories as developed by people such as Sigmund or Anna Freud, Alfred Adler, Otto Rank or Melanie Klein, the nondirective or client-centered therapy of Carl Rogers, the work of Virginia Axline in the Rogerian context, the use of learning theory as evidenced by the use of conditioning procedures, and so on. The modalities used would include individual, group, or family therapy, alone or in combination. An important principle determining choice of therapy involves the question of how can we do the most with the least. Consideration must always be given to the reality of time and cost but never at the expense of the human being in trouble. Geographical area and availability is a built-in condition that is also involved. Essentially the nature of the therapeutic procedures should be based on the needs and problems of the child. Then a minimal program should be set up that is considered as probably effective. As the process continues changes can be made if necessary by expanding or decreasing the experience depending upon the response of the child.

It has been pointed out that play is a natural way through which the child expresses himself and explores his world. It is also natural, therefore, that play has become a form of behavior that has been developed into a modality or means of treating the child. All behavior is both an expression of the person and a form of communication. For the child, play is essential to his growth. For the adult, it is essential to his sanity.

In individual therapy the therapist will use some combination of talking and playing as a means of interacting with the child. What is most essential is that the therapist use whatever methods will most effectively help him to reach the child. Reaching the child means developing a relationship based on trust and an attitude of real caring. Trust never comes about instantly. In a society of instant coffee, soup, and other gimmicks which are technologically useful, the human relationship still comes about more slowly. The therapist must be able to sense where the child is emotionally and what will help him most to open up and participate in the therapy, which means participating in the relationship. Working out the problem of trust is a critical phase in the therapeutic process, and this takes time and patience.

Some children are more verbal than others but most children can talk. As we all know, talking can be used to conceal or to reveal oneself. It takes time to learn the language of a particular child. Words may not always have the same meanings to a child that they have for the therapist. Also, as with people at all ages, words may send out one message while behavior may communicate its opposite. The therapist's ability to listen and hear the meaningful messages is still most basic to therapy. There are children who are quite surprised to learn that they are being heard and understood. What may be more surprising is that they can be accepted. Children are tuned in more to feelings than to words. Unless the child's disturbance has already resulted in withdrawal and tuning out, he is sensitive to acceptance and rejection. Because of his problem he may fight against the therapist, even though he knows the therapist cares. He may be struggling with his own anxiety about trusting or be so angry as to be rejecting.

Play can take an almost unlimited number of forms. The therapist explores the play world of the child with the child to find a common ground, a place where they can form a bond with each other. The therapist tries to ally himself with the positive forces within the child on behalf of growth and change. He always accepts the child but does not necessarily approve of all the child's behavior. The therapist lets the child know that he is his friend by what he says, the way he says it, and how he plays with him. It is equally important that the therapist respect the child as a person and never diminish or humiliate him no matter how unreasonable the child sounds. Child and therapist can fight with each other, argue, or disagree but the therapist doesn't hit below the belt even if the child does. The child may do a lot of testing out before he will come to trust and accept the therapist.

Play materials may include puppets, clay, table games, blocks, or dolls. It is up to the therapist to use his ingenuity and perceptiveness to pick up the clues from the child, to determine what is best, and to be able to shift when necessary. Play may occur without any materials or objects. It can be done through the medium of acting, role-playing or make-believe activities that only involve the persons of the therapist and child. Parents sometimes wonder why they should pay a therapist to play with their child, particularly if they have an attitude that play is wasteful and only work is worthwhile. Play is more than play when it serves the therapeutic purpose of catharsis or release, when it becomes a special way of connecting with the child and paves the way for healthy change. Through play the therapist helps the child to express feelings about himself and others and attitudes about cooperation and competitiveness. Play helps the child to live through disturbing experiences and reactions that enable the therapist to respond in ways that facilitate resolution of anxieties, unwarranted guilt, or fear. This requires a combination of sensitivity and skill. It is an illustration of the art and science of psychotherapy.

The child doesn't see the therapy experience in the same way as the therapist or parents. The young child particularly doesn't come prepared with a conscious or understanding attitude that purposefully works towards resolution or growth. The decision to be there has been made for him. The child is a much more existential person than the adult. He is less able to deal with tomorrows. He knows what he can sense and touch. The future is an abstraction that has little real meaning. It is more difficult for him to deal with promises for the future and hard to relate his present moment to the yesterdays of his life. The need for gratification has a greater sense of immediacy. The infantile attitude is sometimes expressed by "I want what I want when I want it."

The methods used in individual therapy are also applied in group psychotherapy with children. The major difference in the group is that the child interacts with his peers as well as with the therapist. He moves out beyond the realm of the basic one-to-one relationship to the social world of his existence. He now has to relate to several one-to-one relationships and find his place in the larger world. In addition to talking and the various forms of play mentioned, the therapist now uses each member of the group as an agent of change for the others. The social scene is now in view and provides a setting that is comparable to both the family and the social relationships of each child. Each child is unique and will interact in ways that reflect his past experiences, his attitudes, his concerns, and his wishes. In individual and in group therapy the therapist makes interpretations not just by what he says but by the way he responds.

The therapist becomes a model, a surrogate parent, a friend, and someone the child can use to try out new ways of being that can take him beyond his self-defeating forms of behavior and enable him to become more of what he is. Once the child changes via the therapeutic process he can transfer these changes in himself in relating to his outside world. However, there is a time lag between experienced changes in personality and the ability to use them outside. Also the process is not a smooth one; as in life there are ups and downs.

When the family is used as the group in child psychotherapy, each member is worked with in relation to each other. Each member of the real or nuclear family is used as an agent for change. Destructive forms of relatedness to which various members have become accomplices are worked through. More creative and productive paths are explored to deal with old problems.

Let us now summarize some of the essential aspects of child psychotherapy whatever form it takes. When the child enters therapy it is not to be assumed that he requires no introduction or explanation because "he doesn't understand or know any better." As in any therapy it is necessary to be honest but uncomplicated. The child may not understand his troubles or his worries but he is curious. A simple and honest explanation can go a long way towards alleviating anxiety about the therapy. The child is aware of his feelings and his pain. Simply acknowledging the feelings of the child and expressing a wish to help him can be a sufficient condition for beginning the therapeutic relationship. However society views the behavior or symptoms of the child, the therapist must be willing and able to accept him as a worthwhile person. And whatever modality or techniques the therapist uses, he must make primary use of himself, his own person.

The therapist talks with the child, plays with him, struggles with him, but never rejects or diminishes him.

In life there are always ground rules that are spoken or unspoken. In a healthy situation the child knows where he stands. Disturbed children often come from experiences in which they received double messages or were uncertain or confused about their place and the expectations imposed on them. In therapy the therapist lets the child know where he stands. He begins on the right foot by being straight. The rules are made clear and simple. Generally the child is not permitted to behave in ways destructive to himself or others. Such behavior is not approved of but doesn't jeopardize the therapeutic relationship. The child is not threatened with rejection or abandonment. Openly expressed words, thoughts, feelings, wishes, or fantasies are not regarded as destructive. Physical violence or attacks on persons or property may be considered as destructive and necessary limits are set when needed.

Promises are never made; they are too easily broken. There is only the commitment to work together, to help, to be supportive, and to care. The therapist does not engage in magical thinking, mind reading, or creating illusions that can only lead to disappointment and disillusionment. The therapist is a real person working with and on behalf of the child.

13

The Adolescent
as Patient

Traditionally, developmental psychologists have studied and discussed human behavior in terms of major age groups. Childhood includes the period from before birth to approximately age twelve. The adult group includes late adolescence, from approximately seventeen to about sixty or sixty-five. The group over sixty-five is considered gerontological. The adolescent age period from twelve to about seventeen lies between late childhood and early adulthood. Recently psychologists have become concerned with adolescence as a separate and distinct period of growth with its own problems and its own processes.

The psychotherapist working with the referred adolescent requires a clear understanding of what constitutes emotional disturbance and what is reasonable protest or rebellion. Often these are confused by the observing adult. What may be considered by parents and authorities as emotionally disturbed behavior may be the adolescent's response to the perceived irrational restrictions of the family and society. Therefore, psychotherapists working with adolescents must have a clear picture of what they consider emotional disturbance as distinct from reasonable, emotionally constructive rebellion.

One of the sources of information for these standards is a review of constructive rebellion as an historical phenomenon. Every adolescent who comes to the attention of the authorities, either for nonconforming behavior at school or at home, or does not do "what is expected," is not by definition emotionally disturbed. At times the demand to conform or the recommendations of treatment are used to limit reasonable rebellion.

Many psychotherapists and developmental psychologists are uncertain as to whether adolescence is late childhood, a transition stage, early adulthood, or its own distinct period. Concurrently, there is a further division into early and late adolescence. Some workers will go further and consider early adolescence, middle adolescence, and late adolescence as distinct periods of grace. One of the accepted definitions of late adolescence is that period during which the individual makes the transition to adulthood. At times the adolescent is expected to understand certain ideas or concepts simply because he has the intellectual capacity to do so. Many of these ideas are emotionally toned as part of the adolescent's life and the adolescent is familiar with some of the ideas or can grasp them intellectually. However this is not a sufficient reason for assuming emotional readiness or acceptability. The specific chronological age is not the crucial aspect. The emotional age, or the individual ability to assume self-regulation, responsibility, and self-direction, is more important.

Most adolescents do not enter the psychotherapy process by choice. In fact, it is rather infrequent that an adolescent will request psychotherapy voluntarily. When this does occur, it is an indication that the adolescent is aware that he is frightened, desperate, severely disturbed, or that he has sufficient health, insight, or courage to admit the need for help. The therapist in such instances accepts the adolescent's self-judgment to facilitate his immediate entrance into the psychotherapy process. The majority of adolescents are coerced into the psychotherapist's office, often against their own conscious wishes, by parents, school systems, the family physician, or other authorities. Thus the adolescent may well enter the psychotherapy process with a resistance to the entire procedure. At times, this resistance becomes overt and the adolescent makes it quite clear how unaccepting he feels of psychotherapy. Adolescents often feel that people see something wrong with them and that their problem is unique rather than being part of a larger problem which might possibly exist within the family or in the adolescent's relationships to the other individuals in his group. Often adolescents are not informed of the reasons for the referral. They are simply told to see the psychotherapist, or else! The psychotherapy process would actually be enhanced if the adolescent was considered as an understanding and aware individual and given some explanation. Often this capacity for understanding and acceptance is sadly underestimated by parents, the referring authorities, and sometimes even by the psychotherapist.

One of the aspects of working with adolescents is their legitimate reluctance to become involved in psychotherapy. All negativism is not psychotherapeutic resistance. It may be part of the reaction the adolescent has to being coerced into doing anything. This resistance might best be recognized and accepted as part of the ongoing psychotherapy process. Thus the psychotherapist works with the realistic reluctance as well as the resistance posed by the emotional aspects of the psychological disturbance.

There are several therapeutic factors which although not specific to adolescence are important at this period of development. Honesty between the therapist and the adolescent is as important if not more so than between the therapist and patients of other ages. The therapist must respect the adolescent's desire for privacy as well. The adolescent is not an extension of the family or other social group, but an individual in his own right. The therapist does not side with or against the adolescent. When working with adolescents it becomes even more important that the therapist be perceived by the patient as an independent and impartial individual, rather than an extension or representation of the authorities. The well-trained therapist does not adopt the values of the family and attempt to have the adolescent conform to the expectations and demands of the family unit. Neither is the adolescent encouraged to expect the therapist to take his side against the perceived oppressive authority figures. This approach may provoke some conflicts in working with parents, school officials, and some legal authorities. Respecting the adolescent's privacy means that the therapist makes no report to the parents or to the officials as to what the adolescent is saying and doing. The adolescent learns that what he discusses with the therapist remains within the framework of the therapeutic relationship. This is also an important procedure in working with adolescent groups. The adolescent, although often advised not to, may describe anything about himself to an outsider but is prohibited from discussing or even mentioning other members of the therapy group. The patient, adult as well as adolescent, may be advised to avoid discussing his therapy outside the session for two reasons: (1) emotional reactions often change as the therapy progresses, and (2) the outside discussion may serve to dissipate anxiety which should be brought into and discussed during the therapeutic session. There are times when it is extremely difficult for the therapist to maintain the privacy of the adolescent against the demands of the parent and involved officials. A comment often made by parents is that they have a right to know everything that happens or is discussed because they are both legally responsible for the adolescent and they are paying for the therapy itself. The appropriate limits of these arguments have to be explored with the parents, at times with the adolescent present, or therapy may well become either ineffective, or even counterproductive.

There are occasions when the adolescent, either by omission or commission, will mislead or modify the facts. The adolescent will avoid the truth in an attempt either to circumvent investigation or in the fear that this material will be used against him. This behavior becomes part of the therapeutic process and therefore no different than when the therapist becomes aware that any patient is omitting factual material. A patient may avoid discussing either aggressive, sexual, or other experiences that he thinks the therapist will not approve of.

The therapist focuses on what he feels the adolescent can work with at any point in the therapeutic process. There are times when the adolescent can tolerate a higher level of anxiety and distress than at other times. With adolescents it is often advantageous to use indirect rather than direct avenues of investigation and discussion.

Adolescents tend to change the intensity of their emotions more rapidly than the duration of the emotional reaction. The therapist is aware that what might appear to the onlooker as an extremely intense emotional reaction may be of a short duration. Knowing this, the therapist is in a more advantageous position to gauge accurately the level of anxiety and the degree of stress tolerance. As indicated earlier, the adolescent often avoids discussing problems, specific individuals in his life, and specific aspects of emotional disturbance if a direct approach is used. Often the approach is by means of a hobby, sports, or another interest such as music. These topics may then be used to lead the adolescent into the more revealing, more personal aspects of his life. Important here is the therapist's level of knowledge relating to the subject matter under discussion. The therapist needs the knowledge of what is going on in the adolescent's world. This might include information concerning the current musical scene, various sports, the type of reading, and the level of interest of a given adolescent. One aspect of this is the danger of "playing the expert" when the therapist actually has little if any knowledge of the material under discussion. When the adolescent recognizes, and he does rapidly, that the therapist is being pompous and erroneous, trust and confidence are sharply limited if not altogether eliminated. The adolescent may then merely tolerate the therapist or inwardly laugh at the therapeutic process and the therapist involved. The adolescent will usually respect the therapist's honesty in saying that he lacks specific knowledge and then requesting information, rather than attempting to cover up.

There are times when confrontation is important in the therapeutic process. However, this should be handled with extreme sensitivity or avoided with adolescents unless the confrontation is crucial for the therapeutic process at a specific point. For example, the question of misstating the facts in a situation, a refusal to discuss specific areas or individuals in the adolescent's life, or a refusal to explore the private areas of his world. The adolescent does not respond to authoritarian demands in a positive way.

The adolescent will attempt to test the therapist in many different ways. He will play games, such as posing problems and puzzles, in an attempt to "get to" the therapist. Working with these situations on the therapeutic basis usually proves to be rewarding for both, but ignoring the process may be detrimental.

There are several areas which are important in the world of the adolescent. Although these may be important in working with the child as well as the adult they are critical in disturbances of the adolescent. Where intellectual ability is not in question, academic disturbance and academic effectiveness will be reflections of emotional disturbance. While school phobias are more frequent among younger children, there is a second period of school phobias in early adolescence. The phobia may reflect the more specific present attitudes or experiences in the school, as well as a carry-over of an earlier school phobia. An adolescent who is already intellectually capable may respond to an emotional disturbance with severe learning disabilities. There may be either a sharp drop in response to a learning situation or an inability to learn new material. The problem posed by the questions of both "Who am I?" and "Where am I going?" may be another area of conflict for the adolescent. Dangling between childhood and adulthood, he, is experiencing the extreme burden of evaluating his own identity. Under the most favorable conditions there are difficulties in deciding where he fits into society and who he actually is. The search for identity is central to the world of adolescents. This is not to say that every adolescent with an identity conflict is by definition emotionally disturbed. However, many disturbed adolescents do have a serious problem of their own identity. Concomitant with this are the dual problems of the relationship to authority and aspects of sex and delinquent behavior. With the changing standards and mores of both sexual behavior and acceptable response to the demands of the authorities, the adolescent is strained when making the necessary decisions regarding sexual activity and rebellious behavior. He is confused as to how these behaviors fit into his world. The adolescent is ordinarily in conflict, as when he attempts to work out a balance and to find himself in the larger world around him. He distinguishes rather sharply between rational authorities, where limits are understood and appropriately responded to, and the irrational authority in which the limits are seen as restrictive.

There are times when delinquency is emotionally motivated. The adolescent uses delinquent behavior as a way of expressing himself against society. At times sexual behavior may be used in a similar way. However, most adolescent sexual activity is exploratory. It is an expression of a reaching out in an effort to develop interpersonal relationships. Most organized religions hold that overt sexual activity must be confined to married couples of the opposite sex. However, the biological drives in the developing human do not recognize marriage as a necessary condition for sexual activity. The adolescent today is more open in his curiosity in terms of sexual behavior, drugs including alcohol, and many

other experiences that the adult authorities consider either antisocial or at least morally questionable or totally unacceptable. The
therapist finds it necessary to understand whether the behavior
involved is a reaction to an emotional conflict or part of an
exploratory pattern on the part of the adolescent. Deviant behavior is not necessarily an indication of emotional disturbance in the
adolescent.

The adolescent may well question whether he is an integral
part of the adult world. In recent years any group that felt itself
unjustly limited by restrictions has reacted strongly. The adolescent's plea for rationality in the use of a basic resource such as the
air and water has not been an expression of rebellion. There is a
growing clear recognition that there are limits to the things the
adults may consider limitless. Society may be faced with the
destruction of part, if not most, of the world. Some adolescents
may select lifestyles different from the norm. An adolescent
making such a choice marches to the beat of a different drummer.
He may decide he does not want to fit into society as it is currently constituted. Or he may want to become part of a "fringe"
society. He may choose to be involved in a commune, an organic
group, or in a type of life that may be questionable to the adult. It
may be important for the adult as well as the therapist to clarify to
himself what is or is not reasonable or rational. The adult may
almost immediately respond to the adolescent's questions as a
challenge rather than a seeking of information.

There are clear differences in the behavior of the early and
late maturing adolescent. Depending upon the sex and the social
group there are differences in the concerns of the early and late
maturing adolescent. Since physical development plays an important role in life the early enhancement of this in female and male,
or the lack of it, becomes important. We base most of our
responses to other people on the idea that everyone is "average."
Often there is a lack of recognition that deviations from the
average impose possible conflicts on the developing adolescent.
The therapist's responsibility includes the recognition of the
differences and awareness of the emotional difficulties which may
be more frequent in either the early or late maturing adolescent.

The therapist is interested in the various sources of valid
information about the adolescent himself. While this may take

some time and as indicated earlier may have to be done somewhat indirectly, the primary source should be the adolescent. Parents do provide specific information but they also see and present this information in their own way. This does not necessarily mean that their views are distorted, or that they misinform. It does, however, raise questions about their particular set or bias. Information gained from the parents may be used to understand the adolescent's earlier development and experiences as well as to help recognize the attitudes of the parents as significant influences in his life. Often other patients who know the adolescent are a good source of information about him. These other patients, particularly in a group setting, may offer information about the individual and this may then facilitate the adolescent's direct expression about himself. Other sources may be adults, teachers, and friends of the adolescent, as well as other individuals who may be both interested in and concerned with the adolescent. Any information obtained is carefully evaluated and compared with the adolescent's own presentation. The therapist makes every effort to be open-minded and accepting. What is required is a constant process of cross-evaluation, sifting, and cross-validation. This process continues until the final psychotherapeutic session.

Psychological evaluations are an important source of information concerning the emotional state of the individual. There are several projective techniques that are useful in working with the adolescent. It is important that the therapist or diagnostician be cautious in applying the results of the projective material in the instance of a specific adolescent. The adolescent is in a period of extremely rapid change. There are changes in mood, changes in the individual's perception of the world, and rapid changes in overt behavior. What may well be applicable at a given moment may not be so three or six months later. Thus the results of the projective material may be applicable at a given time but may not be so later. A contribution of the projective material is to help distinguish between aspects of functional disorders as compared with neurological or organic difficulties. There are instances where the effects of birth injuries—minimal brain damage—may be initially noted in the psychological material, rather than through the school's records or the individual's overt behavior.

Many of the methods used with the adolescent in

psychotherapy are similar to those used with children or adults. There are some additional adaptives which are of interest. For example, in individual therapy the adolescent may ask to bring in a friend, a member of the same or opposite sex. The friend may help the adolescent directly or may have information that the adolescent cannot bring out. The therapist often remains flexible and is able to include these individuals in the therapeutic relationship when indicated. A group setting may be more productive when working with some adolescents. The adolescent finds support and reassurance in the presence of others his own age and so is often able to respond more effectively to the therapeutic process. The group may be an activity group organized to include physical or intellectual activity as a bridge into the therapeutic experience. Group or individual sessions may be focused on a play therapy activity. An adolescent group or an individual may respond well to a sport or similar activity which includes members of both sexes and which will permit self-expression. With the adolescent, as with the child, the office setting poses a number of limitations. The adolescent, more than the adult, feels constrained by the necessity of sitting or lying in one position or remaining in one place for an extended period of time. He seems to respond more effectively when there is an opportunity to be mobile and to express himself in some physical activity.

The setting of goals for the therapeutic process is important in working with adolescents. Research into the developmental aspects of adolescence has indicated that setting long-range goals tends to be less effective than working towards a reasonable short-term goal as a step towards the long-range goals. Goals are most often dependent on the problem areas involved. Sometimes returning to school, returning to functioning in the community, living with the parents or away from them, may be sufficient as a goal. At other times the adolescent may want to set long-term goals together with a reorganization of his lifestyle. The therapist permits the goals to grow out of the adolescent's increasing awareness of concerns about living and his relationship to the larger group, rather than imposing goals and expectations on the therapist.

The adolescent in general is a difficult individual to work with in therapy. He poses difficulties and complex problems. He moves much more rapidly from one extreme to another. These moods shift erratically and without predictability. The relationships are intense but extremely short-lived. He reacts on the basis of conforming with his own group rather than with the larger social group. What is required of the therapist is patience, flexibility, and a recognition of adolescence as a difficult period in growing up for both the adolescent and the adult. The effective therapist recognizes that it is an especially difficult time because there are no clear and simple answers to the problems of growing up in a complicated and complex society during a very troublesome period. There are times when the therapist agrees with the adolescent's refusal to become involved in a psychotherapeutic process. Forcing the adolescent to continue may well be detrimental rather than helpful. As the door to returning to therapy is always left open, the adolescent may recognize somewhat later that he may benefit from some experience in exploring himself and his world. He may then decide to return on his own, rather than be coerced into the process. If adolescence is thought of in emotional rather than in chronological terms then some young adults may be thought of as late adolescents, some older children as early adolescents, and some late adolescents as early adults.

14

Psychotherapy
with Adults

When people consider psychotherapy such questions as to *why*, *when*, *where*, and *how* usually arise. There is also the question of whether or not some form of therapy benefits everyone. "After all, everyone has problems," is a phrase often heard. There are many conditions in life which lead to disturbing and sometimes distressing difficulties. However, people do have the capacity to develop means of coping with conflicts. The methods and levels of effectiveness in resolving these conflicts are related primarily to the individual's earlier life experiences. Sometimes genetic or developmental factors contribute to the problem. Everyone continues to develop by learning and acquiring new experiences. Those who have developed high levels of frustration tolerance and adequate life experiences usually are able to overcome temporary adversities. For these people psychotherapy may offer a new learning experience. There are some people whose life experience patterns have either precipitated or reinforced a withdrawal from reality as a means of coping with anxiety-provoking conflicts, for example, hallucinatory experiences and delusional symptoms. The inability to establish effective communication with individuals in this state may sharply limit psychotherapeutic benefits.

The majority of people living in the present industrialized society are aware of the realities of life. However, for various reasons they may have developed and reinforced inadequate methods of dealing with conflict situations. They are victim to painful and energy-robbing anxiety and are thus unable to develop and effectively utilize their potential for creativity, intellectual growth, and emotional security. They derive little satisfaction and enjoyment from their daily experiences. These are the individuals who may profit most from psychotherapy.

The *why, when,* and *where* of psychotherapy have been elaborated. The *how*—what happens during the process of psychotherapy with adults—may now appropriately be discussed. The description and illustrations will focus on psychoanalytic oriented psychotherapy. Also, psychotherapy with adults is often general enough to apply to the psychotherapeutic treatment of all age groups.

The problems presented by adults seeking psychological help may range from vague to specific. A person may experience uncomfortable pressures which may arise from either internal or external sources. He may express feelings of distress related to conscious or unconscious anxiety-creating experiences. These problems may be related to emotional or physical pain, disturbances in intellectual functioning or thought processes, symptoms of physiological illness, or disruption of marital, familial, social, or work relationships. Often problems are complex and multicausal. A disturbance in both marital and work relationships was expressed by a man of forty-two who described vague apprehension of losing his job. His efficiency at work had deteriorated and he was experiencing a great deal of pressure from his boss. He stated, "I really don't think things are that bad, but my wife threatened to leave me if I didn't get some sort of professional help. I haven't sensed it, but she says I have become extremely irritable at home. I know I've been having a helluva time with the kids lately, but they're always creating some problem or other. My wife has also been bitching that I haven't been very affectionate and that I haven't come close to her in bed lately. Well, that part's true. I haven't felt any sexual desires for the last couple of months and I don't believe you ought to force yourself to have sex if you really don't feel like it." Continuing to describe his situation he mentioned, in an offhand manner, that he had consulted a heart specialist because "I have been having some heart palpitations." The cardiologist found no organic basis for the symptoms and had told him not to worry.

A nonspecific complaint was offered by a twenty-seven-year-old woman who had been having periodic episodes of mild depression. She described her life as being "pretty much routine. I seem to function pretty well. I get along well with my family and friends. I also have a part-time job which keeps me pretty busy. My boss often tells me I'm irreplaceable. I can't put my finger on anything that's really wrong but everything seems to be lacking something. My friends see and speak of my marriage as ideal and very often tell me they envy my ability to get along with people and do so much. Yet, I don't feel myself experiencing any real satisfaction or enjoyment out of life. I feel something must be out of kilter and that I need some professional help to work this thing out."

A diagnostic evaluation is helpful in clarifying the basic problem(s). The complaint may encompass the basic problem(s) or it may be a means of concealing the underlying conflicts disturbing the individual. The method of evaluation depends on the therapist's training and philosophy of psychotherapy. Some therapists contend that the diagnostic information will evolve from their interaction with the patient and focus their efforts towards the development of an interpersonal relationship from the start. Other therapists tend to follow a more traditional procedure, directing their initial efforts towards a tentative diagnosis formulation. In the process a detailed summary of the individual's life history is taken. The information includes as complete a developmental picture as can be obtained from the patient or other members of his family. Information about the parent's occupation, education, and social standing may throw light onto environmental influences which have affected the individual. Social and interpersonal relationships with the immediate and nuclear family and peers may also reflect conflicts which originated in childhood and continue to the present time. The individual's intellectual development may be assessed by his academic progress, achievements, and aspirations.

The preliminary diagnostic evaluation goes further than obtaining historical data. To aid in formulating the individual's emotional-psychological status, standardized psychological assessment techniques may be utilized as a method of gaining additional information regarding reaction patterns and intellectual functioning processes. Projective techniques permit the individual to respond to ambiguous stimuli with feelings and thoughts which help reveal possible behavioral responses to real life situations. Intellectual and achievement tests provide an indication of potential as well as of the degree to which the person has developed his capacities. These psychological methods may be administered by either the psychotherapist who has received training in these specialized techniques, or by another psychologist as a means of obtaining an independent evaluation. Sometimes the therapist's schedule doesn't permit adequate time for diagnostic testing, which is time consuming.

Physical and neurological examinations may be of value in determining what role organic conditions may play in affecting the emotions and behavior of the individual. There are some symptoms which may be the result of either emotional or physiological conditions, or a combination of both. Emotions and physiological conditions rarely operate independently of each other. Emotional stress often weakens resistance to infection or may intensify an already existing organic condition. Individuals under emotional stress are more likely to catch colds. The intense pain of a headache may be the result of persistent emotional pressure or of an infected sinus condition. Experience has shown and demonstrated that fainting or blacking out may be an individual's means of escaping from an intolerable conflict situation, while the same reaction by another person may be primarily the result of a brain lesion. Emotional stress may intensify the effects of the brain lesion resulting in more frequent blackouts. Another example is epilepsy; it may be a result of organic factors and/or psychological factors. However, the frequency and intensity of epileptic seizures are often affected by the psychological status of the individual. Therefore, a history of past illnesses and knowledge of the individual's general health, including his present condition, is important.

Consultation, with the consent of the patient, with members of the family, close friends, and other significant persons in the patient's life tends to shed additional light and aid in understanding his difficulties. As previously indicated, a person may be unaware of the significance or indirect effects of his behavior. The same can be said regarding memory of past events. The blanks in one's recall of past experiences are rarely due to organic factors.

These lapses usually are selective and related to extreme anxiety-provoking experiences. The need to minimize the pain of the related anxiety results in an unconscious repression or conscious suppression of the experience(s). Although some psychotherapists rigidly avoid contact or communication with family members or other significant persons in the patient's life, there are others who welcome this opportunity. Some psychotherapists who believe in obtaining all the help they can get in understanding and evaluating the patient may restrict these contacts to the preliminary diagnostic evaluation period or may maintain contact throughout the psychotherapeutic process, depending on their orientation to therapy.

After obtaining sufficient information the psychotherapist formulates what might be described as a schematic diagram or rough sketch regarding the nature of the individual's difficulties. The emotional status of a person may have resulted from a severely disturbing experience, or the conflicts may be related to maladaptive behavior which began in early childhood.

When formulating a treatment plan there are many facets which are considered by the psychotherapist. In addition to understanding the nature of the individual's problem, the therapist evaluates and determines whether one or more persons should be directly involved in the treatment procedure. Although a single individual may be referred and seek psychotherapy, there is usually the question of whether the goals of the treatment may best be reached working with only that person or in combination with others.

The following are single examples of emotional reactions and disturbing personality problems.

A young woman, Mrs. K., was referred for psychoanalytic psychotherapy because of her persisting feelings of depression, an inability to perform adequately in daily routine activities, and an inability to enjoy her husband after a happy marriage of five years. Approximately four months prior to the initial interview, Mrs. K's two-and-one-half-year-old son had died as a result of falling out of the window of their sixth floor apartment. Playing alone in the living room, the child had climbed onto the sill of an open window. Mrs. K., seeing the child in the window, shouted that he should get down. The child, in a playful, giggling mood, began to shake the guard rail. For some undetermined reasons the bolt securing the guard rail came loose and the child plunged out the window. Mrs. K. accused herself as being responsible for the child's death. The evidence consisted of (1) leaving the child alone in the room, and (2) shouting at the child while he was standing in the window. This was used to condemn herself, resulting in severe guilt and then depression.

Another situation involving intense feelings of depression was Mrs. J., a forty-eight-year-old married woman with two married daughters. The youngest daughter, aged twenty, had recently married and left the parental home. The description of Mrs. J.'s life revealed feelings of personal inadequacy which had existed from early childhood. Mrs. J. had been an only child whose efforts never quite fulfilled her parents' expectations. Any experience of successful achievement was readily destroyed by either her mother or father. They lessened her achievement by comparing it unfavorably to that of a cousin or friend. Even Mrs. J.'s marriage to a personable successful attorney was viewed by the parents as a fortunate accident. Her husband wanted children and she "bore him two beautiful daughters." Mrs. J.'s adult life had been devoted to performing her "wifely duties" to her husband and "a mother's obligations" to her daughters. The youngest daughter's marriage came when Mrs. J. was going through menopausal changes and was pictured as "adding insult to injury." Menopause was experienced by Mrs. J. as the destruction of her only claim to womanhood and value to her husband—fertility. At the same time, the daughter's marriage robbed her of the only useful activity she felt capable of performing—mothering.

Although Mrs. K. and Mrs. J. suffered from the same emotional reaction—depression—the reasons for each were quite different. Thus the psychotherapeutic procedure or what is professionally referred to as "treatment plan" would be quite different for these two women. The psychotherapeutic effort for Mrs. K. would be directed towards helping her understand and realize that the sudden traumatic loss of a love object is followed by a period of mourning which helps the bereaved adapt to the loss. She would be helped to see that she had no appropriate justification for assuming the guilt and thus condemning and punishing herself for this unfortunate accident. She would also be helped to understand that assuming responsibility for the act was related to her inability to direct her anger to the child for his action. The loss of a loved one may result in a temporary retreat into sadness, but it should not terminate one's ability to establish and enjoy other love relationships.

The treatment procedure for Mrs. J. was quite different. Although her feeling of depression was precipitated by her daughter's leaving home, the basic cause was related to a lifelong feeling of unworthiness. The therapeutic process here included the recall of early childhood emotional reactions to "being put down," with the ensuing feelings of inadequacy. Gaining awareness of how her self-demeaning attitude developed and was reinforced provided the opportunity to judge the validity of her parents' value judgments. Exploration of her attributes and reevaluation of her past endeavors also provided an opportunity to experience successes when appropriate. The therapist offered appropriate encouragement and aided her in developing potential attributes which had been curtailed by doubts concerning herself. The interpersonal relationship developed within the psychotherapeutic milieu allowed for personality growth and development.

In the second illustration given above, although Mrs. K's difficulties included her marital relationship with her husband, the nature of the problem was related to her self-condemnation and guilt. In this instance Mrs. K. had to work out her feelings towards herself. Therefore, although the husband might on occasion be the subject of discussion, his direct involvement and presence in the therapeutic situation would be unlikely to enhance the treatment process.

There are occasions when the resolution of disharmony in a marital relationship would be accelerated with both husband and wife appearing together. Marriage is an interpersonal relationship formalized by a legal contract. The relationship between two people develops, with rare exception, as a result of each seeking and anticipating from the other gratification of some needs or desires. As long as the needs for receiving gratification mesh the interpersonal bond will continue. The interpersonal relationship between the couple may be of a constructive or destructive nature, depending upon the respective needs for which each is seeking gratification. For example, mutual attraction will arise and flourish between a dependent individual who needs someone upon whom to lean and a person who has a strong need to dominate others. Anxiety-provoking conflicts will occur in such a relationship only if the needs of one of the partners change. If either partner is unwilling to tolerate the resulting anxiety, the two may terminate the relationship or seek means of reestablishing equilibrium, for example, a return to the old pattern or the development of a new complementary relationship. If psychotherapy is sought as a means of reestablishing a harmonious relationship, the therapeutic effort might best be served if both partners actively participate. If a formerly overdependent partner develops feelings of strength, self-confidence, and a desire to be more self-sufficient, the dominant partner must be able to relinquish some of his needs in order to maintain or reestablish a compatible relationship. Therefore, if the degree of change in one partner continues as a result of psychotherapy while the other partner's needs remain constant, the lack of compatibility with concomitant conflicts intensifies. The likely result of this severe conflict is termination of the relationship.

Psychotherapy as a means of resolving anxiety-arousing conflicts in interpersonal relationships is not restricted to married couples. The bond between the couple may be a premarital or nonmarital relationship. It may be heterosexual or homosexual with no legal or religious sanctions. Or, the relationship may be between friends or business partners.

The effects of psychotherapy may be considered as not limited to the individual in the psychotherapeutic relationship. Changes which occur within the patient influence others who have a relationship with him. Here again the people not in psychotherapy who may be affected include parent, child, and spouse, as well as friend. For example, after a trip together a friend of a patient who had never had any direct contact with the psychotherapist wrote the following letter:

Dear Dr. X:

First of all, I would like to tell you we both had a wonderful time on our trip to Tahiti and you are to blame for it was all your fault! Though I never met you, I feel I know you as I do understand your

kind—and I'm mad, through and through. I too
began being "open," had dates with men, and now
am vulnerable for both pleasure and pain.

Let me explain—then you'll understand what
you did to me. First off, I was planning a retreat to
the country during Mary's absence—alone and
away from everybody and everything—with the
companionship of a cat, and the woods across the
street. Unable to afford the trip, I went anyway—
for "it was good for me—and a way of taking care
of myself." That was how it all began. Rather than
sitting on sandy beaches, meditating and
relaxing—withdrawing from people—I let them
see the real me—not the clown, hell-bent on
having everyone enjoy themselves—but the quiet
me—the one who on occasion feels like withdrawing and being alone—the gentle me—the vulnerable one. Oh! You know exactly what I mean!

What happened is another story. Two beaux—
not one. From motorcycles to Mozart. Both
tripping over themselves, vying for my attention—for me—and what they could do for me. I
had continuous lunch and dinner dates, nightly
nightclubbing, dancing, and even romantic mid-
night dates (which I did not pursue). A real threat
too, as they both live in Long Island—and I'll see
them I know.

Now, most people would say—gee Doctor X,
thanks a lot, but not me! I was content to attend
New York University, and had a missionary, Mes-
sianic zeal to help others—look after their needs,
"You know what I mean?" Though lonely, I was
getting used to my little cocoon—and felt SAFE.
Now, I am a female—relating to men. I always felt
like shit and thought I was only good when I could
do for others—but not for me. Now this has
changed too. I want to be wanted for me. I bought
things in Tahiti—but mostly for me—and I didn't
stint either. And, finally, I want acceptance for me.

Yes I am mad. I too am vulnerable now—for
pain and ecstasy. I am not your client not undergoing analysis and just look at what you have done
for me!

Nina Z.

This letter sharply points up how far-reaching are the results of
psychotherapy.

The psychotherapeutic setting is an important factor to be
considered in the treatment plan. The choice of treatment setting,
which is also thought of as the modality, should be one most
conducive to progress. The setting may be a dyad, a relationship
consisting of a single patient and a therapist. Or the individual
may participate with other patients in a psychotherapeutic group
with one or more therapists. The person might participate in a
dyadic as well as group experience with the same therapist
(combined therapy) or with two different therapists, one for
individual and another for group (conjoint) therapy. Both the
dyadic and group setting have advantages and disadvantages.
Therefore, the setting choice would depend upon the emotional
status, the personality behavior pattern, and the anticipated
although tentative goals of the patient. The originally selected
setting may or may not be appropriate for the entire period of the
individual psychotherapy. For example, an individual may initially
be seen alone by the therapist. At a later time he may be seen in
combined psychotherapy or by two different psychotherapists in
conjoint therapy. At even a later time group psychotherapy alone
might be considered the exclusive treatment of choice. When a
couple is involved in treatment procedure there are additional
possibilities. The couple may be seen by the psychotherapist in a
triadic relationship or be participants in the same psychotherapeutic group. Each partner may be seen in a dyad, combined, or
conjoint therapeutic group setting. At times there may be a
combination of two or more of any of these treatment settings.

Each treatment modality has advantages as well as limitations
regarding the therapeutic process of any individual. These advantages were elaborated in the discussion of the different modalities.
For example, an individual may require the feeling of close intimacy with another important person in his life. At the same time,

this individual's emotional growth may require involvement with peers in order to work through his competitive feelings and anxieties in interpersonal relationships. Combined individual and group psychotherapy would be the choice for this person.

Therefore, the treatment of choice, which differs for different people, may change during the course of psychotherapy. The preferred treatment that is considered best for the individual(s) is determined by the existing emotional status, personality behavioral pattern, and anticipated goals of the individual.

The goals of psychotherapy may be viewed from two perspectives—those sought by the patient, and those considered appropriate by the therapist. Generally the patient seeks psychological aid with the primary aim of having his uncomfortable feelings and pressures relieved as soon as possible. Magic, miracles, or similar acts on the part of the therapist are often welcome. Many people enter therapy with the idea, some expressing it verbally, "Doctor, you are my last hope . . . I put myself completely into your hands!" This search for relief is usually accompanied by a desire to reestablish or develop more adjustive patterns of behavior. The results initially sought from psychotherapy may or may not be realistic. Frequently the goals initially sought become modified as the therapeutic process continues. The goals may expand when both the patient and the therapist become aware of existing potential for personality changes brought about by psychotherapeutic character reconstruction. This latter process is referred to as *intensive* or *depth* psychotherapy which utilizes psychoanalytic techniques. The objective of mature emotional and personality development is achieved by relinquishing neurotic defense patterns. However, there are individuals whose defenses, which had previously sustained them, crumble as a result of relatively intense stress. Although character reconstruction for these persons might be ideal, the emotional strength required for this process is often lacking. Therefore the most appropriate therapeutic goal may be that of supporting and rebuilding defense patterns so that the individual may reestablish a means of adapting to everyday stress situations.

The ultimate goal of psychotherapy is the development of optimal economy in the expenditure of energy and the experiencing of physical, emotional, social, and intellectual satisfaction as a result of one's endeavors. Some people may use psychotherapy to attain these ultimate goals, while others settle for less. The therapist is responsible for formulating a treatment plan which will direct the course of psychotherapy towards the tentative goals determined from the evaluation of the individual's personality and existing emotional status. The treatment plan might be compared to an itinerary of a voyage. The itinerary may be for a short trip using only one means of transportation, or it may include an extensive voyage which includes many different modes of transportation, experiencing joy and stress in the exploration of many regions, arriving at a number of ports of call and finally arriving at the originally determined point of destination. The itinerary is a recommended guide. The voyage may be shortened, extended, or changed as to the mode of transportation, the ports of call, or the final destination. The psychotherapeutic plan plots the intermediate goals which will eventually lead to the ultimate goal. The means of achieving these goals include the setting and techniques considered most appropriate. The goals, setting, or techniques may be modified when considered appropriate and to the benefit of the patient.

As stated earlier, what happens during the course of psychological treatment will depend upon the needs and desires of the patient as well as the therapist's philosophy of personality development and psychotherapy. The therapist is the *change agent* who provides the direct and indirect influences and conditions which the patient may use to alter his behavioral and emotional reactions. Therefore, the relationship between patient and therapist becomes the essential force in the psychotherapeutic endeavor, regardless of the goals set or the approach taken. Although the actual development of this relationship begins when the patient and therapist first meet, there may be preconceived notions or images before there is any direct personal contact between the two. There are occasions when a prospective patient develops an anticipated relationship before ever meeting or seeing the therapist. This may develop from data obtained from one or more sources—hearsay or published information, observing changes in friends or relatives who have been in treatment with the particular therapist, hearing or reading some of the therapist's professional work, seeing or hearing the therapist at a social, civic, or scientific occasion, and so forth. The anticipated relationship may become a reality to be modified or be completely altered during or after the initial meeting.

The first session is usually a "feeling out" period used by both patient and therapist to evaluate the other and to gauge the probable outcome of working together. The therapist's approach in this endeavor is two-fold—to evaluate the patient's emotional status, and to develop a psychotherapeutic relationship. The emotional status and a tentative diagnosis are obtained by questioning and exploring the meaningfulness of the patient's ostensible problems, lifestyle, historical data, and goals sought, as well as quantity and quality of the patient's responses and interactions. During this procedure the therapist is also responding and interacting to verbal and nonverbal communications from the patient. His responses will be determined by what he considers the overt and covert needs of the patient. He may answer directly or, when appropriate, react to the underlying meaning rather than the overt question. He may perceive and respond to nonverbal cues which indicate the presence of anxiety, anger, or other emotions which have not been openly expressed. During this procedure the patient is also evaluating the therapist, although not always deliberately or consciously. There is an extensive range of attributes from which the patient may select. "How perceptive or sharp is the therapist in picking up what I mean?" "How interested is he in me as a person rather than a case file?" "Is he warm and personable or cold and distant?" "Is he really understanding or is he patronizing?" "Is he accepting, approving, merely tolerating, or condemning either my behavior or me as a person?" All individuals who seek psychological help cannot or might not be willing to work effectively with the same type of therapist. Some people will seek and initially respond only to a therapist who is overtly warm and interacts freely. There are those who will seek and will achieve their psychotherapeutic goals effectively with an authoritative figure who continues to interact in an impersonal manner. There are others, however, who may require a psychotherapist who can be both objectively distant or warm and personal depending upon the appropriateness of the situation.

The first session usually ends with some clarification of what has taken place and an agreement between patient and therapist.

Clarification may range anywhere from a verbalized description of the patient's diagnosis and psychotherapeutic needs to a declaration that the patient and therapist working together will not bring about the desired results. The formulation of the tentative diagnosis and therapeutic needs may require several sessions. The agreement reached may be a therapeutic contract which includes the establishment of the fee, time schedule, and psychotherapeutic approach. The therapist and patient may agree to continue on a tentative basis in order to assure themselves that each is willing to work with the other or decide that they will not continue together. The therapist may refer the patient to someone else or the patient may decide to seek someone else on his own. If the therapist and patient agree to work together a tentative goal is usually considered by the therapist. This goal may or may not be discussed with the patient but is important in regard to the frequency of visits and the psychotherapeutic techniques which will be employed. The goals set may include one or more of the following forms of psychotherapy:

   1. *character reconstruction*, which is often referred to as *depth psychotherapy* and *psychoanalysis*. Character reconstruction is a modification of the individual's personality brought about by alterations of persisting attitudes developed in childhood as well as emotional response patterns.

   2. *conflict resolution*, which involves the exploration of anxiety-provoking opposing drives within the individual or prohibitions from the environment. As the individual gains in understanding of the derivation and meaningfulness of the conflict(s) he is in a position to establish priorities, as well as to develop options regarding emotional and behavioral responses.

   3. *supportive therapy*, which is directed towards decreasing the negative effects of anxiety and thus enabling the individual to function better. To accomplish this goal the therapist aids the patient to shore up or reestablish previous emotional and behavioral patterns, as well as develop new ones.

4. *guidance,* which is primarily guiding the individual in obtaining resources from which he may
draw in order to improve his method of functioning. This last procedure is often used with parents
who are having difficulty with their children. The
therapist aids them in understanding the child's
normal as well as deviant behavior and helps them
learn how to influence the child's development.

Once agreement has been reached by the psychotherapist and
patient that they will work together, the therapeutic process
continues to evolve. Using his knowledge of personality development, the therapist continues to explore and seek understanding
where the natural process of development was blocked, side-
tracked, or impeded. With rare exceptions, every person is born
with potential for developing into adulthood with the ability to
utilize optimally his endowed capacities.

The agreement between therapist and patient also includes
the setting in which they will work, as well as the question of who
will be involved. Basic conditions of the relationship are established, for example, confidentiality of communication, including
with whom and when outside communications will take place and
under what conditions.

Following a mutual acceptance of the therapeutic contract, the
therapist-patient interpersonal relationship becomes the medium
in which changes may take place. An adult usually comes into
the psychotherapeutic situation with a well-defined personality
structure which includes consistent behavioral and emotional
reaction patterns. The existing personality structure and reaction
patterns have been an outgrowth of the person's early struggle for
survival in his environment. The Western culture tends to be
problem solving and success oriented. This orientation fits in with
society's needs to comply with the established work ethic philosophy. Thus the individual from early childhood experiences a
prohibition against internal drives for pleasurable and enjoyable
experiences. At the same time he is encouraged and directed
towards competitiveness and the seeking out of problems which
may then be solved. There is always the clear assumption that
there is a solution to any problem. The individual develops

attitudes and adopts a functional role which, at least minimally, has allowed him to cope with his inner needs and the demands experienced as coming from his outside world. If unresolved childhood conflicts persist into adult life, the person's perceptions and reactions tend to be distorted by unconscious early feelings which have been inappropriately retained. Thus the person has little conscious control over his emotional and behavioral reactions. In essence he has become subject to the feelings related to his unconscious conflicts. Relationships with others are directed towards those who complement this adopted role. When the person is forced into a relationship of noncomplementary roles, the conflict and stress which are provoked lead to intolerable anxiety. Thus one or the other adopted roles must be altered so the relationship can continue without major disruptions or terminations.

In psychotherapy the patient will attempt to establish a relationship consistent with his adopted role. He will expect the therapist to complement and fit into this role, which is important in maintaining an anxiety-free relationship. The therapist has his own personality structure which should include reality-oriented attitudes, value systems, and reaction patterns. At times the patient's needs and usual means of gratifying those needs do not bring the desired or expected results, when the therapist does not conform to the rules of the patient's adopted role. Thus some modification is required of the patient. The patient ventures into unfamiliar, possibly threatening areas of functions. The degree of anxiety generated in the patient may be influenced by the therapist. Frustration of expectations will tend to increase and gratification will tend to decrease anxiety. Another way of decreasing an anxiety-provoking conflict is the modification of the relationship. If the therapist maintains his position and the anxiety increases, the patient will either change to a more adaptive approach or rely upon some previously successful protective reaction pattern, such as withdrawal, hostility, or somatic symptoms.

The therapeutic relationship fosters a bond which helps the patient in therapy even though the anxiety intensifies. This bond may be considered a dependency but not necessarily a relationship of nurturance. The dependence is based upon the therapist having something the patient wants. The therapist fosters and reinforces this bond by offering understanding and when appropriate, satisfaction of certain of the patient's needs. The therapist helps the patient explore the meaningfulness of frustrated demands and the origins of exhibited nonadaptive behavior, as well as exploring more effective means for coping with underlying needs. The patient withstands and, in so doing, develops a greater tolerance level for anxiety. This process occurs because the breaking of the bond with the therapist is experienced as more threatening than the existing frustrating condition. Thus, when the anxiety of the known is less than the threat of the unknown, a person will risk exploring new, unfamiliar areas. This procedure brings about change within the patient as he reestablishes an equilibrium with the therapist and thus maintains the relationship. This is the basis of the therapeutic process.

As described above the process of changing appears to be rather uncomplicated. Undergoing this procedure, however, may be relatively slow and at times painful. The adopted role, even though limited in its effectiveness, has provided the individual with a *known* pattern of behavior which he has learned to depend upon for many years. To change is invariably threatening to the individual as it makes the future unknown and untried. Thus although the individual may overtly want and desire change, the threat of the unknown becomes a counterforce to this effort. This counterforce is referred to as "resistance" in psychotherapy. The therapist must time and again guide the direction of change towards attainment of the individual's intermediate goals. He continually assesses the patient's ability to tolerate the existing anxiety. In so doing the therapist strives to prevent experiences which may overwhelm, panic, and emotionally immobilize the patient. All of the therapist's understanding of personality development, sensitive perception, and psychotherapeutic tools are put to use. A phenomenon which is most helpful to the therapist is that of "transference." This is the relationship in which the therapist is endowed with attitudes and feelings originally experienced with regard to significant persons in the patient's past, such as mother, father, brother, or sister. This is an unconscious process which is not under the control of the patient nor directly produced by the therapist. The individual carries within himself unfulfilled needs and conflicts connected with these early significant figures which are perpetuated throughout his life. The transference phenomenon is thus a recreation of the unresolved emotional relationship with a substitute for the early significant figure. This potential may be compared to a reckless driver who stimulates the thought, "There goes an accident looking for someplace to happen." In a different situation, when the therapist does anything to provoke a particular response or situation, the results are *induced* reactions or relationships rather than transference.

The therapist may use the patient's transference reaction in two ways. First, the patient's reactions reveal the experienced relationships which led to unresolved emotional conflicts and nonadaptive reactions. Secondly, and perhaps most important, is the use of the relationship as a medium for the patient's resolution of those early conflicts. In so doing he develops personality strengths and alters previously unrealistic attitudes, as well as modifying nonadaptive behavior patterns. The patient has the opportunity to use the therapist in the same fashion as other significant figures in his present and past life. The therapist, reacting according to his understanding of the transference rather than as the original person did, provides experiences which the patient may use to resolve inner conflicts. Overcoming the barriers, the patient is in a better position to develop his own potential for healthy emotional growth.

The psychotherapeutic process begins with the initial meeting and continues until completion of the patient-therapist relationship. The process includes the continual exploration of the origin and development of emotional and behavioral patterns as they relate to significant people in the patient's life and as they coincide or vary from normative, healthy growth. There are many techniques which may be employed by the therapist to guide the patient towards the intermediate and final goal. These therapeutic tools, as described in Chapter Six, most often include the following: (1) connecting present emotions with past events, (2) exploration of events and conditions which bring enjoyable as well as disturbing emotional reactions, (3) encouraging the seeking and developing of new and more effective options from which the patient can set up priorities and select more adaptive reactions, (4) exploring the meaningfulness of daytime fantasies and dreams, and (5) differentiating reaction patterns based on the therapist's guides by focusing the patient's attention along the previously described path towards healthy personality development and emotional maturity.

The last segment of the psychotherapeutic process is the terminal phase. The completion of psychotherapy is evaluated on the basis of the patient's relative ability to act and react to the realities of the present rather than continuing to function in line with unresolved conflicts. When the person has progressed to this level of development the therapeutic relationship with the therapist is brought to a close. This procedure may be accompanied with varying degrees of separation anxiety. The therapist has played a significant role in the patient's life. Although completing a period of personality growth can bring intense feelings of satisfaction, the anticipated separation from an important person in one's life may provoke intense anxiety. Therefore, this separation should be experienced as another goal towards emotional maturity and not as a loss, desertion, or rejection. This can be accomplished by a clarification of the differentiation of the patient-therapist relationship from those with other significant persons in the patient's past. The patient's progress has placed him in a position where he is able to continue his personality development without continued professional aid. When he is able to recognize and accept the growth, strengths, and abilities which he has developed and to withstand internal and external stress in independent pursuit of further goals, the patient is ready to conclude psychotherapy. He then leaves the professional situation, with or without anticipation of future contacts with the therapist. The patient during his continued development may occasionally stumble and at times even fall. The sign of continued progress is the ability of the person to pick himself up after stumbling or falling and continue in his chosen endeavor.

Sometimes a person may decide to leave psychotherapy for one or more reasons before reaching the long-term therapeutic goals. Although financial reasons are often given, money is rarely the cause. There are rare occasions where the patient moves out of the geographical area and continuation with the therapist is impractical. Also an individual may have reached an intermediate goal which provides rewarding living experiences and may want to test his progress. He may say, "I feel good. Everything seems to be going pretty well and I'd like to try things on my own for a while."

On occasion the therapeutic progress may reach an impasse despite all efforts on the part of the therapist and patient. If this occurs referral to someone else or discontinuation of psychotherapy might be recommended. Most often, however, premature leaving is a disruption of the therapeutic relationship as a result of intense resistance. The individual has reached a point in psychotherapy where the risk of change is more threatening than the discomfort of the existing anxiety.

There are a few occasions when cessation of the therapeutic relationship, regardless of reason, is seen as completion. This may occur when the therapist has an extremely negative reaction which has to do more with his own personal needs rather than the therapeutic situation. Usually the therapist leaves the future open, assuring the patient that he is available for consultation or further psychotherapy if the occasion arises. The parting is on friendly terms with either person open to seek out the other in the future.

A question often arises about psychotherapy with an elder person. Does the person who has reached the age of sixty, seventy, or older have the same type of emotional problems and can he undergo the same psychotherapeutic process as the younger adult? This area of concern deserves elaboration and should not be sidestepped with a mere "yes" or "no" answer. The next discussion is designed to clarify the emotional development and therapy for this age group.

15

Treatment of
the Elder Person

The elder person, defined as over the age of sixty-five, constitutes approximately ten percent of the American population. The current cultural emphasis on youth as the most highly valued stage of the life cycle has led to a view that only the young—people under thirty—possess vim, vigor, vitality, and value. Although most individuals may have reached a developmental level of emotional maturity and integration in their fifties, most commercial, educational, governmental, and institutional enterprises have arbitrarily set sixty-five years or younger as the age of mandatory retirement. The present value of a person's worth as equated with an ability to produce is rooted in the history of the industrial revolution. As people began to leave the farm for the factory town, their way of life began to change. The ample living space of the country was replaced by limited quarters.

The agricultural setting encouraged multigenerational and extended families. The elder person as head of the farm was accepted and used for his wisdom while maintaining a role of authority. As patriarch he owned and was the titular manager of the farm which was a chief source of family wealth. The elder mother maintained a role as matriarch and was also revered for her wisdom resulting from age. The status of the elder person in the urban community tended to diminish as his/her value as a producer of material goods decreased.

The subculture of the elder person today consists primarily of an unemployed population. The publication *Working With Older*

People published by the U.S. Department of Health, Education, and Welfare offers an explanation as to why the age of sixty-five was selected for retirement. The aged population is considered primarily a retired population. This is a reflection of a highly technological society in which the accent has been placed on youth. The policies and customs that have established age sixty-five as the time of retirement have roots in history. In the late nineteenth century Germany's Chancellor Bismarck established a pension system for persons aged sixty-five or older. At that time however, relatively few persons survived to that age. Age sixty-five for retirement was confirmed in the United States by the Social Security Act of 1935. This legislation represented in part an attempt in the depression to open up jobs for the younger worker by encouraging retirement of the elderly, and in part an attempt to support the often unemployed worker.

Biological, nutritional, and medical research and advances have significantly increased longevity. Census data reveal an increasingly older population distribution throughout the world. The percentage in the age sixty-five and older group in the United States has more than doubled from 4.07 of the total population in 1900 to 9.9 in 1970. The U.S. Department of Commerce, Bureau of the Census, provided population estimates and projections for age sixty-five and older in the United States.

U.S. POPULATION DISTRIBUTION

YEAR	POPULATION 65+	TOTAL POPULATION
1970	19,799,000	205,357,000
1985	25,474,000	249,248,000
2000	28,837,000	300,789,000

The numerical and proportional growth of this age group has resulted in an increase of individuals who have attained wisdom and potential value which may be utilized for the benefit of society as a whole. Regrettably the potential benefits have tended to be neglected by Western cultures because of the emphasis on youth and on denigrating stereotypes of the elder person. These negative attitudes towards aging people tend to prevail as much to the detriment of the younger as to that of the elder person. There are a number of myths about elder people. "Old people are not able to make decisions." "Old people are always sick." "Old people are rigid and fixed in their ideas." And, most popularly, "Old age is second childhood," and "All old people are alike." Although there are some elder persons who might fit into one or more of these categories the same might be said of some individuals in any age group.

Here is an example of the ill effects of negative attitudes towards elder people. In fact, the person described had not reached the age of fifty. She was a forty-five-year-old woman who sought continued advanced education in order to fulfill her desired career goals. She had already achieved a master's degree and was performing a highly specialized service for children in a public school setting. Her efforts to enroll in a doctoral program met with no success for several years because of her age. The prevailing attitude was that her age limited the number of productive years following the doctoral training program. Her experienced frustration and provoked feelings of diminished worth resulted in intense anxiety and depression. With the aid of psychotherapy she was able to differentiate her actual worth and continued value from the societal stereotype that aging is synonymous with degeneration. This woman was then able to pursue her original goal, attaining acceptance in a desired program as a result of her attributes rather than age.

Character traits are formed and personality is relatively well shaped long before one reaches the elder years of life. The biological, socioeconomic, and psychological factors which influence one's behavior bring additional and concomitant stress in crisis periods of the various life stages. The common denominator of aging is the developmental process itself. Everyone has needs, drives, strengths, weaknesses, potentialities, and defenses. As one grows older the environmental and internal stresses tend to increase and proliferate. The degree of importance of the individual's drives increases in proportion to the degree that these are threatened. A strong desire and drive for independence appears during the early years and most often continues throughout life. Distinctive crises of the elder person, such as death of a spouse, loss of a job, or illness, often occur together and are experienced as grave threats to the individual's independence, security, and physical well-being. There is also a tendency for the elder person to internalize society's low esteem of the old. The denigration of one's self-image is likely to result in a rapid increase in the process of deterioration. Thus, where the person is unable to utilize his established intellectual and physical abilities in appropriate and self-benefiting ways, this person becomes a so-called "vegetable" exhibiting what may be labeled "functional senility."

Differences in personality types vary as much among elder persons as young and middle-aged adults. After all, aging is a continuum and the elder person's character structure and personality were developed during earlier years of living. There are, however, some common factors which affect this age group in varying degrees. The elder person may be compared to the adolescent in that both are going through periods of development which are characterized by physiological changes as well as cultural pressures. These may provoke difficulties when the person is called upon to cope with both strange inner stirrings and alien realities of society. During the early and middle adult years, the individual is in a stabilized physiological state. He usually has a great sense of his own adequacy and tends to function more habitually and consistently than during earlier as well as later stages of development. The elder period of life is generally accompanied by a decrease of energy level which tends to limit the physical activity of the individuals in this age group. The body of the elder person generally is unable to withstand the physical abuse tolerated during the younger years. However, with the exception of those who have developed chronic physiological handicaps such as heart trouble, the elder person is usually able to pursue activities which require some degree of physical exertion. There are many persons in their sixties, seventies, and even eighties who regularly play tennis, golf, squash, and are involved in water sports.

As discussed earlier, the ego may be described as a bridge between the individual and the outside world. It functions as an inhibiting force which controls the position of the person in the outside world. This is accomplished in a process of selectively receiving perceptions and selectively allowing discharge to instinctual drives and impulses. Otto Fenichel, a disciple of Freud, describes how the ego develops abilities with which it can observe, select, and organize the stimuli and impulses to which the five senses respond. These abilities thus serve the ego functions of judgment and intelligence. The ego also develops methods of keeping rejected and unacceptable impulses from being put into action by use of mental and physical energy which has been stored for this purpose. In other words, the ego blocks the tendency to carry out impulsive actions by changing them to selective actions. Changes of impulsive drives and efforts at control may become especially pronounced during the elder years because of the cumulative effect of environmental forces. These circumstances in the environment which are generally exclusive to this age group often include: (1) changes brought about by retirement and the resultant inactivity which requires new orientation and adjustment, (2) the death of a marital partner, close friends, or relatives, and (3) cultural stereotyping of appropriate behavior for the elder persons, which intensifies the taboo effect of sexual impulses which have already been conditioned as dangerous early in life. Under these conditions the demands on the ego may be experienced as too severe. Thus the ego may no longer be able to cope with strong impulsive drives resulting in feelings of inferiority, insecurity, and guilt. These feelings may become reinforced by preexisting and chronically unsolved conflicts of earlier life which had been repressed during the adult years but which have become reactivated by the stress of this elder age.

Excessive frustration and anxieties may result in neurotic actions as a means to relieve the pressure. An example of the latter is a sixty-seven-year-old male who sought psychological help because of his feelings of loss and depression. He described his adult life as being relatively successful and happy until approximately six months prior to seeking psychotherapy. He and his wife had operated an exclusive dress shop and reared two daughters. Both daughters had married and had children. At the age of sixty-four he and his wife had decided to retire and had sold their business. Since that time, he said, "things began to go down hill." When he relinquished the role of head of a business with the sale of his store, the strong dependency relationship with his wife began to emerge. Feelings of frustration and inadequacy replaced the happy experiences of visiting with his daughters. His feelings of authority and control with regard to his children were suddenly terminated. When the children were younger and living with him, he experienced himself as a "guiding light" and as head of the household. "Then," he said, "my word was law, but now, not only do I have to watch every word I say, but also how I say it." Whenever he offered a "word of advice," his daughters reacted with what he experienced as contempt. They would frequently tell him to "bug off" and on two recent occasions had told him that if he could not refrain from telling them how to live their lives, he had best stop visiting them.

The feelings of diminished status resulting from retirement and the change in his role as father reactivated early feelings of inadequacy. Describing his early life, he revealed feelings of inadequacy which had led to a marriage with a rather strong motherly woman. The success of the dress shop had been the result of his wife's efforts, but his role of "boss" had provided status and an aura of competence. His role as father and the ability to control small children also contributed to a feeling of power which aided in the suppression of his feelings of inadequacy and dependency. Thus his present emotional state was not of recent origin but the reactivation of earlier unresolved conflicts.

Complaints of depression, feelings of neglect, and unsubstantiated somatic symptoms are rather common in the life of the elder person. The feelings of neglect and the hypochondriasis appearing alone or in combination often are reflections of feelings of isolation. This isolation may be attributed to separation from family, spouse, or children as well as a loss of opportunity to fulfill society's criteria for worthiness, that is, productive work. There are also times when the isolation may be related to a reduction in perception of environmental stimuli. This latter may result from one or both of two factors: (1) decreases in visual or auditory acuity, and (2) a defense against the weakening of the ego strength. As mentioned earlier, an important function of the ego is to perceive and integrate internal and external stimuli. Thus, when the elder person experiences environmental stresses as excessive he may begin to exclude stimuli from awareness. That is, the elder person is likely to withdraw his attention from the various details of daily life which have no direct bearing on his personal situation. He becomes less concerned about acquiring new information regarding what is occurring in the world about him. He becomes more introverted and more concerned with his inner emotional problems.

Depression may occur at any age. In fact, infants who are deprived of emotional caring develop a type of depression. If this deprivation persists over a long period of time, the depression will affect the development of the child, resulting in intellectual and emotional retardation. Various types and intensities of depression may occur in childhood, adolescence, young, and middle adulthood. During the elder years of life the frequency and depth of depressed episodes tend to increase. The development of this pattern may vary from individual to individual and is usually related to one or more of the following factors:

1. The death of love objects such as spouse and friends.

2. Feelings of neglect and rejection. The elder person who has repressed childhood or adolescent hostile feelings towards his own parents may at this time experience himself in the role of the younger generation, as a child. The result is to direct inwardly the earlier repressed hostility towards himself, the parent. This turning inward of the revitalized hostile feelings results in depression.

3. The loss of self-esteem resulting from the elder person's growing inability to maintain a posture of worthiness, to gratify sexual drives, or to defend himself against threats to his security. This limitation may be caused by a decreased efficiency of the body function, loss of an adequate social role, financial insecurity, or a combination of these.

4. Self-blame and condemnation for "being a failure" by not achieving all the aspirations of earlier years or goals ascribed by society.

The frequency of somatic symptoms, that is, bodily dysfunctions, is relatively high. Many of these complaints and subsequent visits to physicians are based upon natural weakening or deterioration of bodily organs. However, a relatively large number of elder persons tend to find that somatic symptoms are a means of establishing or continuing interpersonal relationships which would otherwise be denied to them. Reacting to society's general attitude that they are "old and antiquated," they are unable to experience the realistic worth of the wisdom gained through many years of varied experiences. They conform to the dependent, ineffectual role fostered upon them by society rather than pursue a desired independent role at the anticipated expense of being totally rejected. Physical ailments thus become an effective topic of communication. When asked, "How are you?" the elder person responds by describing physical symptoms, allowing the younger person to do his good deed by sympathizing with the "deteriorating old man." Visits to the physician offer to some elder persons the only opportunity to experience overt signs that someone is taking an interest in them.

Psychotherapy for the elder person as a specialty has developed relatively recently. There is a continuing shortage of professionals working in this area. Most practitioners working with this age group tend to limit their efforts to crisis intervention. This is understandable in light of the usual psychotherapist who prefers to concentrate his efforts with age groups offering the greatest potential for growth and development, such as the child, adolescent, and the younger adult. Many practitioners' attitudes have been biased by their experiences which have been limited to severe problems of aging persons. This bias has been reinforced by the unfounded negative cultural attitudes towards the elder person. These attitudes tend to overlook the potentiality for growth and development existing in the older adult as well as the possible sharing of the acquired wisdom of this age group. Regrettably some psychotherapists tend to encourage the elder person to adopt the cultural role of being "shelved" and provide guidance in accepting and adjusting to the experienced frustrations. This approach merely reinforces the diminishing self-image of this age group.

Psychotherapy with the elder person may take place in one or a combination of several different settings. These include individual psychotherapy, a mixed group which includes young adults, a group limited to a minimum age of sixty, family sessions which include adult, children, and combined group psychotherapy consisting of both group and individual sessions with the same therapist. As in all therapeutic endeavors the selection of the treatment modality is dependent upon the specific needs of the individual. Selection of the therapist for the elder person, however, might be limited to one who has training and experience with this age group. Perhaps even more important, the selected therapist should envision the advanced years of life as a continuum in the developmental process and recognize that the elder person has potential to enjoy giving, receiving, and sharing experiences with others.

Varying degrees of success have been attained in all the above settings of psychotherapy. Jack Krasner has noted, however, that continued experience has demonstrated that the psychotherapeutic choice for these patients is combined individual and group psychotherapy with the initial group constellation often restricted in respect to age. The question may be asked, "What are the advantages of combined individual and group psychotherapy over a single type or form of psychotherapy?" In actual practice the two different therapeutic settings may be used in a complementary fashion, or either modality may be used as an adjunct to the other. The degree to which any particular therapist will emphasize a certain approach in combined therapy is usually determined by his individual orientation, personal and professional circumstances, motivation, and his belief as to what form of combined therapy will best fit the needs of the patient. When utilizing the individual session to further adaptation within the group, he is primarily concerned with working through resistances which prevent spontaneous interaction and verbalization in the group sessions.

The group setting is ideal for the development of transference and multiple transference relationships. These in turn enhance the modification or reprogramming of emotional reactions, and an understanding and integration of feelings and attitudes as they relate to situations and significant others. These processes lead to more effective and adaptive methods of coping with personal and interpersonal conflicts.

When the individual sessions are the primary setting for the psychotherapeutic process the interactions among the group members are utilized primarily for the exposure of conflicts and maladaptive emotional and behavioral reactions. These may then be worked through in the individual sessions. When the two modalities are used as complementary sessions for the psycho-therapeutic process, the dyadic relationship offers the patient an opportunity to develop the necessary transference relationships and work through personal needs requiring a one-to-one relation-ship. The group provides the opportunity to develop multiple transference relationships. It is also helpful in working through interpersonal and intrapsychic conflicts facilitated by or requiring the presence of a familylike constellation.

The utilization of two different settings in combined psychotherapy provides additional opportunity and allows flexibil-ity for patients to adopt different roles necessary for working through their conflicts. Also, the rich active fantasy life is more readily revealed in individual sessions by some, while others experience the group session as a more amenable setting for exposing their "secret life." For example, a man in his middle sixties expressed little affect in the group sessions and constantly defended himself with a deprecatory attitude towards the female patients. In the individual sessions his behavior and manner were those of a shy little boy. When alone with the therapist the patient openly expressed his feelings of inadequacy and described fan-tasies and fears of being a female. Acceptance on the part of the therapist enabled the patient to explore his fantasies and fears in the individual sessions resulting in more trust and openness in the group setting. Multiple transference reactions became more meaningful. They revealed that his behavior in the group had been an attempt to conceal the expectation that his needs would not be taken seriously in the family, or group. Once able to express himself more freely, he recognized and worked through feelings of rejection related to envy of his sister, whom he had experienced as the preferred one in his family.

A woman, Mrs. G., assumed the role of "the nice little old lady" during the group session. She exuded an air of saccharine sweetness and was helpful to all of the other group members. During the individual sessions, however, she expressed sexually aggressive fantasies which had been projected onto the therapist. During one individual session, she revealed her fear of these sessions as "the opening of old wounds." The central theme of the session became her fear of abandonment. When she was a small child her family experienced severe economic poverty and the family sent her to an orphanage. In the group sessions she denied having feelings of bitterness towards her parents and frequently described her stay at the orphanage as the happiest period of her life. Her revelations during this particular individual session focused the source of some of her intense anxiety.

MRS. G. *(to the therapist):* You know me . . . since April (six months). Is it better to be in group or individual therapy?

THERAPIST: Apparently you have given the therapy a great deal of thought.

MRS. G.: I think analysis is too deep for me. *(silence)* . . . I have regressed since June . . . I feel depressed . . . I sleep badly . . . My childhood . . . was very painful . . . It's dormant . . . to bring it back . . . would bring back pain and misery. Of course . . . my daughter *(patient referred to recurring problems in her present life with her daughter. She then recalled having a severe depression the previous summer before entering treatment. Her associations to dreams following group sessions revealed the underlying cause of the depression as being the rage she experienced at figures upon whom she is dependent, primarily husband and therapist. She then continued):* Thursday night a terrible dream . . . I screamed . . . It would never happen . . . never come to the surface. I'm like in a daze. I dreamed I was riding in a train . . . I met with an accident. A doctor standing over me . . . I didn't like him . . . the way he handled me. Even now as I tell it I feel so irritated . . . He (doctor) was leaning over me trying to help me . . . I suppose. His behavior was very repulsive to me. The dream seemed to last a lifetime. I screamed. I was stretched out, maybe sick. The doctor was all dressed in black. *(Mrs. G. then associated thoughts and feelings related to the dream).* I thought of telling you (therapist) the real story . . . what happened . . . how you can still love a mother who makes you prisoner. The same night I thought of telling you the story . . . then I had that dream.

Mrs. G. thus initially stated her fears of reexperiencing the past and her wish to avoid the painful memories. The dream portrayed that the expressed attitude of dependency on the therapist during the group sessions was a defense against hostile, aggressive reactions to her experienced treatment in the group.

The remainder of the dream also revealed that she must "tell a story" to conceal her true feelings towards the mother who sent her to an orphanage when she was a child. The dream also revealed underlying sexual desires with resultant feelings of repulsion. Following the exploration of the dream during the individual session, Mrs. G. was able to react more spontaneously in the group. She began to examine her ambivalent feelings towards her mother and her aggressive sexual feelings towards the therapist. As the psychotherapy continued combined individual and group sessions offered Mrs. G. complementary settings in which to work through the early trauma which had resulted in the intense fear of abandonment and rejection which she had continued to experience in the seventh decade of her life.

The interaction among members within a psychotherapeutic group setting elicits and more readily exhibits the various forms of the characteristic defenses which have become life patterns with each individual. Relating dreams and associations in the group reveals and aids in the understanding of intrapsychic drive and conflicts. Analysis of the interactions among the patients and their respective reactions to the therapist in the individual and group settings exposes and clarifies the behavior patterns that have been developed as attempts to cope with personal and interpersonal conflicts. Continued focusing by the therapist and analysis through discussion by the group members help individuals become aware of which efforts have been an ineffectual repetitive means of coping with anticipated and experienced anxiety. The mutual use of each other in the group to identify, to project, to increase, and to exemplify the experienced positions in the original family constellations without being rejected provides a setting for the continued development of ego strength, emotional growth, and psychosexual maturity. The continued development of ego strength increases each person's ability to relinquish ineffective defense mechanisms. The elder person is then better able to understand his problems and to develop behavioral patterns which are consonant with reality. As a psychotherapeutic process progresses, the individual may develop an acceptable as well as an appropriate self-image, and a growing sense of autonomy within a mutually interdependent relationship with others. Once this has occurred, the elder person may be placed in a group with younger people. This may offer an opportunity to work through conflicts which have been a barrier to enjoying appropriate adult-child-parent interpersonal relationships.

The psychotherapeutic effects on the elder person from the exclusive use of individual sessions, as well as psychotherapeutic groups initially with young adults have been successful. There are, however, hazards in these procedures which necessitate extreme sensitivity and skill on the part of the therapist. The one-to-one relationship in individual sessions tends to foster the development of an inverse transference reaction. With rare exceptions the patient experiences the therapist as a "child" from whom he is now forced to seek aid and comfort. This feeling of dependency on the child tends to reinforce the existing feelings of inadequacy, generating intense feelings of hostile aggression or intense guilt resulting in withdrawal, isolation, and depression. Therefore, this experienced *parent-patient* relationship to the *child-therapist* must be worked through if any therapeutic benefits are to be achieved. In many group settings with the young adult, the elder patient is often easily induced to assume a parental role. When this occurs the patient's efforts are directed primarily towards proving himself as a "good parent." The development of other transferential relationships becomes thwarted when this parental role tends to become fixed. Also, in his attempts to ward off hostile attacks from the younger members, the elder person assumes a defensive role. This setting offers increased opportunity for the elder person to be confronted with persons whom he experiences as trying to destroy him, that is, deprive him of his rightful role in society. Critical responses may be experienced as rejection and often provoke retaliatory aggressive acts or withdrawal. These phenomena and the related intense negative effects usually are worked through more readily in combined therapy where the group constellation is limited to persons of sixty or over.

Excerpts from sessions of a psychotherapeutic group illustrate the intense anxiety-provoking effects of losing someone to depend on, the fear of anticipated death, and how these feelings are displaced from early familial figures onto others. A co-therapist joined a group that had been in existence for several years. This addition led to fantasies of abandonment and loss of the original therapist by the group members. For an extensive period of time the major topics of discussion during the sessions were death and separation. Intense feelings of dependency and rage were manifested by feelings of depression, loneliness, and for some patients, anxiety and panic reactions. During one session, the original therapist (parent surrogate) and two of the original patient members were absent. One of the charter members of the group had an intense reaction to the therapist's absence. Encouraged to share her feelings she described having a strange feeling about the group as well as the office setting. "It no longer seems friendly but cold and depressing." Elaborating, she said, "I feel alone with new people; my family is not here." A member who had recently joined the group expressed more positive feelings which resulted from the absence of the other members. She would now have more time with the therapist who was present. The first patient reacted by expressing her rage at the original therapist "for leaving me to N." She experienced Betty as her sister who was more comfortable with and preferred by the mother. The overwhelming anxiety she experienced resulted in a strong desire to take flight from the group in an attempt to save herself. Focusing on her reaction, the group was able to bring about some insight into her fear of anticipated death resulting from the loss of the absent therapist (mother) and the related rage provoked by fantasies of abandonment.

The development of increased ego strength enables the group participants to further explore the cause and need for perpetuating their basic dependency. Revelation of respective life histories and understanding of past conflict situations results in the patient's development of self-identity and in the growth of the self-image. This therapeutic process also tends to reinforce the continuing increase of ego strength. The patients exhibit changes in attitudes which decreased resistance to psychotherapeutic change. Previously repressed material begins to be expressed more readily through dreams and associations as well as in the interactions within the group setting. The members begin to express and accept their dependency needs and to seek effective means of coping with them. The concept of death and related fears and conflicts are more openly expressed and members are able to deal with these on a more realistic level than in the past.

One group session was started by Evelyn B., who gave an

account of fainting at the office and her fear that she was about to die. The other group members reacted to this open expression of the fear of death by denial. Their attitudes became philosophical. The therapist focused on this situation by relating Mrs. B.'s fear of death to Selma L.'s reaction to the absent members during the previous session. Mrs. L. responded "it was intolerable . . . I couldn't stand it . . . I felt trapped." She then openly expressed anger at the previously absent members and spoke of the intense feeling of resentment experienced by the "family" abandoning her. As she spoke Mrs. L. continued to express feelings of helplessness towards the fantasized departure of the original therapist (mother), saying that she had neither choice nor control regarding his leaving the group.

As Mrs. L.'s feelings of anger and helplessness were brought to conscious awareness and verbalized, the other group members began to express their own great depth of feeling related to their experience of the death of parents and loved ones. The separation anxiety provoked by the absence of the original therapist, and the presence of the co-therapist (foster parent) in conjunction with an unacceptable death wish towards the original therapist, were uncovered as underlying thoughts and feelings of which the group members were unaware. The overt attitude of unconcern and accompanying denial of death resulted from the need to deny such unpleasant ideas and feelings. Exploration and analysis of this content revealed how intense feelings of anger and rage at parental figures were displaced onto others such as spouse and therapist. The need for a mothering life preserving figure and the anticipated annihilation resulting from separation were being provoked by the fantasized loss of the original therapist. These experiences had been relived within the projected familial setting of the psychotherapeutic group.

During personal discussions regarding this age group, Viktor Frankl also emphasized the importance of the elder person experiencing meaning to his life. He described the various possible accomplishments which the person might achieve during the many years of living. Having reached this period of life the elder person was entitled to and should enjoy what society and nature has to offer, for example, the pleasures of the theater, art, music, and a beautiful sunset. This concept has merit but tends to fall short of both the needs and usefulness of the elder person. A self-image based solely upon the glories of past deeds or exclusive feelings of nostalgia are inadequate substitutes for feelings of vitality and a self-image of worth. A healthy emotional state at any age is the individual's ability to utilize himself as well as others in ways which are mutually beneficial and provide continued development. Although the aging process during the advanced years of life brings limitations, the potential for continued development exists. For the elder person who is unable to continue the emotional development process, psychotherapy may provide an opportunity to recognize and eliminate the barriers created by cultural attitudes. It can help to achieve a reevaluation of unresolved conflicts which were repressed during earlier years. The ultimate goal of psychotherapy with the elder as well as with younger people is the development of the individual's optimal potential to enjoy the use of one's self and others.

16

Psychotherapy with the Dying Person

Psychotherapy with the dying person and the others who are involved with him is an effort to aid in the acceptance of death as a natural process, regardless of its causality. Acceptance is different from resignation. Henry David Thoreau poignantly spoke of resignation as a "quiet state of desperation." An effective psychotherapeutic endeavor requires both knowledge and understanding of the possible meaningfulness of death. The concept of death has qualitatively different meanings depending on various philosophies, religions, ethnic and cultural backgrounds.

There is a facetious yet negative idea that life may be characterized as a terminal illness precipitated by birth whose major symptom is reflected by aging. In a more sublime description the noted philosopher Martin Heidegger portrays death as a fundamental modality of living, that is, the aspect of concrete existence. He believes that every action, impulse, or storing of life may be viewed appropriately only in the light of a constituted ordering towards death. This may be compared to the predetermined developmental process of the plant from an unblossomed bud to the ripe fruit at its completion. The personalized meaning of death that has been exemplified in religious training may also be an important influence in determining how an individual conducts himself in life. For example, Hindus are taught that karma, their position in the next life, is dependent upon their deeds in the present life. Thus life is viewed by the Hindu as completion, ripeness, and fulfillment. During the interim period called life, the individual may mature in his sense of being an independent, responsible person with his own meaning until he is capable of making a final complete statement of himself as a person. Psychic environment widens until the individual is ready to ascend into the transcendent mystery of a superpersonal being. The freedom within continues to develop until he is ready to let go of the enfeebled outer shell. At this stage of development the individual has achieved sainthood in the Hindu sense and is prepared for nirvana. Those who do not achieve this stage must return in reincarnated form in order to pursue the ultimate. Medieval Christian theology posited the existence of purgatory where the continued "sins" of the individual are ameliorated. In the Jewish faith, the apocryphal second book of Maccabees says that it would be a "whole and wholesome" thought to pray for the dead so that they may be "loosed" from their sins. On the other hand, there are some people who believe that death is a finality with no existence afterward.

In the youth-oriented Western culture death is viewed as the ultimate obscenity. Death is the absurdity which contradicts one's whole attitude towards life. For some people death is taken as the ultimate proof of the nonexistence of an intelligent creator of the universe. Others such as Whitehead, however, have declared that death is essential to the normal ebb and flow of reality. The stubborn resistance to the cessation of consciousness and the cry for personal immortality are believed to be the result of unrealistic human egocentrism. Elizabeth Kübler-Ross, a distinguished psychiatrist who has worked with dying people over a period of many years, has noted that "in terms of the unconscious, we cannot perceive of our own death. I can only conceive of it as a malignant intervention from the outside. . . . If I have to die, I can only conceive of it, in my unconscious, as being killed. I am not afraid of death per se, but rather the destructive catastrophic death that hits me from the outside when I am not prepared."

Thus the interpretation and meaningfulness of death varies and is eventually determined by the specific individual. The enigma regarding the definition or concept of death is aptly noted in P.W. Bridgeman's comment that death cannot be experienced, for if it were, the individual would not be dead.

Dr. Kübler-Ross has most lucidly described five stages in the struggle to accept death as experienced by most people who are incurably ill. These five stages have become somewhat standard for those who are involved in the professional exploration and treatment of the dying person. The struggle includes shock and denial, anger, bargaining (attempts at postponement), depression, and acceptance and decathexis (desensitization).

The realization of a limited future is anxiety-producing. The awareness that one cannot do all he planned or hoped for usually comes as a shock at any age. The shock may occur in childhood, adolescence, adulthood, menopause, at the prospect of retirement, or during the aging process when the person becomes aware that the decline in physical vitality is more rapid than his resources allow him to compensate for and adapt to. When the shock is sudden, intense anxiety about one's total existence often arises as a result of the experienced disappointment and frustration. This often causes a distortion of the individual's perception of his environment which leads to intolerance and, often, isolation. Shock is quickly followed by denial which is frequently a necessary defense to maintain some integrity of the ego. This is the "no, not me" stage. The duration and intensity of this stage (a few seconds to a few years) vary depending on the emotional stability of the individual. As he rebounds from this initial reaction he may be versatile in choosing different people from among his family members with whom he may discuss his illness and impending death. If he is in the hospital, the staff will likely become his family. The person may pretend to get well with those who cannot tolerate the thought of his dying.

Gradually, as the need for the denial diminishes, or the defense is found to be inadequate, anger and rage become manifest. This stage sometimes takes the form of extreme dissatisfaction and resentment. During this "why me?" stage the individual becomes hard to manage, critical, and most uncooperative. Regrettably for all, those around the dying person attempt to counteract the anger, making the patient feel even more isolated and rejected. This stage is also marked by irritability, narrowness of interest, overevaluation of the past, physical symptoms, and withdrawal. The individual may get "stuck" at this stage. The dying person may unconsciously attempt to retaliate for a cruel fate and in so doing drive everyone away from him. He is then isolated with no one with whom to express or share his anger. The third stage is primarily concerned with bargaining. It produces such statements as "Yes, me, but . . ." or "If you give me one more year, God, I promise . . . ," and so forth. One or many promises are made in exchange for some extension of life. The content of the promise usually proves totally irrelevant because the promise is used as an attempted lever and typically is not kept. This process, however, is most significant in the emotional progress as it is generally the first time that the individual acknowledges what is happening to him.

When the efforts at bargaining dissipate the individual enters the fourth stage. This is the phase of depression, that is, the turning of the anger back upon oneself with resultant feelings of guilt and self-deprecation. The person now perceives the approaching loss of all that he has known with an accompanying experiencing of extreme psychic pain. Suicide, arising out of both rage and depression, may be a real danger if maladjustment is severe. The suicidal attempt may be a "last ditch effort," a means of retaliation, self-punishment, a reaction to the feelings of powerlessness and wrath by taking over control of one's own life and death. Most often, however, the dying person possesses a strong superego or conscience which does not allow for such aggressiveness, even against himself. Studies have shown that the degree to which a dying person, especially the elder, has intimate emotional involvements and available affectionate relationships has an inverse effect on the length and intensity of the depression. Greater involvement will also decrease the degree of physical discomfort that the patient experiences. It is at this stage that the dying person often experiences the universal need to review his life. This review may either contribute to his moroseness or help him find identity and meaningfulness in his existence.

Eventually the dying person may enter the final stage, that of acceptance. This phase appears to be devoid of feelings but is not one of resignation. It may be considered one of victory. Through all of this the person tends to retain hope, a sense of the basic trustworthiness of life and being. This is often exhibited in a terminal patient's feelings that a last minute cure will be found to save him. This appears to be more than the postponement sought by the defense mechanism of denial. Eugene Minkowski describes this stage as that which "separates us from immediate contact with ambivalent feelings" and then allows the person to be free enough from anxiety to open his heart to the mystery of the "transcendence of life." The dying person is then able to develop a sense of dignity while gradually allowing the process of disengagement and decathexis to take place without severe pain. W. Bromley also notes that when the dying person learns the art and meaning of "lived synchronism," that is, the ability to flow with time and life, he then experiences an identity and being which transcends it and remains continuous. With elder persons, the individual may rise above his physical life. He may live many years quietly and gracefully while he disengages from previous responsibilities in proportion to his strength, health, and interest.

Psychotherapy associated with a terminal illness has characteristically focused on the dying person. Other significant persons such as family members and close friends are often neglected to the detriment of both the dying person and those who survive. Some dying persons who might otherwise be relatively anxiety-free may inadvertently be provoked by the anguish experienced by the prospective survivors. Family members, close friends, and professionals tending to the care of the dying person are all involved in the death process. How a person faces death most often depends primarily on the reactions towards death which are conveyed by the observers and survivors. The possible negative attitudes which have detrimental effects on the dying person are not restricted to those expressed by members of the family and friends. There are some studies which reveal that physicians rank highest among professionals in their reluctance to discuss the subject of death with their patients. In fact, Kübler-Ross notes that the more training a physician has the less readily is he able to become involved in a discussion of death with his patient. An article "Explorations in Death Education" by Robert Meale suggests a lack of humaneness in the training of the physician. He emphasizes that physicians are like most other human beings who tend to face death with an attempt at denial. They carry an additional burden, however, in that they look upon death as a personal enemy who snatches away the victory of their cure.

The reluctance of the physician to admit "failure" often leads to conflict when the time comes to inform the patient that he is dying. The irony is that most dying people have some awareness of their impending death whether or not they have been informed. The "failure" actually is in the avoidance of sharing and discussing impending death with the dying person. This avoidance tends to reinforce the defense mechanism of denial which most people tend to use when they encounter the unpleasant.

A major effort in psychotherapy with the dying person is to help the individual recognize and admit this developmental stage, whether it is brought about by aging, internal disease, or externally caused injury. The psychotherapist may then provide the dying person with an opportunity to vent his anger and rage. Inability to express the rage and anger outwardly may result in more intense feelings of rejection and isolation. During this phase the dying patient is often extremely provocative in his condemnation of society, significant people in his life, and even God. The importance of being accepted and acceptable to someone during this period of time cannot be overemphasized. Reports from the Nazi concentration camps and from American prisoners of war in Japanese hands during World War II have indicated that when a prisoner experienced a feeling of alienation, that is, had no one to whom he felt personally significant, he became apathetic and quickly died. These reports further emphasize that a sharing relationship is more effective than a sense of personal adequacy in coping with anxiety. Thus the psychotherapist should maintain his own relationship with the patient. At the same time he should encourage effective relationships between the dying patient and other significant persons in his life. Sharing feelings and guiding the dying patient is often extremely provocative in his condemna-his fears and encourage the development of his ability to anticipate death with dignity. Sharing and relating are involvement in living. And living is the best preparation for dying.

Another important element to be considered in these psychotherapeutic endeavors is to provide what most people might need—permission to die. Dr. Eric J. Cassell, clinical professor of Public Health at Cornell University Medical School, encapsulated the plight of health professionals when he described them as spending their lives "fighting sickness, regression, disability, and death." The controversy as to whether to maintain life at any

cost or to allow the dying to die continues to polarize the professional and nonprofessional population. Cassell emphasizes that a
time arrives when efforts to maintain life must cease. Accordingly,
severely ill and aged patients need to be helped to develop the will
to die by suggesting to them that the time for dying has arrived.
He states that "It is necessary to reassure the patient that it is all
right to leave and that it is not going to hurt." The individual is
reassured regarding the unknown and is encouraged with the
knowledge that things rarely hurt as much as anticipated. When
this is explained to a patient, one is amazed to discover that he
becomes more peaceful. If pain is present it becomes less severe
and more bearable and within a relatively short time the patient
dies. Cassell emphasizes, "Sometimes teaching the aged how to die
turns into teaching the dying how to live." Rather than exhorting,
cajoling, or even suggesting the idea of getting better, the individual is given permission as well as encouraged to accept his dying.
Thus the individual is able to allow himself to die with a sense of
integrity rather than failure. What is most important is that he is
able to live until he dies.

Death may occur from one or more of many forces besides
automobile accidents and suicide. The most common and popularly
considered causes of death are aging, heart disease, and cancer.
There are over 600,000 deaths each year from heart disease. The
general estimate is that forty percent of all people who suffer a
heart attack will be dead within five years. The causes of heart
failure are varied. Research studies have continued to produce
conflicting evidence as to the possible causalities. The Inter-
Society Commission for Heart Disease Resources publication
"Cardiovascular Diseases—Guidelines for Prevention and Care"
lists and discusses a variety of danger signs indicating the high
probability of a heart attack. The major risk factors emphasized
include high blood levels of cholesterol and/or triglycerides, and
hypertension as manifested in high blood pressure, diabetes,
cigarette smoking, and hereditary factors such as having parents
with heart trouble. Persons with multiple danger signs have a
greater risk of developing heart disease than those with one or no
signs. These danger areas create psychological difficulties for the
patient with a bad heart. A 1969 comparison study of myocardial
infarction cases with cancer patients reveals some interesting

differences. The heart attack patient had greater hopes for recovery and was better informed of his condition. He was more concerned about what was going on in the outside world and in getting back to work. On the other hand, the cancer patient associated his illness with imminent death and more often was not told of his condition. The cancer patient tended to be more worried about survival and separation from the family. Later studies, however, reveal that most people find it easier to talk with cancer patients than with the cardiac patient. This appeared to be related to the fear of inducing a coronary attack and possible death. The same anxiety has been revealed by families of heart attack patients as compared to families of cancer patients. The heart attack victim is often more susceptible to intense anxiety than someone suffering from external symptoms of a disease. Uncertainty of deterioration of unseen inner organs may be quite terrifying. Also the individual who feels quite well may experience embarrassment in having to be immobilized. Anxiety, denial, and depression appear to be the most frequent reactions to heart disease. In a clinical study the occurrence of overt depression was higher for patients in their middle fifties than for any other age group. White collar workers tend to worry more about their illness than do blue collar workers. Also the cardiac patient may experience the intensive care unit as a necessary horror chamber. With lights blinking and dots blipping the individual may experience a loss of his state of effective being, as he finds himself hooked up to a machine with all of his functions, from breathing to feeding, taken away from him. He tends to feel alone, anxious, and likely depressed. He may be seized with guilt and anger as he fears that he may have unwisely postponed treatment. If surgery is recommended and the patient does decide to undergo the operation, the doubts persist as to whether he made the right decision. This example illustrates the existence of anxiety and other emotional factors resulting from the idea and the process of dying. Psychotherapeutic efforts have achieved and will continue to achieve beneficial effects in such situations.

The essence of psychotherapy with the dying is the relationship between patient and the therapist and those fostered between the patient and significant others in his life. Marjorie Lowenthal and Clayton Haren reported the findings from a study of 280 aged men and women which may be applied to all situations where death is imminent. They found that satisfaction or depression was directly related to whether or not the individual had a close confidant and was unrelated to the number of social roles or the level of social interaction. According to Lowenthal and Haren, "The maintenance of a stable intimate relationship is more closely associated with good mental health and high morale than is high social interaction or role status, or stability in interaction and role," to the degree that those persons so blessed could suffer disengagement without loss of morale. The writers believe that this study confirmed the theory that "existence in the thought and affection of another is a real concrete level of existence." Maintenance of this is "the crux of our existence from the cradle to the grave." Lowenthal and Haren propose that this need may be a "more basic instinctual force than all or even nursing needs." The greater sensitivity of women to close relationships and their greater versatility in object choice could be a contributing factor to their adaptability for survival.

While the focus of attention here has been on the dying person, other members of the family should not be forgotten. There have been studies which have revealed the existence of what is called the "broken heart syndrome." People in a state of intense grief have a much higher death rate than others. For example, among widows and widowers, twelve percent of the surviving spouses die within a year of their respective partners. In the control group, the group without grief, the death rate was one percent! Edoardo Weiss suggests that "We cannot possibly understand a dead person empathically. The realization that a living person can be transformed into a lifeless body is traumatic for everybody. Such a realization is often repressed or ignored or dealt with in various defensive ways." Conflicts which are related to dying usually begin at the onset of a serious illness. These conflicts tend to produce a lack of communication between family and patient. There is a tendency for everyone to repudiate everyone else. Family members, although remaining physically present, tend to draw away emotionally from the dying person. Many dying patients have complained that family members have withdrawn emotionally, thereby leaving them in a state of alienation. Family members and friends usually are afraid to talk to the dying person for fear of provoking anxiety. This fear tends to have a contagious effect often resulting in the dying person's fear of provoking anxiety in family members and friends. Kübler-Ross emphasizes the importance of such communication between husband and wife. She indicates that difficulty in communication is generally limited to the first occasion: "Instead of increasing alienation and isolation, the couple finds themselves communicating in more meaningful and deeper senses and may find a closeness and understanding that only suffering can bring." Feelings of intense anxiety related to unresolved guilt are frequently experienced by the surviving spouse. The wife, and sometimes the husband, assumes the blame for not taking steps which might have saved the spouse's life. The surviving spouse may on occasion even experience intense anger resulting from feelings of being deserted by the dying person. One of the major difficulties may arise after the individual has accepted his impending death. His spouse and other family members may need psychological assistance in order to learn how to let go of the dying person.

Death in contemporary times may pose a special problem for children. The avoidance of the child's exposure to death may have adverse rather than protective effects. Children who have been shielded from parents or other significant family members with terminal illness may experience anxiety-provoking guilt fantasies. Many adults who were "protected" from participating in the death process of a parent during childhood have developed fantasies of being directly or indirectly responsible for the death of the parent. A child should be informed of the facts related to the death of a significant person at the time of occurrence. It is also important that physical causes of death be explained. Otherwise the child may experience fear and develop guilt over the loss. The child might best be allowed and at times even encouraged to express his feelings towards the dying person. This process is especially important if the child has ambivalent feelings. Such ventilation increases the possibility of clarity and resolution of conflicting feelings while decreasing the opportunity for the development of guilt-laden fantasies. The idealization of or placing the dying or deceased person on a pedestal may result in the child's need to repress any negative and thus unacceptable feelings. If the child is capable of understanding the significance of the occasion, he might be provided with the option of participating in the funeral procession. This procedure tends to allow him a choice which may eliminate the feelings of coercion or guilt.

Death is as much a part of life as is living. The earlier one learns of death, its possible meanings, causes, and effects, the more readily the person will be able to develop the "will to die" when the time arrives. Thus the child may gradually be made aware of the consequences of terminal illnesses and the aging process. The illness or death of a family pet may be used to help the child understand the process of dying. Whenever possible it is better that the child be exposed to this process as a general concept before meeting death as an emotionally charged personal loss. The parents on their own or with professional help may thus help the child to become familiar with and be better able to accept rather than deny the one inevitability in the life process—death. The purpose of such acceptance is to help the person develop his ability to enjoy, that is to achieve satisfaction and fulfillment during life. A thought worthy of repetition is that to enjoy is to live. Learning to live, in turn, becomes the best preparation for the acceptance of death.

17

Research and
Future Development

Let us look at how the process and results of psychotherapy are evaluated and where psychotherapy appears to be going.

Research is basic to any understanding of psychotherapy. Therapists must know the effect of procedures and techniques on patients and whether these techniques are teachable and will have similar effects if used by other therapists. The area of research may be approached from a number of viewpoints. The first is to be concerned with what has already been done. A second is to evaluate what is being done currently. The third would refer to the directions for the foreseeable future. The obtained results are important as they provide help in understanding the various aspects of what is happening in the field of psychotherapy.

Over the years, there has been a sequence of research orientations which have begun with the focus on the patient as the major factor in psychotherapy. Whatever took place in the psychotherapeutic process was seen to be the responsibility of the patient. If a patient cooperated the psychotherapy went well. If psychotherapy was not successful this was because the patient was either resistant or not a suitable candidate for that particular mode of psychotherapy. There was a thorough examination of types of patients, of the various characteristics of the patients, and of the many aspects of the patients' behavior in psychotherapy. This approach is a thing of the past and now there is less focus on the patient as the only primary agent in the psychotherapeutic process.

Research into the outcome of the psychotherapeutic process was a second approach. The result, as measured by success or failure, of the therapeutic procedure was the focus. The criteria included the level or degree of cure and the degree of response to the psychotherapeutic procedures. The procedures were collected and certain techniques of therapy were considered more successful than others because they were reputed to have a higher percentage of "positive" outcomes.

A more recent approach has been on the process of psychotherapy. Research workers focused on what was specific to the techniques themselves and their effect on therapy. For example, group was contrasted with individual therapy, verbal compared to nonverbal techniques, analytic compared to behavioral.

A more current focus has been on the characteristics, personality, strengths, and weaknesses of the therapist which may affect the process, the patient, and the outcome of psychotherapy. The current emphasis is on the interactional process between the patient and the therapist. Behavioral approaches emphasize the techniques and the resultant behavior of the patient. In the dynamic approaches a patient in the literal sense is anyone seeking help. The view today is that there is an ongoing process between the provider of help and the seeker of help, that involves an interrelationship between the two. This relationship may include a group, a laboratory, and in fact any approach which involves a provider and a seeker. Even where there is an intervening aspect such as in token economy, the token, the investigator, and the results are all interwoven. In this approach the tokens are rewards given for certain desired behavior. The patient may accumulate the tokens and then trade them in for something of value to him. Any one aspect of the therapeutic experience cannot be separated from another in an adequate and comprehensive understanding of the total process. The problem of criteria and difficulties in developing adequate experimental models of psychotherapy are many and complex, such as whether the focus is on relief, or cure, or a change in lifestyle. There are therapists who feel that a relief of symptoms *is* the cure. There are others who feel that the relief of symptoms is but one aspect and that what is considered a change involves more. There are psychotherapists who have not discussed the idea of "a cure." They discuss remission, a restructuring of one's life, or the exploration of growth and the individual ability to self-actualize. In this latter the goal is to enable the individual to fulfill his potential to the best of his ability. Because of the complicated and variable nature of the human being and the inevitable multiplicity of theories, experimental research is a highly problematic matter. As a result, empirical research which is based on experimental data, often provides us with much of our information.

There are also questions of new learning and a pattern of newly learned behavior. These may be compared to those therapies which are directed towards changes in the style of living, not in the modification of symptoms. In counterdistinction to learning results, the humanistic psychotherapists insist on changes in a style of living and on an increased level of self-awareness and satisfaction with one's life.

If a person has adjusted to or is coping with unreasonable demands of living, is he to be considered as cured or is this a positive response to psychotherapy? There are those psychotherapists who focus on the growth of the self, and on the process of how one best realizes one's potential. The concern is not with whether a symptom is or is not present, but how a person lives his daily life. These psychotherapists may be concerned, for example, with how one thinks of death, and how one adjusts to the ultimate demand of death. The investigators in the learning and behavioral approaches are not concerned with this area, but are concerned with whether a person's phobia about death is alleviated, or socially unacceptable behavior such as aggression is modified.

A further area of dispute is the use of quantification—statistics—in evaluating the results of research in psychotherapy. The use of statistics is more a concern in American than in European schools. There are investigators who insist that all research must be quantifiable. That is, that everyone must be reduced to percentages, tests of significance, or probability levels. There are concerned psychotherapists who feel that the demand for quantification is not reasonable, as this approach is not applicable to the field of psychotherapeutic research. An attempt at combining the more regular statistical approach with clinical work has resulted in the emergence of the *experimental clinician* who is involved in the attempt of assessing the results, process, and other factors in psychotherapy from a more rigorous point of view.

There are those theorists and psychotherapists who feel that research interferes with ongoing psychotherapy. The attempt at evaluation and quantification during psychotherapy interferes with the natural flow of the process itself. The use of assessment methods, or attempts at evaluation, introduces factors which then alter the process and possible outcome of psychotherapy. Investigators have found it extremely difficult to assess the effects of these factors on the psychotherapeutic process. These investigators also contend that psychotherapy is an art, and while there are elements of science involved, much more depends on the art of the individual and on the individual's ability to relate to another human being. The emphasis is on the personality of the therapist and the interactional process. As soon as any attempt is made to assess this, these psychotherapists contend that the fabric of the relationship has been disturbed. However, psychotherapy must be both teachable and replicable. The research that satisfies the major groups in psychotherapy must be done so that the process can be taught and the results assessed.

There are several directions for research at the current time. John Wolpe and his behavior modification followers feel that therapy should have a goal of changing the individual's behavior in the direction of the accepted social norm. Here, the goal sought in psychotherapy influences both the selection of process and the techniques. Therefore, one of the choices includes consideration of man as machine, as contrasted to man as man. Many learning theorists consider man as a complex machine and contend that he may therefore be manipulated, modeled, or maneuvered in any direction decided upon by the modifier, who is the behavior therapist. Being human, the psychotherapist feels he is to help the other humans find their own way in life. Whether this direction conforms to requirements of society is secondary to the individual's realization of himself as a person and his ability to live life as he desires it. Until the question of the philosophy of psychotherapy is clarified in each experimental procedure, there will be confusing, contradictory, and complicating results.

Some of the more recent changes in technique include the use of video tape and the utilization of instant playback in the psychotherapeutic session. Usually the therapist and patient have had to rely on memory or on notes that have been taken on what occurred during the session itself. Now, through the use of the instant video playback, one can immediately respond to what took place, either verbally or behaviorally. Research can now be done with a body of information that is on a video tape. There is no need to rely on memory, notes, and other subjective methods. There is some question, of course, as to the impact of the camera on the therapeutic relationship. The more comfortable and accepting the therapist is of the equipment and the idea that everything is being recorded the less this affects the patient and the ongoing process. One of the possible outcomes of research utilizing this material is to attempt to unify the concepts of learning as used by the behavior modification adherents and that used by the therapists of the dynamic schools.

In the field of psychotherapy there also has been a strong movement away from the medical towards the psychological learning model. This movement holds that man is not victim to an illness or disease process but rather is involved in learning patterns of behavior in responding to the demands of daily living. In this point of view the individual is thought of as an active participant in a life process rather than a passive host of disease. The person is trapped by his own history but can determine his own destiny. The question of responsibility then has become part of the human behavior pattern. O. Hobart Mowrer and Karl Menninger have written recently on a concept of sin and guilt as concerns of the human condition. The field of dynamic psychology has shifted the emphasis from the exploration of unconscious processes for their own sake to the area known as ego psychology. The dynamic approaches are now concerned with some of the current social and personal conditions of life. The concerns are not with the patient's history but with how the individual is coping with the demands of his life.

The dynamic psychotherapist has emphasized learning as one of the important aspects of development and therapy. Within this framework there is a wide range of dynamic psychotherapists. There is a concomitant wide range of approaches under the overall term "behavior therapy." This group includes the radicals who reject the ideas of dynamic therapy and who steadfastly cling to their original formulations in both theory and therapy, and the moderates who base their theory and methods on social learning, cognitive processes and experimentally verified behavioral principles. Many, but not all, of the important behavior theorists and therapists have broadened their approach to what one might consider "eclecticism" of techniques and understanding. They still reject the idea of an amalgam of dynamic and behavior therapy, but this may have to do more with the problems of language than of substance. Russian psychologists have been among the most emphatic in supporting the idea of working with overt behavior and using physiological explanations for their work. Recently, they have published a number of articles exploring the idea of an "unconscious" which they feel is necessary in order to explain and understand the totality of human development and behavior.

Approximately twenty years ago the field of psychotherapy was strongly affected by the introduction of chemical agents. These included tranquilizers, energizers, antidepressants, and other chemicals. Initially these were thought of as curatives and the answer to emotional disturbance. Nathan Kline at Rockland State Hospital in New York considered the tranquilizers the answer that would empty the hospitals. This has not been the result. The chemotherapeutic agents are sometimes effective adjuncts to the psychotherapy process and they offer aid in the procedure itself. They have not, and are no longer expected to, replace psychotherapy as a sole agent for change.

Recently there has been more research into the neurological and neurophysiological aspects of human behavior. Steven Rose, in his book on the conscious brain, has elaborated most of this research. José Delgado, a neurophysiologist, has indicated that certain kinds of behavior can be controlled by implanting electrodes in various parts of the brain and introducing a mild electric current to these areas. He has been able to affect certain types of aggressive behavior in this way. This approach is in the early stage of development and may provide fruitful information to help the clinician understand more of human behavior. Exploration in these areas involves ethical and moral issues with which researchers have not been concerned until recently. Sleep therapy is being explored in Russia and other countries in Europe as a method of treatment for specific emotional states. Recently work was begun at Stanford University into computer programmed psychotherapy processes. The computer is programmed with all the information available about a given individual, as well as many of the more typical psychotherapeutic responses. This approach is also in the early stages of development and, as yet, has not been particularly effective.

With the ever increasing number of people who find that they are in need of help for emotional problems there has been a demand for more effective use of limited psychotherapeutic personnel and time. This has resulted in an increasing focus on community psychotherapy. There has also been the development of psychotherapeutic "paraprofessionals" who function under the supervision of the more experienced, trained therapist. The one-to-one relationship in the office has come to be time-consuming, expensive, and limited. There are many people in need of help who do not receive it. There is also the expansion in emergency and crisis-oriented psychotherapy approaches. In these, the therapist is available on an emergency basis at the moment of crisis, for example, an attempt at suicide, a threatened breakup of a family unit or marriage, an adolescent threatening to run away from home or doing something drastic to gain attention or relief. To wait for a scheduled appointment would be unrealistic and less effective than having the therapist available at the moment. In addition to the therapist being available, the individual involved must be willing to utilize his services. Through increased understanding and a more positive attitude on the part of the general public there is continuing expansion and utilization of these services.

The overall view, then, is that the direction of the future is towards greater utilization of both the traditional and the innovative approaches of psychotherapy. Expansion continues in many directions, with the focus on providing the most effective and efficient aid to the greatest number of individuals, families, and groups.

Reviewing a mass of studies and information often tends to confuse as much as enlighten the reader. There are a number of facts that the reader becomes aware of as he goes through the literature of research on psychotherapy. More and more, psychotherapy is being approached as a group of theories and methods, without the idea that one or the other is either the "right" or the "wrong" theory or method. There seems to be strong evidence that there is some type of psychotherapy for just about everyone with emotional problems. Although these approaches may not be as successful, or as brief and inexpensive as we might like, overall psychotherapy does work. The individual who is having trouble facing and coping with some of the problems of living does have someone to turn to who is able to offer help.

Enjoy!

Glossary

Aberration, mental. Pathological deviation from normal thinking. Mental aberration is not related to a person's intelligence.

Abnormal psychology. The study of deviant and maladaptive behavior.

Abreaction. A process by which repressed material, particularly a painful experience or a conflict, is brought back to consciousness. In the process of abreacting, the person not only recalls but relives the repressed material, which is accompanied by the appropriate affective response.

Acting out. An action rather than a verbal response to an unconscious instinctual drive or impulse that brings about temporary partial relief of inner tension. Relief is attained by reacting to a present situation as if it were the situation that originally gave rise to the drive or impulse.

Active therapist. Type of therapist who makes no effort to remain anonymous but is forceful and expresses his personality definitively in the therapy setting.

Activity group therapy. A type of group therapy developed and introduced by S. R. Slavson and designed for children and young adolescents, with emphasis on emotional and active interaction in a permissive, nonthreatening atmosphere. The therapist stresses reality-testing, ego-strengthening, and action interpretation.

Actualization. Process of mobilizing one's potentialities or making them concrete.

Adaptation. The dynamic process by which an individual responds to his environment and the changes that occur within it. The ability to modify one's behavior to meet changing environmental requirements. Adaptation to a given situation is influenced by one's personal characteristics and the type of situation.

Affect. Emotional feeling tone attached to an object, idea, or thought. The term includes inner feelings and their external manifestations.

Affective disorder. Disorder of mood or feeling with resulting thought and behavioral disturbances. Chief forms are manic-depressive psychosis and psychotic depressive reactions.

Affective interaction. Interpersonal experience and exchange that are emotionally charged.

Aggression. Forceful, goal-directed behavior that may be verbal or physical. It is the motor counterpart of the affects of rage, anger, and hostility.

Alienation. Condition characterized by lack of meaningful relationships to others. May result in depersonalization and estrangement from others.

Ambivalence. Presence of strong and often overwhelming simultaneous contrasting attitudes, ideas, feelings, and drives towards an object, person, or goal. The term was coined by Eugen Bleuler, who differentiated three types: affective, intellectual, and ambivalence of the will.

Analysand. A patient in psychoanalytic treatment.

Analysis. A common synonym for psychoanalysis.

Analytic psychodrama. Psychotherapy method in which a hypothesis is tested on a stage to verify its validity. The analyst sits in the audience and observes. Analysis of the material is made immediately after the scene is presented.

Analytic psychology. The system of psychodynamic psychology created by Carl Jung.

Antidepressant drugs. General term for a number of drugs used to relieve depression and to elevate mood.

Anxiety. Unpleasurable affect consisting of psychophysiological changes in response to an intrapsychic conflict. In contrast to fear, the danger of threat in anxiety is unreal. Physiological changes consist of increased heart rate, disturbed breathing, trembling, sweating, and vasomotor changes. Psychological changes consist of an uncomfortable feeling of impending danger.

Anxiety, free-floating. Anxiety that is not attached to specific ideas, situations, or activities of the individual. The outstanding symptom of anxiety neurosis.

Anxiety neurosis (anxiety reaction, anxiety hysteria). A neurotic disorder characterized by persistent and diffuse tension and apprehensiveness, which on occasion may reach the proportion of panic.

Apathy. Want of feeling or affect; lack of interest and emotional involvement in one's surroundings. It is observed in certain types of schizophrenia and depression.

Assessment. Information-gathering aimed at the description and prediction of behavior. Assessment specialists study the tools of assessment themselves, and such problems as the effectiveness of treatment programs.

Aversion therapies. A group of behavior therapies which attempt to condition avoidance responses in patients by pairing the behavior to be extinguished with punishing stimuli (electric shock, social criticism, drugs that cause vomiting).

Avoidance conditioning. Conditioning procedures in which an organism learns to respond so as to avoid an unpleasant stimulus.

Behavior therapy. Includes several techniques of behavior modification based on laboratory-derived principles of learning and conditioning. Behavior therapies focus on modifying overt behaviors with minimal reference to internal or covert events.

Behaviorism. A school of psychology whose adherents contend that the study of overt and observable behaviors is the only legitimate source of scientific data. Covert events, such as consciousness, are disregarded or considered to be only mediating processes between stimulus and response contingencies.

Biophysical viewpoint. The general position that maladaptive behavior and psychological disorder are caused by genetic, biological, and constitutional factors of the human organism.

Castration anxiety. Anxiety due to danger (fantasied) of the loss of the genitals or injuries to them.

Catharsis. A method used to obtain abreaction. Discharge of strong emotions intended to achieve abreaction. Psychodynamically oriented clinicians assume that by bringing emotionally laden fears and problems to consciousness, therapists can deal with them. A major tool of psychodynamic psychotherapy.

Cathexis. An affective or emotional charge attached to an object, idea, or action; one's investment in a type of object, idea, and action.

Character structure (personality structure). The arrangement, group, or pattern of individual traits, needs, and motives which form a relatively stable and enduring configuration.

Client-centered psychotherapy. A form of psychotherapy, formulated by Carl Rogers, in which the patient or client is believed to possess the ability to improve. The therapist merely helps him clarify his own thinking and feeling. The client-centered approach in both group and individual therapy is democratic, unlike the psychotherapist-centered treatment methods.

Client-centered therapy. Carl Rogers' therapeutic approach, which views the subject matter of psychotherapy as the client's world of immediate experience that should be approached from the client's own frame of reference. In the Rogerian system. the main task of the therapist is to create the opportunity for the individual to achieve a reorganization of his subjective world, and self-actualization.

Clinical psychologist. A psychologist, usually with a Ph.D., and with special training and skills in the assessment and treatment of maladaptive behavior.

Cognition. Thinking; the process of knowing, thinking, and reasoning.

Collaborative therapy. A type of marital therapy in which treatment is conducted by two therapists, each of whom sees one spouse. They may confer occasionally or at regular intervals. This form of treatment affords each analyst a double view of his patient—the way in which one patient reports to his analyst and the way in which the patient's mate sees the situation as reported to the analyst's colleague.

Community mental health center. A community-based facility or complex of facilities for the prevention and treatment of mental illness.

Community psychology. A branch of applied psychology concerned with man's behavior and position in a social system and how both the individual and the structure may be modified to produce optimal benefits for both. Community psychologists are often primarily interested in preventing maladaptive behavior.

Compensation. An ego-defense mechanism erected against feelings of inferiority and inadequacy. An attempt to substitute or compensate for a real or imagined defect by emphasizing a more positive trait, skill, or attribute.

Complex. Generally, any grouping of related elements in the psychic organization. Groups of emotionally charged attitudes, memories, and motives which have been at least partly repressed may give rise to deviant or maladaptive behavior.

Compulsion. Irresistible and repetitive act or behavior which the individual recognizes as irrational but which cannot be easily gotten rid of. Often viewed as a defense against obsessive thoughts.

Conduct disorder (disturbance). An adjustment reaction of childhood, manifested primarily as disturbances in social conduct or behavior. Behaviors classified as conduct disturbances include truancy, stealing, or destructiveness and are often explicable in terms of an unfavorable environment.

Conflict. A condition of opposition between responses, impulses, needs, or desires which are mutually exclusive.

Conjoint therapy. A type of marriage therapy in which a therapist sees the partners together in joint sessions. This situation is also called triadic or triangular, since two patients and one therapist work together.

Consciousness. The process or state of being aware of or comprehending what is happening around one. In psychoanalysis, events of mental life that are currently in awareness. These events are on a continuum ranging from conscious to preconscious to unconscious.

Conversion. An unconscious defense mechanism by which the anxiety that stems from an intrapsychic conflict is converted and expressed in a symbolic somatic symptom. Seen in a variety of mental disorders, it is particularly common in hysterical neurosis.

Corrective emotional experience. Re-exposure, under favorable circumstances, to an emotional situation that the patient could not handle in the past. As advocated by Franz Alexander, the therapist temporarily assumes a particular role to generate the experience and facilitate reality-testing.

Co-therapy. A form of psychotherapy in which more than one therapist treats the individual patient or the group. It is also known as combined therapy, cooperative therapy, dual leadership, multiple therapy, and three-cornered therapy.

Countertransference. Conscious or unconscious emotional response of the therapist to the patient. It is determined by the therapist's inner needs rather than by the patient's needs, and it may revive the patient's earlier traumatic history if not checked by the therapist.

Cyclothymic personality. A personality disorder characterized by mood swings alternating between euphoria and despondency. May be persistently euphoric, depressed, or cyclic.

Decompensation. Deterioration or disorganization of the personality in response to excessive stress.

Defense mechanism (ego defense). Psychoanalytic term for a number of psychic operations used by the ego to avoid awareness of unpleasant and anxiety-provoking stimuli. The ego selectively utilizes the various defense mechanisms to ward off anxiety which arises from the id, the superego, or dangers in external reality.

Déjà vu. The feeling that a new situation is familiar and has been experienced before.

Delusion. An incorrect belief that is maintained even though clear evidence exists to the contrary.

Depersonalization. Feelings of unreality, a loss of personal identity, often experienced as being someone else or as watching oneself as if in a movie.

Depressive neurosis (neurotic or reactive depression). Reaction characterized by apprehension, self-devaluation and feelings of guilt and worthlessness, dejection, and a rather pervasive pessimistic outlook. Does not involve drastic loss of the capacity to engage in reality-testing.

Determinism. The doctrine that everything is entirely determined by a sequence of causes.

Deviancy. Refers to behavior which differs from some norm or standard.

Diagnosis. A classification of behavior disorders in terms of relatively homogeneous groups based on similar behaviors or correlates. A shorthand description of the behavioral and personality correlates associated with a particular classification. In medicine, the act or process of deciding the nature of a diseased condition.

Disorientation. A loss of orientation; a condition of mental confusion with respect to time, place, and the identity of persons and objects.

Displacement. Defense mechanism in which the object of an emotional attitude is altered and the attitude is transferred to the substitute object.

Dissociative reaction. Any of several types of neurotic reactions in which alterations in states of consciousness are the primary defining feature. Includes amnesia, fugue states, somnambulism, and multiple personality. May include feelings of depersonalization and periods of stupor.

Double bind. A type of conflict created when a person is confronted with mutually contradictory messages and demands. Believed to be especially characteristic of communication in families of schizophrenics.

Dream work. The process by means of which the true meaning of a dream is distorted and concealed by the operation of defense mechanisms.

Drive. An energizing or motivating state which gives impetus to behavior.

Dynamic. Refers to the interplay of forces. Term applied to psychological theories which emphasize drives and motives, internal events, and/or cause-and-effect relationships.

Dysfunction. Refers to a disturbance or impairment in normal functioning.

Ego. In psychoanalytic theory, the part of the psyche which makes up the self or the "I." It is that part of the psyche that is conscious and most closely in touch with reality, functioning as the "executive officer" of the personality, to integrate the impulses and strivings of the id with the moral and inhibitory directives of the superego in conjunction with the demands of external reality.

Ego psychology. Refers to several dynamic psychologies derived from orthodox psychoanalysis. Ego psychologists place less emphasis on the importance of unconscious and instinctual mechanisms than did Freud and are more concerned with the adaptive and ego functions that are independent of drives and conflicts.

Ego structure. Refers to the various coping and defensive processes, attitudes, traits, etc., which make up the relatively stable components of the ego or self.

Emotion. A feeling state which is consciously perceived, such as anger, anxiety, etc.

Emotional support. Encouragement, hope, and inspiration given to one person by another. Members of a treatment group often empathize with a patient who needs such support in order to try a new mode of behavior or to face the truth.

Empathy. A projection of one's own personality into the personality of another in order to understand him better. Ability to put oneself in another person's place, get into his frame of reference, and understand his feelings and behavior objectively. It is one of the major qualities in a successful therapist, facilitator, or helpful group member.

Encounter group. A form of sensitivity training that emphasizes the experiencing of individual relationships within the group and minimizes intellectual and didactic input. It is a group that focuses on the present rather than the past or outside problems of its members. J. L. Moreno introduced and developed the idea of the encounter group in 1914.

Etiology. Assignment of a cause. Scientific study of causes and origins of maladaptive behavior.

Existential analysis. A psychotherapeutic method aimed at helping relieve the client's inhibitions in order to aid him in reacting spontaneously to his environment with a greater sense of personal freedom. Emphasizes the sense of self-direction and the need for a personal meaning for one's existence.

Existential psychology. The view that psychological activity should be limited to the observation and description of the existing contents of experience and that inner drives and conditioning procedures cannot explain the behavior of man. Man viewed not as a machine but as a responsive decision-maker.

Family therapy. A specialized type of group therapy in which the members of a given family constitute the group.

Fantasy. A mental image as in a daydream. Fantasies are forms of imaginative activity which resemble reveries. They are usually pleasant and represent a sort of wish-fulfillment. Escapist fantasy has been viewed as a defense mechanism which functions to permit a temporary escape from reality, providing need gratification through fantasied achievements.

Fixation. An inappropriately strong attachment for someone or something. Often refers to an abnormal attachment developed during infancy or childhood which persists into adult life as an inappropriate constellation of attitudes, habits, or interests.

Flight into health. A transference cure relinquishing a neurotic response, not because the psychodynamic problem has been solved, but rather as a defense against further probing by the therapist into painful unconscious material.

Free association. A basic technique of the psychoanalytic method by which a patient expresses his thoughts as freely and in as uninhibited a manner as possible. Free associations provide a natural flow of thought processes unencumbered by interruptions or explanations.

Freud, Sigmund. Austrian neurologist who founded psychoanalysis as a theory and method of treatment upon which modern psychiatry is largely based.

Frigidity. Sexual inability of the woman to achieve orgasm through intercourse.

Frustration. Blocking or thwarting of an ongoing, goal-directed sequence of behavior.

Fugue state. A flight from reality in which the individual may leave his present environment and life situation and establish a new life style in another geographical location. The person is usually totally amnesic concerning his past life, although other abilities remain unimpaired and he may appear essentially normal to others.

Functional disorder. Maladaptive behavior having no demonstrable organic basis and precipitated primarily by psychological and social factors.

Geriatrics. The study of the health problems of the aged.

Gerontology. The scientific study of knowledge embracing all aspects of the process of aging.

Gestalt psychotherapy. A form of therapy that stresses the here and now. The therapist's task is to restore the client's personality to an organized whole. Emphasis is placed on self-actualization and fostering creative solutions to actual problems of living.

Group therapy. Psychotherapy of several persons at the same time in small groups.

Hallucination. A sensory perception in the absence of an external stimulus. Hallucinations are usually visual ("seeing things") but may occur in other sensory modalities as well.

Hedonism. Excessive orientation towards personal pleasure and need gratification.

Heterogeneous. Composed of unrelated or unlike elements or parts; varied, miscellaneous.

Holistic. Viewing man as a unified, biological, psychological, and social organism whose total configuration must be studied.

Homeostasis. Maintenance of equilibrium and constancy among the bodily processes.

Homogeneous. Composed of similar or identical elements or parts; uniform.

Humanistic approach. Theories characterized by an emphasis on self-fulfillment and social systems in which everyone has equal opportunity to become fully human through realizing his individual potentials.

Hypertension. High blood pressure, usually considered a psychophysiologic disorder.

Hypnosis. An altered state of consciousness induced by suggestion. Ranges from mild hypersuggestibility to deep, trancelike states.

Hypochondriacal neurosis (hypochondriasis). A neurotic reaction in which the chief feature is an excessive concern and preoccupation with one's physical health.

Hypomania. A mild manic condition characterized by excitement, impatience, and euphoria, but which does not generally incapacitate the individual.

Hysterical neurosis (conversion reaction). Primarily involves organic symptoms in the absence of any observable organic disturbance. Some classifications include the dissociative neuroses in this category.

Hysterical personality. A constellation of generalized personality or character traits rather than a specific hysterical symptom, such as conversion reaction. The hysterical personality is a disordered personality characterized by personality traits of oversuggestibility, emotional lability, general immaturity, excitability, and often a propensity for self-dramatization.

Id. In psychoanalysis, that division of the psyche which is a repository of all instinctual impulses and repressed mental contents. Represents the true unconscious or the "deepest" part of the psyche.

Identification. An emotional tie unconsciously causing a person to think, feel, and act as he imagines the person with whom he has the tie does. Viewed as both a developmental process and as a defense mechanism.

Identity. Generally refers to that constellation of traits, values, and attitudes which form a person's relatively stable perception of "self." May be thought of as a product molded by the processes of identifying oneself with various others and integrated with other life experiences.

Identity crisis. Erikson's term for conflicts occurring primarily in adolescence during which the individual seeks to define himself and his place in the world.

Impotence. Inability of the man to achieve an erection and orgasm in the sexual act.

Impulse. An impelling or drive force. A tendency or readiness towards action.

Inadequate personality. Personality disorder characterized by inadaptability, poor judgment, poorly developed social skills, and general ineptness.

Inferiority complex. Adler's term, which refers to self-perceived deficits and weaknesses for which the individual attempts to compensate by various means.

Inhibition. Restraint or control exercised over an impulse, drive, or response tendency.

Insight. Self-knowledge. Understanding the significance and purpose of one's own motives or behavior, including the ability to recognize inappropriateness and irrationality.

Intellectualization. Defense mechanism related to isolation. The emotional bond or link between symbols and their emotional charges is broken by this process.

Introjection. The incorporation of the values, attitudes, or behaviors of another person (e.g., parent) or group into one's own ego structure. Absorbing of aspects of the external world into oneself. Generally synonymous with the term **identification** but often used in a more limited or specific sense. The process by which a child incorporates the moral and ethical values of the parents.

Isolation. Defense mechanism by which inconsistent or contradictory attitudes and feelings are walled off from each other in consciousness. Similar to repression but different because in isolation the impulse or wish is consciously recognized but is separated from present behavior (in repression neither the wish nor its relation to action is recognized). Intellectualization is a special form of isolation.

Jung, Carl. Early student of Freud who broke with the psychoanalytic movement and founded an approach called analytical psychology.

Labile. Easily changeable; unstable; rapidly shifting in emotions.

Latent dream content. The underlying symbolic significance of the manifest content, which reflects the "true" meaning of the dream. It is one of the purposes of the dream work to disguise this meaning.

Libido. A psychoanalytic term referring to the general instinctual drives of the id. A motivational force related to the concepts of psychic energy or drive. Libidinal energy or drive is composed of libidinal impulses, which Freud felt were genetically determined. In a narrow sense, libido has been equated by some writers with sexual drive, although it more appropriately refers to the organism's total quest for pleasure and gratification.

Life style. Adler's term for the individual's typical coping mechanisms and his active adjustment to his social environment.

Logotherapy. Psychotherapy based on a system of spiritual values and existential analysis.

Maladaptive behavior. Behavior that is deficient or excessive and hinders successful interacting with the environment and dealing with stress; responses that are inappropriate to environmental circumstances.

Manic-depressive disorder. Psychosis characterized by marked emotional lability. Three types have been distinguished. The manic type is characterized by excessive elation, excitement, and overactivity. The depressed type is accompanied by motor and mental retardation, extreme sadness, and frequent suicidal tendencies. The circular type is characterized by periodic alternations between manic and depressed episodes.

Manifest dream content. The ideas and images of a dream as recalled and reported by the patient.

Marathon therapy. A type of group sensitivity training in which participants meet with therapists for continuous periods of one to five days. The group usually remains together at all times, and decisions regarding eating, sleeping, and other activities are jointly determined. The emphasis is on total involvement of all members, and the group interactions focus on the here-and-now, the present lives of the participants.

Marital counseling. Process whereby a trained counselor helps married couples resolve problems that arise and trouble them in their relationship. The theory and techniques of this approach were first developed in social agencies as part of family casework. Husband and wife are seen by the same worker in separate and joint counseling sessions, which focus on immediate family problems.

Marriage therapy. A type of family therapy that involves the husband and wife and focuses on the marital relationship, which affects the individual psychopathology of the partners. The rationale for this method is the assumption that psychopathological processes within the family structure and in the social matrix of the marriage perpetuate individual pathological personality structures, which find expression in the disturbed marriage and are aggravated by the feedback between the partners.

Mood swings. The oscillations between periods of feelings of well-being and those of depression or "feeling blue."

Moral treatment. A technique of treatment of mental hospital patients which prevailed in the 19th century. It emphasized removal of restraints, along with religious conviction and humanitarian treatment.

Motivation. Inner determinants of the strength and direction of animal or human activities. Often referred to as need states, goals, or aspirations. Term is often used synonymously with drive or activation.

Narcissism. Love of oneself; a high evaluation of one's own physical attributes, behavior, and personal qualities.

Narcotherapy (narcosynthesis). A form of treatment accompanied by injection of a barbiturate drug such as sodium amobarbital or sodium pentobarbital. May be used as a "truth serum" or to elicit painful repressed material.

Nature-nurture issue. The argument concerning the relative influences of heredity and environment in the development of individuals.

Need. The needs of the hero in a TAT story. Also, similar to drive.

Need for achievement. Need or drive to attain success generally or in some specified area; reflected in a tendency to work with energy, to persist towards goals, and to attain a high standard of excellence.

Negativism. Aggressive withdrawal which includes the refusal to cooperate or obey orders, usually expressed by behavior exactly the opposite of what is expected, appropriate, or desired.

Neo-Freudian. Pertaining to former followers of Freud who departed in several major doctrinal ways from orthodox psychoanalysis. Whereas ego psychologists view themselves as psychoanalysts, neo-Freudians disagree enough to be classified as not belonging to the camp of psychoanalysis. Prominent among the neo-Freudians are Adler, Jung, and Sullivan. Their writings emphasize the social and cultural determinants of behavior.

Neologism. A coined word made up of condensed combinations of several words, that has meaning only for the person who coined the word.

Neurosis (psychoneurosis, neurotic disorder). A functional personality disorder, usually mild and not accompanied by severe impairment or disorganization requiring hospitaliza-

tion. The neurotic's anxiety restricts his capability for achieving optimal functioning in his social life.

Nondirective approach. Technique in which the therapist follows
the lead of the patient in the interview rather than introducing his own theories and directing the course of the interview.
This method is applied in both individual and group therapy,
such as Carl Rogers' client-centered and group-centered
therapy.

Nonverbal interaction. Technique used without the aid of words
in encounter groups to promote communication and intimacy
and to bypass verbal defenses. Many exercises of this sort are
carried out in complete silence; in others, the participants emit
grunts, groans, yells, cries, or sighs. Gestalt therapy pays
particular attention to nonverbal expression.

Norm. A standard or pattern for a group; may be derived from
statistical averages or group consensus.

Nosology. The study of the classification of diseases.

Nymphomania. Excessive and uncontrollable sexual drive in
females.

Obsession. A repetitive idea or thought which is recognized as
irrational but cannot be easily eliminated.

Obsessive-compulsive neurosis. Reaction characterized by persistent and repetitive irrational thoughts, often of an anxiety-
provoking nature (obsessions) and uncontrollable and repetitive overt acts and behaviors (compulsions). The compulsive
activities often seem to be a defensive reaction to obsessional
thoughts.

Obsessive-compulsive personality disorder. A classification given
to persons characterized by extreme concern with conformity
and adherence to standards and moral dictates across a wide
variety of behaviors. These personalities are generally over-
conscientious, rigid, inhibited, and unable to relax.

Occupational therapy. A form of help to a patient suffering from a
maladaptation of a psychological or physiological nature.
Occupational therapy is conducted with the goal of giving the
patient opportunities to learn skills consistent with his
capabilities.

Oedipal period. In Freudian theory, stage of psychosexual development during which a child must resolve his Oedipal striv-

ings and achieve a harmonious identification with the same-sex parent.

Oedipus complex. Freudian term for a constellation of motives and behaviors, occurring among boys at approximately the fifth year of life, in which an intense fantasied love relationship with the mother is developed and accompanied by the wish to assume the role occupied by the father. The comparable process in the female child is termed the Elektra complex. Both are hypothesized to be resolved by identification with the same-sex parent.

Oral stage. The first developmental stage of infancy, during which pleasure is derived from lips and mouth contact with need-fulfilling objects (e.g., breast).

Organismic. Pertaining to the organism as a whole rather than to particular parts. Organismic theories hold that behavior is an interrelated and interactive function of the entire integrated organism, and the term is applied to this viewpoint. Similar to the holistic approach.

Outpatient. A patient who receives treatment at a hospital or clinic without being an inmate.

Overanxious reaction. Personality disorder of childhood or adolescence characterized by chronic anxiety, excessive and unrealistic fearfulness, self-consciousness, and sleep problems.

Overdependency. Excessive reliance on others when it is not appropriate; the behavior resembles that of the early parent-child relationship.

Overt. Observable; refers to behaviors, actions, and verbalizations.

Paranoia. A rare psychosis characterized by logical and highly developed delusional systems with little or no indications of other psychotic symptoms. The delusional system of grandeur and/or persecution is relatively isolated, permitting the rest of the personality organization to remain intact.

Pleasure principle. Psychoanalytic term for the regulatory mechanism of mental life that functions to reduce tension and gain gratification. The principle which governs the functioning of the id to obtain gratification without regard to reality considerations.

Preconscious. Pertaining to mental events or contents not currently at the level of awareness (consciousness) but easily raised to that level by alterations in the focus of thinking.

Predisposition. Receptiveness or sensitivity; a predetermined characteristic making probable the development or acquisition of specific traits or disorders.

Primary process thinking. The primitive cognitive mode, characteristic of infants and children, which is not based on rules of organization or logic. A characteristic of the id is the presence of primary process thinking—free association in its purest form. Primary process thought is illogical, entirely pleasure-oriented, has no sense of time or order, and does not discriminate between reality and fantasy.

Prognosis. A forecast. The probable course and outcome of a disorder.

Projection. Defense mechanism which involves attributing to others the undesirable characteristics or impulses which belong to but are not acceptable to oneself.

Psyche. The mind, including its functions and hypothesized structures (e.g., ego, unconscious).

Psychedelic therapy. A psychiatric treatment which combines the administration of LSD-type drugs with psychotherapeutic procedures.

Psychiatric nursing. Specialized field of nursing primarily concerned with the care of patients, usually in a mental hospital setting.

Psychiatric social work. Field of social work in which the worker specializes in maladaptive behavior in a clinical, usually medical, setting.

Psychiatrist. A physician with postgraduate training in the diagnosis and treatment of emotional disorders.

Psychiatry. A specialized field of medicine dealing with the diagnosis, treatment, and prevention of maladaptive behavior.

Psychic determinism. A principle of causality, one of the basic assumptions of psychoanalysis, which states that all events, overt and covert, are determined by prior causes that operate on an unconscious level beyond the control of the person involved.

Psychoanalysis. This term has three meanings: (1) a theory of psychology and psychopathology developed by Freud from his clinical experiences with patients; (2) a procedure for investigating the mental life, conflicts, and coping processes, which employs the techniques of free association, dream analysis, and interpretation of transference and resistance phenomena; and (3) a form of therapy that utilizes the psychoanalytic procedure and the theories of personality and psychopathology described above.

Psychoanalytic psychotherapy. Intensive, long-term treatment based on Freudian methods and techniques, aimed at a significant restructuring of large segments of the personality.

Psychodrama. Psychotherapy method originated by J. L. Moreno in which personality make-up, interpersonal relationships, conflicts, and emotional problems are explored by means of dramatic methods. The therapeutic dramatization of emotional problems includes: (1) protagonist or patient, the person who presents and acts out his emotional problems with the help of (2) auxiliary egos, persons trained to act and dramatize the different aspects of the patient that are called for in a particular scene in order to help him express his feelings, and (3) director, leader, or therapist, the person who guides those involved in the drama for a fruitful and therapeutic session.

Psychodynamic. Pertaining to the operation of and interaction among mental forces or energies within the psychic apparatus.

Psychogenic. Of psychological origin; caused by mental conflict.

Psychopathy. Mental disorder conceived in terms of the effects of mental conflict.

Psychophysiological (psychosomatic) disorder. Physical pathology and actual tissue damage which results from continued emotional mobilization of the body during periods of sustained stress.

Psychosexual development. The mental and emotional development of the individual from birth to maturity, culminating in satisfactory heterosexual adjustment.

Psychosis. A group of maladaptive behaviors which involve major distortions of intellect and/or affect, often accompanied by delusions and hallucinations, and which often require hospitalization.

Psychotherapy. Form of treatment for mental illness and behavioral disturbances in which a trained person establishes a professional contract with the patient and through definite therapeutic communication, both verbal and nonverbal, attempts to alleviate the emotional disturbance, reverse or change maladaptive patterns of behavior, and encourage personality growth and development. Psychotherapy is distinguished from such other forms of psychiatric treatment as the use of drugs, surgery, electric shock treatment, and insulin coma treatment.

Psychotic depression. Severe psychosis in which profound depressive symptoms are the major feature.

Rank, Otto. Austrian psychoanalyst. He was one of Freud's earliest followers and the long-time secretary and recorder of the minutes of the Vienna Psychoanalytic Society. He wrote such fundamental works as *The Myth of the Birth of the Hero*. He split with Freud on the significance of the birth trauma, which he used as a basis of brief psychotherapy.

Rapport. An interpersonal relationship characterized by mutual confidence, cooperation, and harmonious interaction.

Rational-emotive therapy. A directive form of psychotherapy developed by Albert Ellis, based on the premise that disturbed persons needlessly create anxiety and anger in themselves by accepting uncritically certain irrational hypotheses.

Rationalization. A defense mechanism by which logical, socially approved reasons for one's behavior are presented that, although plausible, do not represent the "real" reasons or motives behind one's action.

Reaction formation. Defense mechanism which enables the individual to express an unacceptable impulse by transforming it into its opposite.

Reality principle. Psychoanalytic term for the regulatory mechanism in mental life which takes into account reality demands and restrictions in obtaining gratifications. Whereas the id functions according to the pleasure principle, the ego operates on the basis of the reality principle in its attempt to integrate the internal, superego, and external demands.

Reality testing. Exploring and evaluating one's social and physical environment, as well as possible future developments, so as to respond effectively to situations.

Recall. Process of remembering thoughts, words, and actions of a past event in an attempt to recapture what actually happened. It is part of a complex mental function known as memory.

Reconstructive psychotherapy. A form of therapy that seeks not only to alleviate symptoms but to produce alterations in maladaptive character structures and to expedite new adaptive potentials. This aim is achieved by bringing into consciousness an awareness of and insight into conflicts, fears, inhibitions, and their derivatives.

Regression. Unconscious defense mechanism in which a person undergoes a partial or total return to earlier patterns of adaptation.

Reinforcement. Any event (stimulus) which, if contingent upon a response made by an organism, increases the probability or likelihood that the response will be made again. Reinforcements may be positive (reward) or negative (aversive, punishing, or withdrawing of reward) and may be presented according to a prescribed schedule (continuous, intermittent). They may also be primary (drive reducing—e.g., food) or secondary (derived from prior association with a primary reinforcer—e.g, money, praise).

Remission. Cessation of the symptoms of a disorder.

Repetition compulsion. The impulse to re-enact earlier emotional experiences.

Repression. Psychoanalytic defense mechanism which involves a "stopping thinking" response or not being able to remember. Traumatic events, intolerable and dangerous impulses, and other undesirable mental affects are actively forced out of consciousness into the less accessible realm of the unconscious by the mechanism of repression.

Response. The behavioral result of stimulation; a movement or activity of the organism.

Resistance. Opposition to therapeutic efforts, especially a defensive reluctance to explore repressed material.

Rogers, Carl. American psychologist noted for developing a self-concept theory and method of nondirective or client-centered therapy. Stressed psychotherapy as an opportunity for self-actualization.

Role playing. In psychotherapy, a technique which requires an individual to enact a social role other than his own, or try out new roles for himself. In sociology, the individual's assumption of the role expected of him in a particular type of situation.

Sadism. A form of sexual deviation marked by the infliction of pain on another person as a means of achieving sexual arousal and release.

Schizo-affective reaction. A condition in which the emotional disturbances of manic-depressive psychosis are combined with the disordered thought and behavior patterns associated with schizophrenia.

Schizoid personality. A mildly deviant personality type characterized by social withdrawal, introvertive tendencies, and extreme shyness.

Schizophrenia. A psychosis that usually has its onset in early adulthood and is characterized by disordered thinking, delusions, hallucinations, social withdrawal, and bizarre behavior.

Secondary gain. Advantages other than the reduction of anxiety gained through a neurotic symptom.

Secondary process thinking. Psychoanalytic concept referring to organized, logical and reality-oriented adult thinking. Whereas primary process thinking is characteristic of the id, and based on the pleasure principle, secondary process thought is an ego function based on the reality principle.

Self. The integrating core of the personality.

Self-actualization. Synonymous with **self-fulfillment.** The process by which the development of one's potentials and abilities is achieved.

Self-concept. The individual's view of himself, including the most complete description of himself which he is capable of giving at any particular time. The self may be viewed as an *object,* the self the person states that he is; or as *inferred* self, the self an observer ascribes to another by inferences from the other's behavior.

Sex role. Differential patterns of attitudes and behavior in a given society that are deemed appropriate to either one sex or the other.

Sexual deviation. Deviant sexual behavior that has legal and/or psychiatric implications.

Shaping. A basic process of operant conditioning involving the reinforcement of successively closer approximations of the desired behavior.

Skinner, B. F. American psychologist who developed the principles of operant conditioning and pioneered the development of teaching machines.

Socialization therapy. Programs of resocialization directed at helping group members gain experience in cooperatively establishing group norms and working towards group educational and vocational goals.

Sociodrama. Dramatization using therapeutic role-playing techniques designed to teach socially desirable behaviors.

Sociopathic personality disturbance. Behavior that is maladaptive in terms of failure to adhere to social requirements and standards. Sociopaths tend to behavior which impulsively and frequently violates social mores and customs. Two subtypes of this disturbance are often distinguished: (a) antisocial reaction (antisocial personality), a term applied to chronically antisocial individuals who are always in trouble, profiting little from experience or punishment, and unable to identify with or maintain loyalty to other persons, groups, or moral codes. These individuals lack judgment and responsibility and often demonstrate remarkable emotional immaturity. This classification includes an older one, *psychopathic personality* (q.v.). (b) dyssocial reactions, a term applied to individuals who typically do not show significant personality deviations except for consistent disregard for usual social and legal codes, often as a result of being raised in a deviant subgroup such as a delinquent or criminal subculture. May be capable of strong loyalties and often strongly identifies with the particular deviant group.

Spontaneous recovery. Reappearance of a response after it has been extinguished.

Spontaneous remission. The disappearance of symptoms or maladaptive behaviors in the absence of therapeutic intervention.

Stereotype. A biased and preconceived set of judgments applied to members of some particular group.

Stimulus. An internal or external event that precedes and causes some change in the behavior of an organism. Physical energy that impinges on a receptor sensitive to that kind of energy.

Stress. In general, an aversive or novel condition to which the organism must make some form of adjustive reaction.

Subconscious. Partially unconscious; in the state in which mental processes take place without conscious perception on the individual's part.

Sublimation. Defense mechanism and developmental concept which occupies a somewhat unique position in psychoanalytic theory. Involves the refinement or redirection of undesirable impulses into new and more socially acceptable channels. Where displacement involves an alteration in choice of object, sublimation alters both the aim (unacceptable drive) and the object to a personally acceptable one.

Substitution. A replacement of one goal or behavior by another. Defense mechanism whereby a person substitutes an alternative activity or goal for an originally desired but unobtainable one.

Superego. Structure of the psyche in psychoanalytic theory which is developed by internalization of parental standards and by identification with parents. Contains two parts, the ego-ideal and the conscience. The ego-ideal represents the total of positive identifications with accepting and loving parents and desired standards of excellent and good conduct. The conscience includes the attitudes and values which are moralistic (good-bad) in nature.

Supportive therapy. A brief form of psychotherapy in which the therapist provides acceptance for the patient and affords him some opportunity to be dependent.

Symbiotic infantile psychosis. Childhood psychosis which appears at the time of a threat of separation from the mother. Usually associated with disturbances in the mother-child relationship which date from infancy.

Symbol. An image or object that represents something else.

Symptom. A form of behavior that indicates the presence of a psychopathological condition according to psychodynamic theories. A sign or indicator of an underlying maladaptive process.

Syndrome. The pattern or grouping of symptoms that characterizes a particular disorder or disease.

Systematic desensitization. A learning-theory-based therapeutic technique in which a client is first trained in muscle relaxation and then imagines a series of increasingly anxiety-provoking situations until he no longer experiences anxiety while thinking about the stimuli. The learning principle involved is reciprocal inhibition according to which two incompatible responses (e.g., anxiety and relaxation) cannot simultaneously be made by a person.

Tension. Physiologically, an increase in muscular strain accompanied by other bodily changes. Psychologically, refers to emotional response with accompanying uneasiness, anxiety, and partly restrained restless activity.

Thought disorder. A characteristic of psychotic thinking in which there is an impairment in the intellectual functions reflected in incoherence, irrelevance, use of neologisms, overinclusiveness or concrete reasoning, "word salads," and unusual syntactical speech constructions.

Trait. Any enduring characteristic of an individual which distinguishes him from other persons. The broad meaning includes somatic characteristics as well as personality traits.

Transference neurosis. A highly developed transference reaction in which the patient becomes so caught up in the transference that it assumes the properties of a neurotic reaction.

Transient situational personality disorders. A group of temporary personality disorders generally manifest as an acute response to stress or a sudden or overwhelming change in one's life. These reactions often seem to occur without apparent underlying personality disturbance. General classification includes gross stress reaction, and adjustment reactions of infancy, childhood, adolescence, adulthood, and later life.

Transvestitism. Sexual deviation in which the individual derives gratification from wearing the clothes of the opposite sex.

Trauma. An injury, something hurtful; a painful idea.

Traumatic neurosis. A neurotic reaction attributable to or following a traumatic situational event. May not involve physical injury but usually has some symbolic emotional significance for the individual.

Unconscious. Out of awareness. Mental contents that can be brought to awareness only with great difficulty (or not at all).

Unconscious motivation. An aim or goal that is not recognized consciously by the individual as reflected, for example, in slips of the tongue or pen, or dreams.

Undoing. Defense mechanism aimed at negating or atoning for some disapproved impulse or act.

Unsocialized aggressive reaction. Personality disorder of childhood or adolescence characterized by overt or covert hostility, quarrelsomeness, vengefulness, temper tantrums, physical and verbal aggressiveness, and frequent lying and stealing.

Validity. The quality of being true, factual, or correct. When applied to tests, the term has several meanings but generally refers to the ability of the test to do what it is intended to do. Several subtypes of test validity are defined, based on the nature of the criteria used to establish validity and the method by which it was obtained.

Value. The degree of excellence or worth attached to an object or activity.

Withdrawal. A pattern of action induced by persistent frustration in which a person removes himself from the realm of conflict and obtains satisfaction in less strenuous ways, i.e., daydreams, sleep, excessive work, etc.

Working through. An internal process of recapturing, rearranging, adjusting and remolding repressed unconscious material and its conversion into conscious thoughts such as feelings and strivings.

Index

To Enjoy is to Live

Psychotherapy Explained

BENJAMIN FABRIKANT, Ph.D.
JULES BARRON, Ph.D. JACK D. KRASNER, Ph.D.

From the reassuring introduction, "Have You Seen a Shrink Lately?" to the compassionate, "Psychotherapy with the Dying Person," **To Enjoy Is to Live** guides the layman and student through the mystique and substance of psychotherapy. The three psychologists were commissioned by the American Psychological Association to write a monograph on psychotherapy. **To Enjoy Is to Live** is an expanded version of that monograph and has been written to explain psychotherapy to the layperson. Wearing both the hat of the therapist and the hat of the patient, the authors give full definition to psychotherapy as a therapeutic process which holds the key to personal discovery, psychological growth, and fulfillment for many, many people.

Throughout the book, psychotherapy is dealt with as a human experience, the purpose of which is to help people find more creative ways of living, along with increased ability to enjoy that creativity. The authors champion the mental health movement but are not blinded to the need for more services, more trained people, and more liberalized attitudes toward mental illness. However, they are convinced that dynamic and necessary changes will come when common misconceptions about psychotherapy are dispelled and when there is more understanding of the field's proliferating theories and techniques.

To Enjoy Is to Live, among other things, serves to take the "crazy" out of "psycho," which generally has been associated with being crazy or insane, when it simply refers to the mind. The authors relate the what, when, why, how, and who of psychotherapy to the treatment